Worship
in Spirit and Truth

Julia A. Upton, RSM

Worship
in Spirit and Truth

The Life and Legacy
of H. A. Reinhold

A PUEBLO BOOK

Liturgical Press   Collegeville, Minnesota

www.litpress.org

A Pueblo Book published by Liturgical Press

Cover design by David Manahan, OSB. Photo provided by the author,
courtesy of Mrs. Marian Tanasse.

Excerpts from documents of the Second Vatican Council are from *Vatican
Council II: The Basic Sixteen Documents,* by Austin Flannery, OP © 1996
(Costello Publishing Company, Inc.). Used with permission.

Library of Congress Cataloging-in-Publication Data

Upton, Julia.
    Worship in spirit and truth : the life and legacy of H.A. Reinhold /
Julia A. Upton.
        p. cm.
    "A Pueblo book."
    Includes bibliographical references (p.   ) and index.
    ISBN 978-0-8146-6220-5
    1. Reinhold, H. A. (Hans Ansgar), 1897–1968.   2. Catholic Church—
Clergy—Biography.   I. Title.

BX4705.R433U68 2010
282.092—dc22   2009037709

In gratitude

to Fr. Hans Ansgar Reinhold, Obl.S.B. (1897–1968)
for his courage, persistence, and enduring witness
to worship in spirit and truth

and

to Nathan D. Mitchell,
Fr. Reinhold's worthy heir,
for his friendship, encouragement, and stimulating ideas
always in the service
of worship in spirit and truth

Contents

Biography illuminates history, inspires by example, and fires the imagination to life's possibilities. Good biography can create lifelong models for us. Reading about other people's experiences encourages us to persist, to face hardship, and to feel less alone. Biography tells us about choice, the power of a personal vision, and the interdependence of human life.[1]

(Matina S. Horner)

[1] Matina S. Horner, preface to Radcliffe Biography series in Robert Coles, *Dorothy Day: A Radical Devotion* (Reading, MA: Addison-Wesley, 1987), ix.

SALVETE to Pioneer Reinhold!

Who shouted his message so bold.
    Some said "He's too fidgety
    About all this litagy." . . .
Yet all has come out as foretold.

They said that the great H.A.R.
In the past was way out, by far.
    When he wrote *Timely Tracts*
    Which gave us the facts,
We were covered with feathers and tar.

Now it's no longer spectacular—
This praying in the vernacular
    Though once a sad sin,
    It's really quite 'IN';
So let's get with the *ipso factor*

In the basement of Holy Name School
Various liturgists played it real cool
    But there was one prophet
    Who wouldn't get off it:
He blasted 'till it's now the rule.

Some thought he was really outrageous;
And others said "All ostentatious!"
    They needed a jar
    From our H.A.R.
(We knew he was true and sagacious.)[2]

R.B.H.[3]

(The above were written in haste in the sprung rhythm with ogdenash rimes)

---

[2] "Some Occasioned Limericks" (Dedicated doggerel for Father Reinhold's Vernacular Society Luncheon), Box 18, Folder 45, H. A. Reinhold Papers, John J. Burns Library, Boston College.

[3] R. B. H. is probably Robert B. Heywood, cited as a member of the Vernacular Society and a student at the University of Chicago in Keith Pecklers, *Dynamic Equivalence: The Language of Christian Worship* (Collegeville, MN: Liturgical Press, 2003), 42. Heywood also served as editor for the Committee on Social Thought of *The Works of the Mind* (Chicago: University of Chicago Press, 1947).

Preface

In academia colleagues often speak devoutly, almost reverently, of their mentors—those who helped them to hone their skills as scientists or researchers. My relationship with this particular mentor, however, is somewhat unusual, because Fr. Reinhold died just as I was coming of age. He first captured my attention not with a memorable course taught by a distinguished professor but with a single paragraph. Working on a research project for Villanova University's Theology Institute in 1997, I was reading deeply into the early years of the liturgical movement in the United States.[1] Writing about the contributions Virgil Michel, OSB, made to the liturgical movement a decade after his death, colleague H. A. Reinhold observed:

> It is almost beyond human comprehension to grasp the completeness with which he absorbed everything that Austria, Belgium, and Germany had to offer. But greater yet was what he did with it. Instead of dragging his find across the border as an exotic museum piece, he made it as American as only an American mind can make it. He had seen the high sweep of German ecclesiology and sacramentalism; he had admired the Belgians for their clear grasp of a new spirituality and their critical awareness of all that stood in the way of liturgical, ecclesiastical piety from traditional carry-overs; he had learned in Austria what the common people could gather from the Church's treasure without fright, but he did not come back to force these foreign and incoherent moulds on the American church. Besides, his clear realism and his burning apostle's heart had one urge none of the great masters in Europe seemed to see: the connection of social justice with a new social spirituality. For Virgil Michel the labor encyclicals of Leo XIII and the liturgical reforms of Pius X did not just by accident happen within one generation, but were responses to cries of the masses for Christ who had power and gave the good tidings. They belonged together.[2]

[1] This paper was subsequently published as, "*Carpe Momentum*: Liturgical Studies at the Threshold of the Millennium," in *At the Threshold of the Third Millennium*, ed. Francis A. Eigo, 103–38 (Villanova, PA: Villanova University Press, 1998).

[2] H. A. Reinhold, "The Liturgical Movement to Date," *National Liturgical Week Proceedings* (1947): 9–20; here 11.

I was stunned! In one beautifully crafted paragraph not only had this writer succinctly summed up the contributions of Michel but he had also underscored the essential link between liturgy and social justice that I had found so consistently missing from more recent liturgical writings. "When I have time, I want to find out more about this H. A. Reinhold," I resolved. Time, as you well know, can be so elusive. One does not find it; one must use it judiciously. What we so often lack is the wisdom to use it well. Fortunately God, the source of all wisdom, compensates for our weaknesses and persistently attempts to get our attention, so I found myself drawn into this research project almost without choice.

Later that summer, while on an excursion to Loome Theological Booksellers in Stillwater, Minnesota, with several other Sisters of Mercy theologians, I was aimlessly wandering through the stacks when my gaze fell upon a set of five books all written by Reinhold—the complete collection of his book-length liturgical writings. "This is for me!" I knew, without giving it a second thought or even looking at the price being asked for the volumes. Something in me knew that whatever the books cost, they would be a priceless investment for me.

That night I picked up one of the volumes, *H. A. R.: The Autobiography of Father Reinhold*.[3] From being captivated by an artist's paragraph I now found myself totally immersed in his intriguing and amazing life, profoundly aware that his contributions to the American liturgical movement had surely shaped my life both as a woman of the church and as a liturgical scholar. Life held other more immediate concerns, however. At that time I was absorbed in caring for my father in his last illness and trying to finish work on another writing project that was nearing completion.[4] Although I finished reading the autobiography for *lectio*[5] over the next several months, despite my growing curiosity I did not find time to investigate Reinhold's work further. I told friends

[3] See H. A. Reinhold, *H. A. R.: The Autobiography of Father Reinhold* (New York: Herder and Herder, 1968). In reality, this is more a brief memoir than a full-length autobiography.

[4] See Julia Upton, *A Time For Embracing: Reclaiming Reconciliation* (Collegeville, MN: Liturgical Press, 1999).

[5] *Lectio* is a monastic practice of sacred reading. Akin to spiritual reading, in *lectio* one spends more time reflecting on and savoring a text, usually Sacred Scripture, always aware of the divine presence in the text and with the reader.

and colleagues about my interest in him, certain this would be my next big project, but the time was not yet ripe.

A big break came in January 1999, however, while I was reading Madeleva Roarke's history, *Father Damasus and the Founding of Mount Saviour*, for *lectio*. An oblate of that monastery myself since 1980 and a friend of Madeleva's as well for all those years, I had long been aware of her interest and research in documenting the history of Mount Saviour. What might seem to others just insignificant facts leaped out at me: Damasus and Reinhold, both natives of northern Germany, had been novices together at Maria Laach in 1922 and remained lifelong friends. In 1966, Reinhold donated his entire library to Mount Saviour and is buried in the cemetery there.[6]

Chills tingled up and down my spine, as if someone had taken me by my shoulders, looked me directly in the eye, and said, "You have been chosen for this work." In that instant my casual yet consuming curiosity was transformed into a serious mission. No questions asked! I knew what was being asked of me, and although I am still filled with awe at the unfolding of the saga, I enthusiastically accepted the responsibility.

I e-mailed Madeleva immediately and told her that I had begun work on a study of Reinhold. She responded with equal enthusiasm, explaining that she would put aside a box of materials from the monastery's archives that I might find helpful, and suggested that I visit soon. Ever eager to lure me back to the monastery for a visit, as a further enticement Madeleva sent me some Xeroxed copies of materials from the archives: obituaries of Reinhold and a copy of his 1967 Christmas letter, written a month before his death. A gold mine! My treasure trove was growing.

Two weeks later, on February 22, 1999, Madeleva died of complications following spinal surgery. With Reinhold she is buried in the oblate cemetery at Mount Saviour, and I trust that they are both enjoying the heavenly banquet and have been urging me on in this collaborative venture.

As I was drawn further and further into Reinhold's life, ministry, and legacy, I gradually came to see that my own life and ministry had quietly prepared me for this project. Not only have I been an oblate of Mount Saviour for almost thirty years, but as I delved deeper into

[6] J. Madeleva Roarke, *Father Damasus and the Founding of Mount Saviour* (Pine City, NY: Madroar Press, 1998), 23–24.

the project I saw that in my work as a theologian I have continually and unknowingly encountered people who knew or worked with Reinhold.

Once I began to immerse myself in his writings, I came to regard him as a mentor. Although I wish that he had been the inveterate journal-keeper that I am, I discovered that by piecing together his personal correspondence with his writings for publication, and then reading them chronologically, I was able to conclude a good deal about what he was thinking and writing.

In 1964 Reinhold left me the best clue of all. Writing the introduction to a master's thesis that studied his work, Reinhold wrote as if to the future: "If there is a chance to put the thesis into the frame of a doctoral dissertation in the future, I would be flattered. The Harvard *Current*[7] in its first issue, if I am not mistaken, and the book of Father Hovda (*The Sunday Morning Crisis*[8]) contain thoughts nowhere expressed in any of my other writings. They would have to be considered in the future with major book reviews and the collection of weekly articles[9] for the Los Angeles diocesan paper."[10] There he was fairly giving me instructions from the grave!

Just assembling all of those materials proved to be a challenge. For example, book reviews are rarely indexed in databases by the author of the review, but rather by the title and author of the book.[11] Tracking down Reinhold's book reviews, therefore, took some interesting and relentless detective work. Some are among his papers preserved in the Burns Library at Boston College thanks to the foresight and diligence

---

[7] See H. A. Reinhold, "The Silence and Singleness of Prayer," *The Current: A Review of Catholicism and Contemporary Culture* (May 1961): 61–64.

[8] See H. A. Reinhold, "Eucharistic Bread," in *Sunday Morning Crisis: Renewal in Catholic Worship*, ed. Robert Hovda, 89–97 (Baltimore: Helicon, 1963).

[9] See H. A. Reinhold, "Worship in Spirit and Truth," *The Tidings*, January 28, 1944, to August 24, 1945.

[10] H. A. Reinhold, "Introduction," in Blane Brehany, "Aspects of the Liturgical Renewal as Seen in the Writings of H. A. Reinhold and the Constitution on the Sacred Liturgy" (master's thesis, The Catholic University of America, 1965), ii–iii.

[11] *Book Review Digest Retrospective*, an online database, now allows one to search H. W. Wilson's *Book Review Digest* from 1905–1982 by the name of the reviewer.

Worship in Spirit and Truth

of Fr. William Leonard, SJ.[12] Many others were assembled by looking in likely outlets and scanning their annual indexes—tedious, painstaking work, but always with interesting detours into other areas of scholarship.

Another approach I took was working with Reinhold's library, consisting of over 1,100 volumes, which had been donated to Mount Saviour in 1966. Some of the books he was sent for review are among them, which provided a few additional clues needed to find the review indexed. Reading the book reviews alongside his monthly columns in *Orate Fratres/Worship* and somewhat regular essays in *Commonweal* and *Jubilee*, while not exactly like reading someone's journal, is a close approximation, especially since Reinhold often wove everyday experiences into his writings. One quickly learns that he was bold as well as erudite, taking graceful, artistic leaps with words and ideas.

Finding those articles in the Los Angeles diocesan newspaper initially posed another serious challenge. It would have been so helpful if he had given even an approximate time frame for when that series was published. Since the Hesburgh Library at the University of Notre Dame is the repository for all of the country's Catholic diocesan newspapers, I set aside some time to begin looking through old issues of *The Tidings* while on a business trip there, selecting what I thought might be a likely period and working my way through each weekly microfilmed issue. After an entire day at that tedious task, I decided that there must be a more efficient approach to the problem, confident that in time an alternate solution would emerge. Eventually it did. While studying Reinhold's papers at the Burns Library, I came across the correspondence between him and the editor of *The Tidings* commissioning a series of articles in 1944.[13] My initial hunt had been off by ten years!

In addition to Blane Breheny's thesis, I have also been assisted in this project by the work of those who previously studied other

[12] Active in the liturgical movement from its earliest days, Fr. William Leonard, SJ, almost single-handedly amassed and curated the "Liturgy and Life Collection" housed at the Burns Library at Boston College.

[13] In a letter dated November 11, 1943, Rev. T. McCarthy invited Fr. Reinhold to write a series of weekly articles under the heading "Worship in Spirit and Truth." "The Tidings," Box 10, Folder 1, H. A. Reinhold Papers, John J. Burns Library, Boston College. As noted previously, the series began on Septuagesima Sunday (January 28, 1944) and continued until August 24, 1945, when it was abruptly terminated by a letter from *The Tidings* editor R. S. Labonge.

aspects of Reinhold's life and mission. One of the earliest of these is a biographical article "H. A. R., Front Line Fighter,"[14] written in 1954 by Warren Bovée, then a journalism professor at Marquette University. I contacted Professor Bovée at the beginning of my research, curious to know if he had met Reinhold while preparing the article. There began a wonderful correspondence, which eventually led to a memorable visit with Bovée and his wife, Gladys, in Milwaukee. Since by then Bovée had retired and given all his papers to Marquette's archives, he accompanied me there, gave me free access to all of his notes and pictures, and regaled me with detailed stories of Reinhold's visit with them. What proved most memorable for both Bovée and his wife was Reinhold presiding at Eucharist at one of the side altars in Marquette's Gesu Church. Bovée's notes read, "those who have been fortunate enough to be in church when Fr. Reinhold is saying Mass can note some . . . effects. He says Mass with such care, such loving devotion that those in attendance might almost be pardoned for considering it a 'unique experience.'"[15]

Two other writers studied specific aspects of Reinhold's contribution to the church. Rev. Joel Garner, O.Praem. completed his doctoral dissertation at Columbia University in 1972 focusing on Reinhold as an educator.[16] Jay Corrin, a historian at Boston University, has published two articles that principally explored Reinhold's political involvements.[17] In his later book, *Catholic Intellectuals and the Challenge of Democracy*,[18] Corrin examined Reinhold's contribution in greater detail.

My research led me to northern Germany, to Hamburg where Reinhold was raised, and to Niendorf and Bremerhaven where he ministered. On a visit to the Abbey of Maria Laach, I had the privilege

[14] Warren G. Bovée, "H. A. R., Front Line Fighter," *Today* 10 (December 1954): 3–5.

[15] Warren G. Bovée, "Father Reinhold Fights On," 1954–1956. Warren G. Bovée Papers (Series 2.4-WGB, Box 2) Department of Special Collections and University Archives, Marquette University.

[16] See Joel Garner, "The Vision of a Liturgical Reformer: Hans Ansgar Reinhold, American Catholic Educator" (doctoral diss., Columbia, 1972).

[17] See Jay Corrin, "H. A. Reinhold, America, and the Catholic Crusade Against Communism," *Records of the American Catholic Historical Society* 105 (Spring–Summer 1994): 47–69; Corrin, "H. A. Reinhold: Liturgical Pioneer and Anti-fascist," *The Catholic Historical Review* 82 (July 1996): 436–58.

[18] See Jay Corrin, *Catholic Intellectuals and the Challenge of Democracy* (Notre Dame, IN: University of Notre Dame Press, 2003).

Worship in Spirit and Truth

of interviewing Dom Burkhard Neunheuser, OSB, then age ninety-seven, who had also been a novice there with Reinhold and maintained contact with him over the years, particularly during his visits to Mount Saviour with their other classmate, Fr. Damasus Winzen.

In the United States I had the opportunity to spend time with the people of St. Joseph's Parish in Sunnyside, Washington, where Reinhold was pastor for twelve years. Even today more than fifty years after he left the parish and more than forty years after his death, the people of Sunnyside remember Reinhold as a quintessential preacher who never failed to challenge or inspire them. When faced with a moral decision they still ask themselves, "What would Father Reinhold say?"

A firm believer in the importance of Catholic higher education, Reinhold encouraged families to dedicate their resources to ensuring their sons and daughters attended Catholic colleges. Believing parents to be the primary religious educators of their children, he did not establish a Catholic elementary school in Sunnyside, which further exacerbated his difficulties with diocesan officials. In his memory parishioners in Sunnyside established the H. A. Reinhold Scholarship Foundation, which for over forty years has been awarding scholarships annually, continuing to serve Catholic students in his original parishes[19] as he would have.

After forty years of actively working in the liturgical apostolate, and living long enough to experience the initial implementation of post–Vatican II reforms of the liturgy, one might expect that a legend like Reinhold would be exhilarated. In one of his last published articles[20] he wrote that although he was "deeply satisfied" with the accomplishments of the liturgical reform of the Second Vatican Council, he believed that what had been achieved to that point was external—only what affects the congregation. "The inner reform is yet to come . . . the visible and audible field of expression will reshape our concepts."[21]

More than forty years later I find abundant evidence that the inner reform for which Reinhold and his colleagues in the liturgical apos-

---

[19] As pastor of St. Joseph's in Sunnyside, Washington, Reinhold's responsibilities included serving churches in Bickleton, Grandview, Granger, Mabton, as well as Sunnyside.

[20] See H. A. Reinhold, "A Liturgical Reformer Sums Up," *New Blackfriars* 46 (1965): 554–61.

[21] Ibid., 560.

tolate worked has indeed begun to occur. Unlike the more immediate simpler tasks, such as revising texts that have been completed, this task of liturgical catechesis remains the ongoing responsibility of a new generation of disciples. It was relatively straightforward to form *consilii* following the council and charge each with a different aspect of the reform. In the last decade there have been several important works published that will be referenced throughout this study. Although they are not the only ones now available, each is unique enough that taken together they form a foundational library for serious study of the conciliar and postconciliar era of reform, consisting of both primary and secondary sources.

Dom Bernard Botte, OSB (1893–1980), was a monk of Mont César and director of the Institute de Liturgie in Paris from 1956 to 1964. In 1973 his memoirs were published in *Le mouvement liturgique: Témoignage et souvenirs*.[22] Unlike all of his other research publications, which were commissioned by various publishers, this work comprises "a message to pass on to the world" because he was "an eyewitness to the beginnings of the liturgical movement, and doubtless . . . the last witness still around."[23] The excitement I felt when I first read his memoir still stirs in me twenty years later. Having come of age during Vatican II and been excited about its liturgical reforms, I was oblivious to the world and intrigue that led up to the council. Botte does not just open the door to that era, he actually takes the reader inside so you feel as though you are reliving the liturgical movement from a European perspective.

Archbishop Annibale Bugnini served as secretary of the preparatory commission on the liturgy for Vatican II from 1960 until 1962, as a *peritus* (theological expert) of the council and its Commission on the Liturgy, as secretary of the Consilium for the Implementation of the Constitution on the Liturgy (1964–1969), and as secretary of the Congregation for Divine Worship from 1969 until its reorganization in 1975. With that unique perspective Bugnini related the complete story of the process of the liturgical reform before, during, and after Vatican

[22] Paris: Desclée et Cie, 1973.

[23] Bernard Botte, *From Silence to Participation: An Insider's View of Liturgical Renewal*, trans. John Sullivan (Washington, DC: Pastoral Press, 1988), xi–xii.

II, including the controversies and intrigue that surrounded the reform and his role in it in *The Reform of the Liturgy: 1948–1975*.[24]

In 1982 a compendium of over five hundred official documents became available to scholars through the International Commission on English in the Liturgy.[25] Published as *Documents on the Liturgy 1963–1979: Conciliar, Papal, and Curial Texts* it remains an important reference for liturgical study, although it does not contain specifically American documents.

The Unread Vision: The Liturgical Movement of the United States of America, 1926–1955 will long remain a classic, for in it Keith Pecklers provides the reader with the social history from which the reform of the liturgy at Vatican II, a vision that is still unfortunately largely unread, emerged.[26]

A true gem is a monograph by Martin Connell titled *Guide to the Revised Lectionary*.[27] He quickly sketches for readers the specific Scripture texts that were not in the Lectionary of the 1962 Missal, responsive to the virtual command in Vatican II's Constitution on the Sacred Liturgy (*Sacrosanctum Concilium*): "The treasures of the bible are to be opened up more lavishly so that a richer fare may be provided for the faithful at the table of God's word. In this way the more significant part of the sacred scriptures will be read to the people over a fixed number of years" (SC 51). Connell helps the reader see how it happened and just how expansive that change was.

The most recent addition to this library comes from Archbishop Piero Marini,[28] who served as Master of Pontifical Liturgical Celebrations for twenty years under John Paul II and Benedict XVI from 1987 to 2007. In *A Challenging Reform* he has given the world a wonderful resource by taking the reader behind the scenes—back to Vatican II

[24] See Annibale Bugnini, *The Reform of the Liturgy: 1948–1975*, trans. Matthew J. O'Connell (Collegeville, MN: Liturgical Press, 1990).

[25] See International Commission on English in the Liturgy, *Documents on the Liturgy 1963–1979: Conciliar, Papal, and Curial Texts* (Collegeville, MN: Liturgical Press, 1982).

[26] See Keith F. Pecklers, *The Unread Vision: The Liturgical Movement in the United States of America, 1926–1955* (Collegeville, MN: Liturgical Press, 1998).

[27] See Martin Connell, *Guide to the Revised Lectionary* (Chicago: Liturgy Training Publications, 1998).

[28] Piero Marini, *A Challenging Reform: Realizing the Vision of the Liturgical Renewal, 1963–1975* (Collegeville, MN: Liturgical Press, 2007).

and its original vision, and into the committee meetings that eventually resulted in the reformed liturgy. After forty years even those of us who lived through the council and the era of reform that followed have forgotten the details and sequence of the reform. Too often those who were born after the council think that the reforms happened with the turn of a switch. Marini was privy to all of that history from the inside and in this book he takes the reader back into the meeting rooms where the drama unfolded. For anyone interested in liturgical history this is essential reading, but for any person interested in how the Roman Catholic Church functions this will provide valuable insight.

Texts are an important and essential first step, and understanding how revisions came to be made is essential for a proper appreciation of the reform, but the process of inner reform is longer than our lives. To assist this generation of disciples, I find that there is yet wisdom and energy in Reinhold's life and writings that remain both challenging and inspiring. His voice needs to resound again in the church. In the preface to a biography of another leader in the American liturgical movement, Msgr. Frederick McManus observed that the "tragic loss of continuity with the great figures of our immediate past . . . is intolerable as well as unnecessary."[29] This book is my humble effort to correct that wrong. McManus also noted that "the writing of biography surely involves some element of *pietas*, of loyal devotion, esteem, and appreciation."[30] McManus was the first person I interviewed for this project, and as it draws near to completion, I hope he would find that this book radiates that "loyal devotion, esteem, and appreciation" that he encouraged as I continued to expand an earlier Reinhold "portrait."[31]

The title chosen for this book had particular significance for Reinhold. As mentioned earlier, "Worship in Sprit and Truth" was the title of a series of weekly articles he wrote for the Los Angeles diocesan newspaper, *The Tidings*, from January 28, 1944, until August 24,

[29] Frederick McManus, "Preface" in Noel Hackmann Barrett, *Martin B. Hellriegel: Pastoral Liturgist* (St. Louis, MO: Central Bureau of the Catholic Central Union of America, 1990), ix.

[30] Ibid., x.

[31] See Julia Upton, "H. A. Reinhold: Architect of the Liturgical Movement in America," in *Benedict in the World: Portraits of Monastic Oblates*, ed. Linda Kulzer and Roberta Bondi, 187–97 (Collegeville, MN: Liturgical Press, 2002).

1945. Also the title of an essay that appeared in *The Way*[32] at the very end of his life, "Worship in Spirit and Truth" (John 4:23) proved to be the overarching goal of his life, a phrase that was woven into many of his other writings, and can be seen as the theme of his ministry in the service of the liturgy—building the church of God.

Although someday I aspire to write a definitive biography of my dear mentor, H. A. Reinhold, this is not that day. It is his voice that I want to have echo in the church again and reverberate in the lives of faithful Christians who strive to worship in spirit and truth. Because his life was so integral to his work, the first part of this book (chaps. 1 and 2) fills out the story that his autobiography only began to sketch. With his life story as a kind of sounding board, in the second part (chaps. 3–6) I turn to the liturgical movement and Reinhold's writings. I do so not as a historian or biographer but rather as a theologian. Again my goal is not to be exhaustive. Although his entire corpus can be found in the bibliography, in this section I draw out some key themes from Reinhold's work that I regard as the essence of his unique contribution to the church of his day and ours: active participation, social justice, and liturgical architecture. The final section (chap. 7) returns us to the present with the blessings and challenges of our own time, to listen for what Reinhold has to say to us about needs of ministry in our own day.

Many others have assisted me in this long research journey. I am particularly grateful to my Benedictine friends: Fr. Martin Boler, OSB; Br. Bruno Lane, OSB; and the monastic community at Mount Saviour who on numerous visits allowed me to have access to their archives as well as to Reinhold's books that have been assimilated into their library. Other members of the extended Benedictine family have also assisted in the project in various ways both directly and indirectly: Joel Garner, O.Praem.; Timothy Joyce, OSB; Abbot John Klassen, OSB; Jane Klimsch, OSB; Linda Kulzer, OSB; Abbot Nicholas Morcone, OSB; Nathan Munsch, OSB; Martin Shannon; and Basilius Sandner, OSB, the archivist at Maria Laach Abbey.

The administration and my colleagues at St. John's University have not only provided me with the time and resources necessary for research, but many have also helped directly in this research effort by providing translations and references as well as encouragement:

[32] See H. A. Reinhold, "Worship in Spirit and Truth," *The Way* 2 (April 1962): 115–20.

Preface

Dolores Augustine, Frank Brady, Maura Flannery, Robert Hendricks, Brian Mikesell, Robert Pecorella, Walter Petrovitz, and Ann Wintergerst. I am particularly grateful to Vasco Lopes, a generous and diligent graduate assistant, and Marina Torre, a most gracious and meticulous proofreader.

Friends and colleagues in the North American Academy of Liturgy and Societas Liturgica, in addition to providing valuable critique, have also given me some important leads: Edward Foley, OFM Cap.; Keith Pecklers, SJ; Fr. Raymond Rafferty; Alexander Röder; Msgr. Wilm Sanders; Msgr. Anthony Sherman; Mike Woods, SJ.

Finally there is a long list of Reinhold's many colleagues and friends who have shared the journey with me. Some have crossed over to the other side and I trust are enjoying the heavenly banquet: Warren Bovée; John Deedy; Fr. Godfrey Diekmann, OSB; Msgr. Paul Lackner; Fr. William Leonard, SJ; Msgr. Frederick McManus; Fr. Burkhard Neunheuser, OSB. Others as of this writing continue to provide assistance: Fr. Edmond Bliven, Msgr. Dermot Brennan, Roger Garrison, Elma Jane Greco, Judy and Vincent Lackner, Justus George Lawler, Robert Rambusch, Jose Ignacio Resendez, William Storey, Marian Tanasse, Kerry Turley, and Fr. Raymond Utz. Their stories and those of many others are woven along with mine here as I introduce you to one of my most intriguing mentors, H. A. Reinhold.

Mount Saviour Monastery
Feast of All Souls
November 2, 2008

Worship in Spirit and Truth

Acknowledgments

Excerpts from *H. A. R.: The Autobiography of Father Reinhold* (New York: Herder and Herder, 1968). Used with permission.

Excerpt from "The Dry Salvages" in *Four Quartets*, copyright 1941 by T.S. Eliot and renewed 1969 by Esme Valerie Eliot, reprinted by permission of Houghton Mifflin Harcourt Publishing Company.

Excerpts from H. A. Reinhold's column, Worship in Spirit and Truth, in *The Tidings* (January 1944–August 1945). Used with permission.

Ruth Duck, "Hope of Abraham and Sarah," copyright © 2005 by GIA Publications, Inc. All rights reserved. Used by permission.

Permission for the following work was still in process at the time of publication:

Excerpt from "The Dry Salvages" in *Four Quartets*, copyright © 1941 by T. S. Eliot and renewed 1969 by Valerie Eliot, published by Faber & Faber.

Chapter 1

Rooted in Germany

It is said that God never asks anything of us for which we have not been carefully prepared, although that preparation usually precedes our conscious awareness of it. If you look back through your own life or through the life of any person in the public record for that matter, you will find that this is often true. Events and people that might once have seemed inconsequential, in retrospect take on increased significance. Looking backward we find a pattern that was never so obvious in the crushing reality of the present. In some respects the past is never really over because it can continue to shape us, in ways both dramatic and subtle, sometimes by our choosing and sometimes not. This was certainly true for Fr. Reinhold when we look back to his remarkable life.

HAMBURG BEGINNINGS

Hans Emil Alexander Reinhold was born in Hamburg, Germany, on September 6, 1897. While southern Germany at that time was predominantly Catholic, the country's northern cities like Hamburg were almost exclusively Lutheran, and more often than not both Catholics and Jews were treated as outsiders if not downright outcasts. Educated in Hamburg's public schools from the fourth grade on, Reinhold and his Jewish classmates were excused from the Lutheran catechism classes, which threw them together in an unusual alliance. Encouraged by his father, during these years Reinhold began to develop lifelong interests in languages, history, art, and architecture. In time all these interests and relationships would both save and shape his life.

By today's standards, Reinhold would be considered an aristocrat. Although his grandfather had emigrated from Headcastle in Hessen to Hamburg in order to make his living as a carpenter, he eventually turned his skill to real estate, which enabled the family to climb out of near poverty. When Reinhold was a lad, his father took him to see the old neighborhood where he had been raised. Reinhold was appalled at the conditions they found there. By then it was a part of Hamburg that had to be demolished because it was so hazardous. "The roads, the streets were so narrow that you could reach from one house to the other house across the street. The buildings were made of timber and brick, wooden beams to support them."[1] Although that section of Hamburg was destroyed during the bombings of World War II, today one such block has been restored, and turned into quaint shops and bistros. With just a slight twist of imagination one can easily see how appalling living conditions there might once have been. By the time Reinhold was born, however, the family lived in a more comfortable part of Hamburg, called Heareeste Hude, so "it was quite a jolt," as he wrote, "for me as a boy to see how my father had lived."[2] It is not surprising, therefore, as we will see later, that throughout his life Reinhold was particularly attentive to those who lived in adverse circumstances and found various ways to be of assistance to them himself and to involve others in the project as well.

Reinhold wrote that he was an "indifferent student . . . high-strung and nervous," but he developed "an avid interest in languages and history, and in art and architecture." The stimulus for all this, he recalled, was his classmates' religion teacher. Students who were not Lutheran were excused from religion classes, which not surprisingly resulted in Reinhold bonding with his Jewish classmates. Once stimulated, however, Reinhold indicated that he became interested in everything, and because his school did not afford him the opportunity to study all the languages he wanted, he took private lessons in Spanish and Italian.[3]

According to Reinhold his father's favorite pastime with him was to visit Protestant churches on Sunday afternoons, and he recalled that one day he saw an Old Catholic baptism, which was celebrated entirely in the vernacular. He also enjoyed the sermons he heard in those churches, which left the family with the impression "that our own priests could have been more solicitous in their preaching, and above all that the music in our Catholic churches was decidedly inferior."[4]

---

[1] H. A. Reinhold, "Manuscript for Autobiography," Box 12, Folder 2, H. A. Reinhold Papers, John J. Burns Library, Boston College, 1. This 121-page typescript was edited down to the first chapter of the published autobiography noted previously.

[2] Ibid., 2.

[3] H. A. Reinhold, *H. A. R.: The Autobiography of Father Reinhold* (New York: Herder and Herder, 1968), 7–8; hereafter cited as *HAR*.

[4] Ibid., 9.

Worship in Spirit and Truth

"Our own parish was an hour away in a slum neighborhood, and had poor sermons and overcrowded, silent Masses. Saint Anthony's was in a working-class district; its furnishings were in appalling taste, but we liked it because the pastor preached well and could always hold our teen-age attention."[5] Elsewhere he stated that the long walk to Saint Anthony's was pleasant and brought the family through lovely gardens and open spaces. "Above all, we could sing to our heart's delight: a lusty hymn while the priest hurried through the beginning of the Mass."[6]

Reinhold's parents searched for good intellectual training for all their children and transferred his two sisters, Kate and Carola, from one private school to another. Reinhold attended Catholic grade school for the first four years, and then transferred to local public school because of the "uninspired" teaching of the priests.[7] "It was my mother's idea, heartily endorsed by my father, that we children should learn the social graces. Dancing master—on weekends. I was at first shy and awkward . . . though with time I overcame this timidity. Still, throughout my youth I was soft-voiced, reticent, and quick to blush—always to the dismay of my parents."[8] Reinhold's parents "created an atmosphere of intellectual freedom in the house," but he also wrote that he had "no grasp of the fine dogmatic structure of Christianity" and knew "virtually nothing of the liturgy." "Only one support of my faith originated from my own inner being. This was the fact that the sacrament of penance was such a strong force in my life. Aside from that, however, my whole experience of faith was external and superficial."[9]

SHAPED BY WORLD WAR I

The family was on a vacation trip through Switzerland, Austria, and the Tyrol in June of 1914 when Archduke Francis Ferdinand was assassinated. Persuaded by government propaganda that Germany had been attacked, the very day he became eligible for military service in 1914 Reinhold joined the field artillery of His Royal Highness, the

---

[5] H. A. Reinhold, "Music in the Church," *Today* 14 (April 1959): 17–20; here 20.
[6] H. A. Reinhold, *The Dynamics of Liturgy* (New York: Macmillan, 1961), 93.
[7] HAR, 6.
[8] Ibid., 12.
[9] Ibid., 18–19.

Rooted in Germany

Grand Duke of Mecklenburg, expecting that military life would satisfy him for the rest of his days.[10]

Erich Maria Remarque's novel *All Quiet on the Western Front* (1929) was released as a film originally in 1930 and rereleased in expanded versions in 1934 and 1939. Based on his personal experience, it tells the story entirely from the perspective of a German foot soldier, shedding light on what the war could have been like for Reinhold since he was one of these. The film has one scene that probably describes perfectly the situation in which young Hans found himself. In the scene, students obviously in a high school classroom are being whipped into an emotional frenzy by their teacher and head directly from class to sign up for military service.

Injured several times in battle and left for dead twice, Reinhold was repeatedly sent back to the front until May 1917 when a shell exploded near his dugout, smashing his right leg. When he was finally released from the hospital in October of that year, military authorities deemed him unfit for front-line service. Therefore, Reinhold applied for admission to language school, hoping to be assigned to army intelligence after training. His language skills were so good, however, that he passed the examinations for English, French, and Italian and was immediately assigned to intelligence work. Although Reinhold found the work ingenious and fascinating, he was also continually confounded. It was obvious to him from the dispatches he translated that the German front was collapsing, but leaders of government, commerce, and industry seemed to be successful in perpetuating an illusion that Germany was winning the war. This conflict forged in him a basic instinct of distrust in government, and probably authority in general as well.

LITURGICAL BEGINNINGS

While recovering from his wartime experiences during the spring and summer semesters of 1919, Reinhold studied philosophy in Freiburg. There he would assist the priest at Mass each morning, take long walks in the pinewoods on the edge of the city, and on free days go mountain climbing on the outskirts of the Black Forest with friends. "It was a great emotional release for all of us after the restraining years of the war. I found peace here."[11] It was during this time that Reinhold

---

[10] Ibid., 23.
[11] Ibid., 38.

discovered Romano Guardini's *Vom Geist der Liturgie*[12] soon after its 1918 publication in Germany, which further enhanced his peace and, as we will see, became a turning point in his life.

Romano Guardini (1885–1968) had been a theology student at the University of Tübingen when he first visited the nearby Abbey of Beuron in 1907. He was deeply impressed by the liturgical celebrations at the abbey, where the Benedictine monks were already leaders in the liturgical movement. Guardini returned to the abbey many times for retreats, eventually becoming a lifelong oblate.[13]

Guardini entered the seminary in 1908, studying for the Diocese of Mainz, and was ordained two years later. He began doctoral studies soon thereafter and received his PhD in 1915. From 1916 to 1918 he fulfilled his military obligation by serving part-time as a hospital orderly. Somehow in the midst of all this he managed to write a small manuscript that focused on the essence of liturgical worship. He showed the manuscript to Abbot Ildefons Herwegen of Maria Laach Abbey, who agreed to publish it as the first volume in the abbey's Ecclesia Orans series under the title *Vom Geist der Liturgie*. It became a best seller in Germany, where there was a genuine hunger for spiritual nourishment.

In seven interconnected chapters Guardini provides the reader with the underlying principles of liturgy, giving shape to communal worship as well as motivation for personal prayer. Reinhold said that when he discovered the book he stayed up all night reading it through twice. "I got so excited about it that I could not sleep that night, my mind being filled with another and deeper view of my church. The legalistic body of restrictions and commandments which I used to have in my mind and which I used to defend in fierce and dull despair had vanished before the vision of Christ's Mystical Body and the incredible beauty of His Mystical Life among us through His sacraments and mysteries."[14] Guardini's book suddenly gave sense to all that he had experienced; it "proved to be a turning point in my life, giving me not

[12] This small book was not available in English until 1930.

[13] See Robert A. Krieg, "A Precursor's Life and Work," in *Romano Guardini: Proclaiming the Sacred in a Modern World*, ed. Robert A. Krieg (Chicago: Liturgical Training Publications, 1995), 19.

[14] Warren G. Bovée, "H. A. R., Front Line Fighter," *Today* 10 (December 1954): 3–5; here 4.

so much new insight into the liturgy as a positive attitude towards Catholic teachings."[15]

Guardini was also a leader in the Quickborn Movement, which was a German Catholic youth movement begun by young people in 1910. Although the church sponsored its leadership, it continued to be organized by young people themselves, and in Guardini they found an amazing spiritual director who helped them to make sense out of the turbulent times in which they were living.[16]

As a teenager Fr. Burkhard Neunheuser (1903–2003), a monk of Maria Laach Abbey, had been involved with the Quickborn Movement, and he told me that Reinhold regularly queried him about his thoughts and experiences. Their activities centered at Burg Rothenfels castle, which they acquired in 1919 and where they were known for regularly hosting moving liturgical celebrations for young men and women. As we will see, these probing discussions were subtly shaping the way in which Reinhold would later minister as chaplain and pastor.

When the student chaplain at Freiburg suggested that he consider becoming a priest, Reinhold admitted that although he had considered this in his youth, he had changed his mind. He no longer thought that he was cut out to be a priest—that he lacked the "strength of will, the character, the ascetic requirements, and so on."[17] Intrigued again by the possibility, however, he mulled the idea over in his mind for a while and then decided to try his vocation. With the chaplain's recommendation, Reinhold enrolled in the seminary at Innsbruck the following year where he enjoyed his studies. Because he believed that he would serve the church better in the South Tyrol, where he had regularly vacationed with his family and where his best images of the church had been forged, he decided to transfer to another diocese. The bishop of Trent, ecclesiastical superior of South Tyrol, accepted him as a candidate and sent him to Bressanone, where German-speaking members of his clergy were trained.

Bressanone (or Brixen, its German name) is located in Northern Italy, nestled in the foothills of the Dolomite mountains between Switzerland and Austria. I remember wondering when I stayed at the

---

[15] *HAR*, 38.

[16] See Mike Tyldesley, *No Heavenly Delusion? A Comparative Study of Three Communal Movements* (Liverpool: Liverpool University Press, 2003), 25–27.

[17] *HAR*, 39.

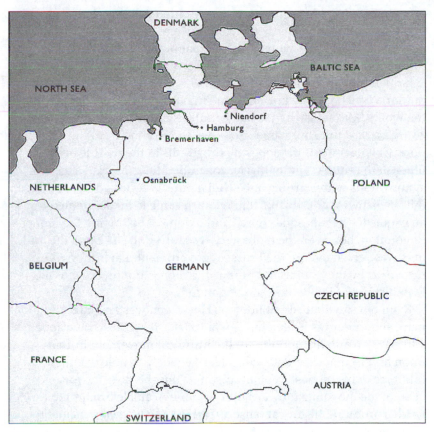

Figure 1

seminary there how anyone could ever be stressed-out living there. The town is encircled by mountains like a scene right out of *The Sound of Music*. Just looking up into the surrounding mountains had an instant calming effect on me.

BENEDICTINE FORMATION AT MARIA LAACH

Reinhold did not stay long at the seminary in Bressanone, for the next great idea to seize him was the desire to be a religious—a Benedictine![18] Reflecting on his first visit forty years later, he admitted that the approach to Maria Laach was "forbidding." "The abbey is located in the crater of an extinct volcano, now filled with a rather large

---

[18] See ibid., 43.

lake rimmed by a dense forest. If you couldn't call this setting gloomy, you would probably choose the word austere. But the spirit inside the abbey was full of life—young life. A great number of novices gave pulsating impetus to the monastic traditions of Maria Laach."[19]

Growing up in Hamburg, Reinhold was acquainted with the name of Maria Laach, "a boy in Hamburg High School . . . we lived with the words 'Maria Laach.' We had countless old copies of *Stimmen aus Maria Laach*, a title, my parents told me, that sprang from the temporary ownership of the abbey by the Jesuits in the middle of the nineteenth century." From this he concluded that "Maria Laach was synonymous with learning and scholarship."[20] Founded in 1093 fifteen miles northwest of Coblenz, Maria Laach came to be dominated by an exquisite Romanesque church and a dome.[21] Following the French Revolution, however, the monastery was forced to close and the buildings were given over to the Prussian government. Later they were recovered by the Jesuits, and in 1892 the monastery reverted to the Benedictines of the Beuron congregation.

Reinhold saw that Abbot Ildefons Herwegen was an extraordinary man, and under his leadership "an air of charity suffused the abbey."[22] Already "an ardent supporter of the liturgical movement in 1907," upon his election as abbot in 1913 Herwegen "was able to enlist the full force of his monastic community and thus became the revered head of the movement toward liturgical renewal. He brought to the work a profound historical sense as well as rich gifts of personality and oratory."[23] "It was a great experience the first time I went to Vespers to see the abbot, at the head of his monks, majestically moving with them up the aisle to the altar to enter choir stalls in grave silence and recollection. Once they began to sing you realized that a new way of life for nineteenth and twentieth century youngsters was indicated

[19] H. A. Reinhold, "Maria Laach Revisited," *Commonweal* 78 (August 23, 1963): 497–500; here 497.

[20] Ibid.

[21] See Burkhard Neunheuser, "Maria Laach Abbey: A Double Jubilee 1093–1993; 1892–1992," *Ecclesia Orans* 10 (1993): 163–78.

[22] Reinhold, "Maria Laach Revisited," 497.

[23] H. A. Reinhold, "Ildefons Herwegen," *New Catholic Encyclopedia*, 2nd ed. (New York: McGraw-Hill, 1967). See also Ildefons Herwegen, "The Liturgy a Pattern of Life," *Orate Fratres* 6 (April 1934): 506–14.

by this service of beauty and profound piety. Only then did I begin to understand the meaning of the liturgy as *Opus Dei*, the work of God."[24]

The next morning in the crypt under the main altar, Reinhold was to have his first experience of a "Dialogue Mass," celebrated facing the assembly by the abbey's prior, Father Albert Hammenstede. By his own admission and later astonishing surprise, Reinhold held a very conservative position at the time and approached the event reluctantly. The experience moved him so deeply, however, that within the hour he was transformed. Not only was he sold on the concept of the Dialogue Mass and Mass celebrated facing the assembly, but he was later to become their prophet and apostle on both sides of the Atlantic.

"I remained about a week and came back to my home town fully convinced that the only place for me in this life would be the Abbey of Maria Laach as a monk of the Benedictine order. Soon I received a letter from the novice master, Father Simon, informing me that I was accepted and could come in April 1922."[25] Before entering the monastery at Maria Laach, though, with his parents' permission Reinhold decided to visit Rome again. "No city ever enraptured me so swiftly or so completely as Rome. I can still feel the awe I had on my first visit to the Vatican."[26] where it was actually the city's architecture that filled him with "limitless fascination." Reinhold spent three weeks touring Rome before his money ran out, but he did not leave the city before visiting with Stotzingen, the abbot primate, at Sant'Anselmo Abbey. After stopping to visit friends at Innsbruck, Reinhold traveled on to Maria Laach.

Reinhold entered Maria Laach as a novice in April 1922 and was given the name Ansgar[27] in honor of the patron of the city of Hamburg and of his home parish. "Most of what I learned of the liturgy and the way of thinking of the liturgical apostolate was given to me in that year," he would later write.[28] "While the liturgical efforts of Maria Laach were directed to the intellectual and the scholar, the intention

---

[24] Reinhold, "Maria Laach Revisited," 498.

[25] Ibid.

[26] *HAR*, 43.

[27] There are variant spellings for Reinhold's patron and religious name. Most often it appears as "Ansgar" but also as "Anscar" and the Latin "Anscarius." Reinhold himself used variant spellings for his own name. For consistency in this volume I have settled on the more common American spelling "Ansgar."

[28] Reinhold, "Maria Laach Revisited," 498.

was that eventually the apostolate of the liturgy would be taken up by the people and their pastors."[29]

The tower of learning in the house at that time was Dom Odo Casel,[30] who had recently developed the theology of *mysterium*, which he discussed at great length with the novices. Reinhold described Casel as a "frail, shy man . . . who might have gone through life as a book-worm, whose scholarly research resulted in turning a few things upside down in the well-tended garden of professional theologians."[31] "The enormous achievement of this quiet monk . . . who never traveled, never lectured, and never produced anything but 'occasional' books, slim in size; who loved solitude and enjoyed company; practiced silence and had more to say than anybody else when he spoke; who preached the glorious pneumatic Christ and was deeply attached to the mystery of the Cross, cannot be measured by me in a short article."[32]

During my own visit to Maria Laach in July 2001 I spent long hours in the crypt, drawn to that simple space more than to the magnificent Romanesque church above. The crypt is a tiny chapel today with little decoration, but in it I found myself surrounded by that great cloud of witnesses from Hebrews 12:1. Their presence stoked my imagination and I gave quiet thanks for all that the Holy Spirit had accomplished through their fidelity.

Neunheuser was so gracious to me during my visit to the abbey and he generously shared both his memories of Fr. Ansgar, as he called him, as well as stories about life at the abbey in general. He thought that Reinhold was "too dynamic" for Maria Laach and that was probably the reason he did not persevere. Reinhold was older than the other novices and had not only seen more of the world than his classmates but also, in the fever of battle, had stared down death. Too dynamic? That could be, but my suspicion is that Reinhold was probably more outspoken than a novice in that era was expected to be.

Although Reinhold left the official formation process at Maria Laach within the year, I believe he never really left the community. He became an oblate of Maria Laach on June 11, 1924, and again took the

---

[29] *HAR*, 47.

[30] See H. A. Reinhold, "Dom Odo Casel," *Orate Fratres* 22 (June 1948): 366–72.

[31] Ibid., 369.

[32] Ibid., 370.

name Ansgar.[33] All of his later correspondence with the community is signed Fr. Ansgar, Obl.S.B. Thus he retained his Benedictine identity for the rest of his life, and the relationships with both friends and teachers that began forming in that year at Maria Laach continued to deepen throughout his life. More important for us, however, in that one year Reinhold had so thoroughly absorbed the liturgical mission of Maria Laach that he continued its work for almost fifty years in a variety of ministries as pastor and author on both sides of the Atlantic and both coasts of the United States of America, among thousands of people, through hundreds of articles, and in several important books.

Wherever he went, Reinhold formed community and empowered the laity through the liturgy. During that year he also formed relationships that would endure throughout his life. His friendships with Casel, Neunheuser, and Winzen have already been mentioned here. During that year others passed through Maria Laach, including Msgr. Martin Hellriegel (1891–1981), later also a leader in the liturgical apostolate. Addressing those gathered for the third Liturgical Week, Hellriegel said, "You know, although I was born in a liturgically inspired home in 1890, I was baptized into the liturgy here at Saint Meinrad's in 1909. I owe my gratitude to Saint Meinrad's for that; but my *conversio morum* took place at Maria Laach. That was in 1922, when I made a memorable visit there."[34]

FORMATION OF THE *SEEMANSPASTOR*

When Reinhold left Maria Laach in September 1922, after a brief visit home he signed on as assistant purser on the SS *Hamburg* of the German–Austral Line headed for Java, Indonesia. During the voyage he kept a journal, "From Hamburg to Piraeos," apparently as a gift

---

[33] Register of Oblates, Abbey Maria Laach, as per letter from Fr. Basilias Sander, OSB, archivist. Records of the exact dates of entrance and exit are not available from that period. Abbey records were partially destroyed at the command of the abbot during the Third Reich, so that during a house search not too much dangerous material would be available.

[34] Martin Hellriegel, "Intervention," *Proceedings of the North American Liturgical Week, 1942,* 142. See also Noel Hackmann Barrett, *Martin B. Hellriegel: Pastoral Liturgist* (St. Louis, MO: Central Bureau of the Catholic Central Union of America, 1990); Barrett, "The Contribution of Martin B. Hellriegel to the American Catholic Liturgical Movement" (doctoral diss., St. Louis University, 1977); Godfrey Diekmann, "Monsignor Martin B. Hellriegel: Holy Cross Church, St. Louis," *Worship* 38 (August–September 1964): 497–98.

to the Benedictine community at Maria Laach, although it might also have been intended for publication some day. The journal is unique because no others have come to light, and I am grateful to the archivist at Maria Laach for sending me copies not only of the journal but also of all Reinhold's extant correspondence with the abbey.

The thirty-page journal not only documents the journey between October and December 1922 but also explains in vivid detail experiences along the way, carefully translating them for the uninformed reader. He drew small maps as well as little sketches of interesting sights along the way as seen in figure 2. As one might expect, Reinhold was particularly attentive to visiting various churches and participating in liturgical celebrations along the way. He also provided searing critique at times of the naïve worldview held by many Germans. This sharp tone is a clue to the struggles that he experienced at Maria Laach and that would haunt him until death. Furthermore, Reinhold's involvement with the seaman's apostolate truly began in these few months, for he lived their life if only for a season.

By the time the spring semester came around, Reinhold was back in Germany, enrolled at the University of Münster and completing theological studies for the diocese of Osnabrück. Ordained a deacon in 1923, he had the privilege of serving as deacon when Abbot Herwegen consecrated the new Abbess Teresia at Herstelle the following year.[35] "Herstelle" is the more commonly used name for the Abbey of the Holy Cross, a community of Benedictine Sisters of Perpetual Adoration in North-Rhine Westphalia where Dom Odo Casel served as chaplain from 1922 until his death in 1948,[36] and Reinhold often made retreat there.

On December 18, 1925, Reinhold was ordained to the priesthood at Osnabrück and the following day sang his first Mass at the Ursuline convent chapel there. Invited to speak at the banquet honoring the newly ordained priests, Reinhold used the psalm text, "In your light, O Lord, we will see light." Its enthusiastic reception was the first indication Reinhold had that he could speak.

[35] Reinhold, "Dom Odo Casel," 368.
[36] See Teresa Berger, *Women's Ways of Worship: Gender Analysis and Liturgical History* (Collegeville, MN: Liturgical Press, 1999), 100–101.

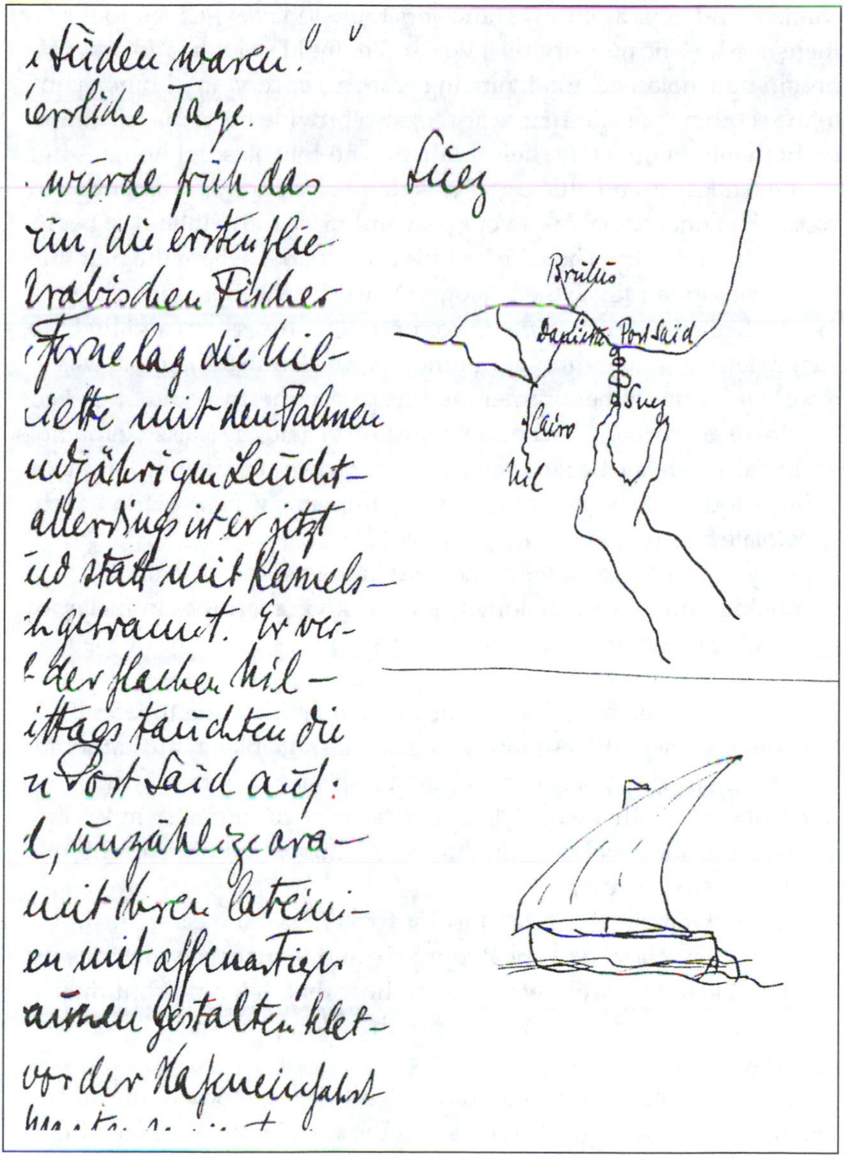

Figure 2

MINISTRY IN NIENDORF

Reinhold's first assignment was to Niendorf, today a charming resort town on the Baltic Sea, reminiscent of many American East Coast seaside villages, although on a smaller, simpler scale. There he served as chaplain to three houses of Franciscan nuns who cared for convalescent children and their mothers. The sisters there today explained to me that theirs is a holistic ministry, as it was in Reinhold's era. In addition to providing wholesome food, nursing care in a cheery, airy home open to the soothing seaside air, the sisters also provide religious education for both the children and their mothers. The convalescent home is right on the Baltic Sea, and although I was there on a sunny summer day in 2003, I imagine that it was a very peaceful place for Reinhold to begin his priestly ministry. There he had his own chapel, where the first thing he did was to introduce the Dialogue Mass. By the following Christmas he had added offertory and communion processions and had the congregation singing throughout the Mass.[37] Because Niendorf was a resort area, during the summer months priest-guests would often vacation there. Since many had never heard of a Dialogue Mass, Reinhold's liturgical apostolate began in unassuming ways at prayer around that inauspicious table of the Lord, in much the same way as Maria Laach's apostolate began in the crypt.

Many Polish seasonal workers were in the area as well, and Reinhold frequently made long trips to outlying farms to minister to them. When he was away overnight, he would stay in one of their barns or in a makeshift bed in the cramped migrant quarters. In the morning he would say Mass on the kitchen table, facing the family. No one thought that these innovations were surprising, but rather just how things ought to be. He also began a special form of ministry to migrant workers that would later characterize his ministry in Washington State and involvement with the National Catholic Rural Life Conference (NCRLC).[38]

Reinhold remained at Niendorf for two and a half years, during which time he learned to speak publicly and to manage what was comparable to a parish. Records also show that Reinhold continued to be a benefactor of the sisters' work there long after he left that ministry.[39]

In the summer of 1928 Reinhold was selected to go to Rome and resume his archaeological studies. On the way, he stopped for a brief stay at Maria Laach and for his first visit to Paris. What he most

[37] *HAR*, 57.
[38] Founded in 1923 the NCRLC has supported rural people, family farms, and local businesses throughout the United States.
[39] See "Donation Records II," Box 20, Folder 9, H. A. Reinhold Papers, John J. Burns Library, Boston College.

wanted to see in Paris was the Carolingian altar in the Cluny Museum depicting three archangels and St. Benedict, with the mysterious inscription beneath: "*Quis sicut hel fortis medicus soter benedictus prospice terrigenas clemens mediator usias*," what he described as a Latin play on a Greek and Hebrew text. Rendered into English the text reads something like "Michael, Gabriel, Raphael, Benedict; gentle intercessor, watch over earth-born beings." Reinhold said that each time he returned to Paris, he visited the museum, forever puzzled by what those words meant.[40] Having spent many years now living within his life story, I suspect that what really attracted him was the artist picturing St. Benedict with the three archangels.

STUDIES IN ROME

From Paris Reinhold took the train to Toulouse, where he transferred to a train heading for Bressanone, where he had once been a seminarian. There he found a small hotel with running water across from the rail station. The next morning, as he related the story, he said Mass in what he thought was the parish church. A "kindly priest" helped him vest, served at the Mass, and then assisted as he unvested. Only later, as they were talking, did the "kindly priest" happen to mention that he was the bishop of Bressanone. Although the bishop pressed him to remain a few days in Bressanone, Reinhold was anxious to get on to Rome to take up his archaeological studies.[41]

Back in Rome, Reinhold was a resident student at the Campo Santo Teutonico, the German Theological College with a high-walled cemetery located immediately beside St. Peter's Basilica. There he enrolled at the newly-established Pontifical Institute of Archaeology,[42] but when

[40] *HAR*, 61.

[41] Ibid., 61.

[42] Originally a commission established by Pius IX (January 6, 1852) "to take care of the ancient sacred cemeteries, look after their preventive preservation, further explorations, research and study, and also safeguard the oldest mementos of the early Christian centuries, the outstanding monuments and venerable Basilicas in Rome, in the Roman suburbs and soil, and in the other Dioceses in agreement with the respective Ordinaries," with the *motu proprio I primitivi cemeteri* of December 11, 1925, Pius XI made the commission pontifical, expanding its powers and establishing the degree-granting institute. See Pontifical Commission for Sacred Archaeology, http://www.vatican.va/roman_curia/pontifical_commissions/archeo/inglese/documents/rc_com_archeo_pro_20011010_pcas_en.html (accessed May 15, 2009).

Bishop Berning asked a few months later that he interrupt these studies to take on a special assignment, Reinhold said he felt no regret. He did not consider the faculty at the institute to be first-rate, found the library holdings meager, and was appalled at the "shoddy approach" to the liturgy. In one of his most honest personal assessments he wrote, "I suppose that at bottom I lacked what the Germans call *Sitzfleisch*—the ability to sit still, a liking for the sedentary life of the scholar."[43]

SEEMANSPASTOR

The assignment the bishop had in mind for Reinhold was an ambitious one—to serve as the bishop's secretary for the seaman's apostolate, responsible for the entire coastal area of Germany. In this capacity he was expected to set up a foundation to support the work and establish a number of seaman's clubs in port cities. Headquartered in Bremerhaven, Reinhold embarked on his new assignment with fervor if not enthusiasm. To the task he brought with him not only his facility with languages, but also his brief experience aboard the SS *Hamburg*, which gave him an intimate understanding of the seaman's lifestyle and mindset.

Although the seaman's apostolate had been established in Germany in 1925, its effectiveness was not ensured until Reinhold's appointment as *Seemanspastor* in 1929. Peter Anson, who wrote extensively about the seaman's apostolate, described Reinhold's holistic approach to the ministry. During a visit to Bermerhaven in early December 1929, shortly after Reinhold had begun his work there, Anson described their conversations in which "Fr. Reinhold expounded his views on the nature of the Catholic sea apostolate. I discovered that they went much deeper than those of the average priest and were based just as much on a profound study of philosophy and theology, not to mention liturgy, as to an immediate sense of the need for purely religious and social work."[44] "Let the seamen pray and sing the Mass, not at Mass—as we do it already in Hamburg," he instructed. "Show them Christ as He is. Teach the sailors to read and meditate on the Gospels."[45]

[43] *HAR*, 62.

[44] Peter F. Anson, *Harbour Head: Maritime Memories* (London: John Gifford Limited, 1944), 176.

[45] Peter F. Anson, *The Church and the Sailor: A Survey of the Sea-Apostolate, Past and Present* (London: Catholic Book Club, 1948), 144.

Today we would say that Reinhold established "base ecclesial communities" among the seamen, but his own words are far more descriptive and cut to the quick. It captures his personality as well as his perspective, which we will see develop throughout his life and ministry.

> A seamen's chapel is not a store-house for cheap plaster statues, oleographs and artificial flowers, with imitation stained-glass windows of stuck-on paper. It is the place where our seafaring brother meets Christ in His Liturgy and a room for private prayer. So do not allow pious but ignorant people to put up images or pictures of their favourite saints—bought in a "Catholic repository"—in every empty space. The one thing necessary all seamen need is the knowledge of Our Lord and vital contact with Him through the Sacraments. There are many good things which are superfluous for our seamen's religious life which is necessarily reduced to the essential and necessary things. So let your chapel be plain and dignified, bright and warm in colours. Bring the sailors close to the altar, so that they may not fail to pray and sacrifice Mass *with* their priest. A "Dialogue Mass" is absolutely necessary if we want to give seamen a firm conviction that Sunday Mass is more than a duty and a legal formality. Dedicate your chapel to the Good Shepherd, Our Saviour, Christ the King (and not to your own pet saint) in order to concentrate all their love and energy to our Lord. Statues or paintings of Our Lady, St. Peter and a local saint will be sufficient for a seamen's chapel, and keep their thoughts on the necessary and fundamental needs of their spiritual life. *Non multa sed multum.*[46]

In every essay Reinhold wrote for those engaged in the seamen's apostolate he emphasized the need for the ministry to "concern itself with the social problems of seafarers, be based on an intimate knowledge of their lives in these times, and attack the evils by an intensive spiritual and educational program." He even visualized retreats for seamen in every large port.[47]

Although Adolf Hitler had not yet come into power when Peter Anson visited Reinhold and his Seaman's Institute in Bremerhaven in 1929, Anson noted that Hitler's "Party" was often spoken about and "one was conscious of a feeling of acute pessimism in the air."[48]

---

[46] Anson, *Harbour Head*, 180–81.
[47] Anson, *The Church and the Sailor*, 145.
[48] Anson, *Harbour Head*, 176.

Although there was no longer a Catholic Seamen's Institute in Bremer-haven when I visited there in 2003, I was able to visit a Seamen's Insti-tute sponsored by the Lutheran Church. The director shared with me what he had learned from his predecessors in the ministry who were active in the apostolate during World War II. It was like hearing an echo of Reinhold's words.

"Everything in Germany was in turmoil at this time," Reinhold ob-served. "Hitler's power was growing, communism was taking root, and the moderate parties had lost control of the government. . . . I was greatly alarmed by the evident progress of Nazism and com-munism in Germany, and foresaw either a civil war or terrible revolution."[49]

Reinhold drew up "naively," as he wrote, a plan in which Catholics would seize the initiative and restore balance in the German govern-ment. "The Church would surrender all properties which were of no direct social use; mansion-like rectories would house the poor; con-vent schools would educate the children of the poor; and the bishops would lead their people in this act of sacrifice by donating large sums of money to impoverished areas."[50] Such idealism and gospel con-sciousness clad Reinhold with a cloak of suspicion, and the govern-ment took covert action to get him out of Germany. Between 1932 and 1935, when he was eventually expelled from Germany by the Gestapo, Reinhold made five all-expense-paid trips to New York, courtesy of the shipping lines. Although he spent most of the trip in the kitchen and below deck, trying to interest the men in the mission, Reinhold spent time aboveboard as well. "The contrast was dramatic. Cham-pagne and sumptuous dinners were served throughout the day, while back home in Germany a depression was ravaging the land and men roamed the streets searching for food. When there is this kind of dis-parity, only calamity can ensue."[51]

For Reinhold calamity struck on January 30, 1933, when Hitler was named chancellor. Because Reinhold was already unpopular with the Nazis, Bishop Wilhelm Berning no longer thought the coastal city Bremerhaven to be a safe place for Reinhold's ministry and therefore

---

[49] *HAR*, 66–67. For a complete analysis of Reinhold's difficulties with the Nazi regime see Jay P. Corrin, "H. A. Reinhold: Liturgical Pioneer and Anti-Fascist," *The Catholic Historical Review* 82 (July 1996): 436–58.

[50] *HAR*, 67.

[51] Ibid., 68.

reassigned him further inland to the port city of Hamburg.[52] There Reinhold continued his work among the seamen for another two years. In his chapel, with an altar facing the congregation, a Dialogue Mass was celebrated every Sunday, with the enthusiastic participation of all. In 1934, when the annual convention of the International Seamen's Apostolate was held in Hamburg, the archbishop of Edinburgh came to celebrate Mass at Reinhold's chapel. Although he was a Benedictine, the archbishop had never participated in such a Mass. Thus, in small but boldly persistent and courageous ways Reinhold's influence and his liturgical apostolate continued to develop in Germany until the inevitable occurred. He wrote, "It was perhaps the saddest day of my life when this hard job after exactly six years of up-hill work was taken out of my hands by five agents of the secret political police on April 30, 1935, and I had to sit down at my own desk to sign the receipt of the decree banishing me from all contacts with the sea and her men 'according to Section I of the Law of the Reich President for the Protection of People and State' under which I had to leave the coast that very afternoon."[53]

Reinhold was instructed to leave the city at once, by way of a particular bridge that would head him toward Munich, which he was instructed was to be his next place of residence. He was given a two-hour reprieve, however, to bid farewell to his mother. On his way out the officer placed a packet containing Reinhold's passport and visa on the secretary's desk, which the secretary concluded was a benevolent hint for Reinhold to leave the country immediately. The secretary, a British citizen, served as a protection while he first visited his mother and then drove to Osnabrück to meet with Bishop Berning, who immediately contacted the Gestapo trying to remedy the situation.

---

[52] According to Robert Krieg, Bishop Wilhelm Berning of Osnabrück and Archbishop Conrad Gröber of Freiburg held favorable views of Hitler. See Robert Krieg, *Catholic Theologians in Nazi Germany* (New York: Continuum, 2004), 6.

[53] H. A. Reinhold, "The Sea for Christ!" *Commonweal* 25 (March 12, 1937): 549–51; here 551.

Chapter 2

Saved for America

LIFE IN EXILE

Within a few days and with the help of a few brave friends, Fr. Reinhold was able to cross the border into Holland and begin his escape to England, with only a toothbrush and a fountain pen. He spent the next few months in England under the protection of friends from the International Apostolatus Maris[1] while he determined where to settle more permanently. Ultimately he wanted to go the United States, but advisors suggested that refugee priests were not readily accepted by American society. Among his advisors was Dorothy Day, who wrote in response to his letter of July 4, 1935:

> If you are banished from port towns, can't you work elsewhere for the time being? It is true that the general feeling here in America is unsympathetic to other nationalities. Also, the people feel that a priest should stay in his own country, on the battlefield as it were, rather than go away somewhere else and leave the people priestless. Also, that he should continue to work under obedience to his Bishop, even though he runs great risk. I have no sympathy for the nationalistic attitude of Americans but with the instinctive feeling of the rank and file that the priest should stay in his own storm-tossed country I do sympathize. Can't you stay in Germany rather than in Switzerland?[2]

Aware that she might have been too simplistic, she concluded the letter: "I am writing your name in my Missal so that I shall not fail to remember you daily in Mass. Please do pray for us too and excuse my

---

[1] See Arthur Gannon, *Apostolatus Maris 1920–1960: The Personal Record of Arthur Gannon* (New Orleans, LA: Apostleship of the Sea, 1965), 25–26. See also H. A. Reinhold, "Don Luigi Sturzo: A Memoir" *Commonweal* 55 (November 30, 1951): 193–95.

[2] Dorothy Day to Fr. H. A. Reinhold, August 12, 1935, Dorothy Day–Catholic Worker Collection (Series D-1, Box 4), Department of Special Collections and University Archives, Marquette University.

presumption in freely expressing my feelings. If I do not know what I am talking about please excuse me."[3]

Despite advice to the contrary and that by someone he deeply admired, that year Reinhold accepted a position as a curate in a parish in Interlacken, Switzerland. Within a month of his arrival, however, he was issued an expulsion order to leave Switzerland within twenty-four hours. When the pastor went to the immigration department with him, even he was treated as a criminal. Only later did they learn that the immigration official had been arrested as a Nazi agent. For Reinhold it was "an instructive lesson on how far spread the nets of the Nazis had been laid"[4] and served to further fuel his desire and efforts to immigrate to the United States with which he had "fallen in love."[5] On August 20, 1936, that dream finally became a reality when Reinhold, aboard the SS *America*, docked in New York Harbor. Freedom at last!

While we might like to think that Reinhold, after being hounded, harassed, and hunted by the Nazis, received a warm welcome in the land of the free and the home of the brave, quite the opposite was the case, just as Dorothy Day had predicted. Within a week of his arrival, for example, the chancellor of the Archdiocese of New York, Msgr. Francis McIntyre,[6] forbade him to give any public lectures. Although he was permitted to say Mass, permission extended no further than that, because the chancellor incorrectly concluded that Reinhold was a Spanish Loyalist.[7] Apparently it was a common presumption in those days that being anti-Nazi was equivalent to being pro-Communist. It would be two years before Reinhold would find a permanent residence and ministry in the United States.

In the meantime, God was preparing Reinhold for the next phase of his mission, for during those two years he made friendships that would endure throughout his life. He took up residence within the Diocese of Brooklyn, at St. Margaret's Rectory in Middle Village,

---

[3] Day to Reinhold, August 12, 1935.

[4] H. A. Reinhold, *H. A. R.: The Autobiography of Father Reinhold* (New York: Herder and Herder, 1968), 94; hereafter cited as *HAR*.

[5] Reinhold, "Don Luigi Sturzo," 195.

[6] Msgr. J. Francis McIntyre later became the ordinary of the Archdiocese of Los Angeles. See Francis J. Weber, *His Eminence of Los Angeles: James Francis Cardinal McIntyre* (Mission Hills, CA: Saint Francis Historical Society, 1997).

[7] See *HAR*, 105–6.

which put him right in the center of a German-speaking community, with easy access to the educational resources of Manhattan. His credentials from the University of Münster enabled him to be matriculated at Columbia University, pursuing a doctorate in history.[8] He also became an integral part of the Catholic intellectual circles in New York and deepened his bonds, which were initially made in his prior visits to New York City, with the Catholic Worker Movement and the *Commonweal* community.[9]

In 1937 Reinhold accepted a position at Portsmouth Abbey School, a residential high school for boys near Newport, Rhode Island, sponsored by the Benedictine community, where he taught dogma and Scripture. While living in New England he was quick to take advantage of the intellectual life of nearby Boston, particularly of Widener Library at Harvard University. "Where Manhattan and Brooklyn were crowded and loud, liberal and progressive, Boston was quiet and by comparison empty, staid and conservative. It was drab and grey, and it made me feel as though I were in Hamburg again."[10] This hardly sounds like high praise to our ears, but for a young man alone and in a foreign land, it probably had the feel of home.

One day, in the sacristy of St. Peter's Church in Cambridge, he met Fr. Emeric Lawrence, OSB, from Saint John's Abbey in Collegeville, Minnesota, who was studying at Harvard. Reinhold was familiar with Saint John's Abbey through the work of Fr. Virgil Michel, whom he deeply admired. It was not surprising, therefore, that Reinhold and Lawrence would develop a long and fruitful relationship.[11]

Through a friend, Reinhold had heard that Gerald Shaughnessy, bishop of Seattle, was looking for a priest who would establish a seaman's apostolate in his diocese. He applied for the position and in the fall of 1938 traveled across America to take up residence in Seattle. Along the way he stopped to visit Saint John's Abbey, where he "captivated

---

[8] Reinhold was admitted to Columbia University in February 1937 and given thirty graduate credits for previous work. (See Box 20, Folder 5, H. A. Reinhold Papers, John J. Burns Library, Boston College.)

[9] See Dorothy Day, "On Pilgrimage—March 1968," *The Catholic Worker* (March 1968): 1, 2, 8. Some of the dates and locations mentioned in this reminiscence of Day's relationship with Reinhold are flawed.

[10] *HAR*, 114.

[11] See Emeric A. Lawrence, "H. A. R.—Death of a Friend," *Commonweal* 87 (March 8, 1968): 686–88.

the young professors, lay and religious," who wanted him to remain at the abbey. Reinhold discussed this possibility with the abbot, Alcuin Deutsch, but the abbot who Reinhold said "welcomed me as though I were his son,"[12] saw that this was in neither's best interest.[13] Reinhold's relationship with Saint John's, however, was not to end there. When Virgil Michel died in November 1938 at only 48 years of age and at the apex of his "influence both in the fields of liturgy and social justice,"[14] Fr. Godfrey Diekmann, who had been serving as managing editor, was appointed to continue Michel's work as editor of *Orate Fratres*.[15] At Lawrence's suggestion, Reinhold was invited to continue writing the monthly Timely Tracts, a popular feature of the magazine originally penned by Michel. Reinhold continued in this ministry for fifteen years.

NORTHWEST PASSAGE

Reinhold's arrival in Seattle on a drizzly day in October of 1938 was unheralded, and from the outset he was regarded with suspicion both by the bishop and his fellow clergy. In those days, as mentioned earlier, his credentials as a refugee from Hitler and opponent of Franco were enough to have him regarded as a leftist and communist sympathizer. By his own admission, Reinhold did not handle this situation well. "I did not have the gift of laughing off my fellow priests' prying questions, but answered honestly and clumsily in my own fashion. I soon became known among the clergy as a dissenter and a man to be treated with great caution."[16]

[12] *HAR*, 124.

[13] See "A," Box 2, Folder 1, H. A. Reinhold Papers, John J. Burns Library, Boston College.

[14] Lawrence, "H. A. R.—Death of a Friend," 686.

[15] Now known as *Worship*, it is published by the monks of Saint John's Abbey, Collegeville, Minnesota. Edited by Dom Virgil Michel, OSB, the first issue appeared on the First Sunday of Advent, 1926. Its primary aim then and for many years thereafter was "to develop a better understanding of the spiritual impact of the liturgy and to promote active participation on the part of all men and women in the worship of the Church." See History of *Worship* Magazine, http://www.saintjohnsabbey.org/worship/worship/page1.htm (accessed May 16, 2009).

[16] *HAR*, 125. Elsewhere Reinhold refers to himself as "blunt and irascible." See Reinhold, "Don Luigi Sturzo," 195.

Before assigning Reinhold to the seaman's apostolate in his diocese, Shaughnessy decided to try him out as a parish assistant to get an idea of what kind of man he was. Staying at the cathedral rectory, with few duties and much free time, Reinhold seized the opportunity to write articles and became active in the liturgical apostolate. Perhaps to stem the tide of that activity, the bishop finally gave Reinhold permission to establish a seamen's club in Seattle the following spring.

Suspicion, however, continued to hound Reinhold, and he was both treated and investigated as a Nazi spy. Despite having to live under this dark cloud, he went about his work among the seamen with enthusiasm, and at the same time became actively involved in the national liturgical apostolate, writing, giving retreats and talks throughout the country, and regularly teaching summer session in various liturgical programs.

In October of 1941 Reinhold was transferred to Yakima, a city in central Washington, about two hundred miles from the coast, but suspicion followed him there and once war was declared in December of that year, he became a virtual prisoner of the rectory. Regarded as an enemy alien, immigration authorities restricted him[17] to a five-mile radius of Yakima and between dusk and dawn he was not permitted to leave the rectory. Since much of the parish at that time extended eighty miles east into the Cascade Mountains, Reinhold's ministry as a parish priest was virtually halted.

Any daytime trip he might want to make first had to be cleared by the enemy-alien control board, but he did manage to get permission to drive to Seattle every other month during 1942. The bishop, however, saw this as Reinhold's failure to cooperate with civil authorities and therefore forbade him to exercise his priestly faculties anywhere but in the Yakima parish church and convent chapel. After a stay of eighteen months, Reinhold was finally able to leave Yakima in the spring of 1943 and return to New York. After lecturing at Mundelein Seminary in Chicago and giving a brief course at Assumption College in Windsor, Ontario, Reinhold settled into Corpus Christi Parish in New York, as the guest of its pastor Fr. George Ford. There in the shadow of

---

[17] A series of presidential proclamations beginning in January 1942 required the registration of "enemy aliens" and increasingly restricted their mobility. See Karen E. Ebel, "German American Internees in the United States during WWII," http://www.traces.org/timeline.aftermath.html (accessed May 16, 2009). See also *HAR*, 129–32.

Columbia University he was able to do the kind of parish work from which he had been prevented all the years he had been in Seattle. During that year he also completed work on an edited volume of spiritual writings, *The Soul Afire*,[18] which had been commissioned by Kurt and Helen Wolff, editors and publishers at Pantheon, who wanted to publish an anthology of mystical writings similar to the German anthology edited by Deitrich von Hildebrand.

Reinhold's return trip to the West Coast, however, was as exuberant as his journey eastward had been labored, because in April 1944 he received a telegram from the Federal Court House in Yakima informing him that he had finally been accepted as an American citizen. Following the naturalization ceremony, he drove to Seattle to see Bishop Shaughnessy, who was exceedingly surprised at this turn of events. Every false rumor about Reinhold had found its way to Shaughnessy's desk, but after carefully examining the citizenship papers, he immediately offered Reinhold a pastorate. "After all that has happened, I am going to have to give you a parish, because I want to make up for what you have been through. I hope you don't mind one of the leftovers. There aren't any fancy parishes around."[19] Reinhold was given the pastorate of St. Joseph's in Sunnyside, which also encompassed the mission churches of Bickleton, Grandview, Granger, and Mabton.[20]

Today Sunnyside lies in the heart of Wine Country in the Yakima Valley, known for its magnificent fruit orchards. When Reinhold arrived there on Labor Day afternoon in 1944, however, it gave all the evidence of being a little village on the edge of nowhere. His description gives us a glimpse of what he found there: "The next morning I went over to the church to say Mass. It was not locked, because there was no key. There was a hole between the front wall and the roof, and sparrows nested there. There was no sacristy, but a small area curtained off from the rest of the sanctuary served as a vesting place. The altar was a home-brew of bad taste and design, and was covered with

[18] See H. A. Reinhold, *The Soul Afire: Revelations of the Mystics* (New York: Pantheon Books, 1944).

[19] *HAR*, 138.

[20] Bickleton, thirty-five miles southwest of Sunnyside, no longer has a Catholic presence; Blessed Sacrament in Grandview, six miles southeast, was established in 1954; Our Lady of Guadalupe in Granger, nine miles west, was established in 1966; and Mabton, seven miles south, is now a mission of the Grandview parish.

dust. The linen was tattered, and the hangers in the closet were rusty. Nobody was at Mass that morning, because no one had expected me to be there."[21]

The parish register had not been updated since 1933. Assisted only by that register and the local telephone directory, Reinhold's next task was to locate parishioners. Although given his experience and interest in the liturgical movement one might expect that he would have begun in earnest to reshape the community, he did not take that approach. Rather, he decided to let the parishioners become accustomed to him and to have the experience of worshiping in pleasant surroundings before he introduced any liturgical changes. By the time Lent arrived, however, he had Dialogue Mass cards printed and encouraged active participation in the Mass. Parishioners responded enthusiastically.[22]

Reinhold was to remain in Sunnyside for twelve years, until 1956, although during the summers he usually took a leave of absence to conduct a school of liturgy on campuses across the country.[23] The parishioners knew of this interest and some also knew of his writings in *Commonweal* and *Orate Fratres*. It was this, Reinhold believed, that gave an "air of respectability" to the innovations he introduced into the parish, which might otherwise have been regarded simply as the "whims of a liturgical avant-guardist."[24]

Reinhold's interests and concerns were not only liturgical, for he continued to make the essential connection between worship and justice. Just as he had done with the seamen, Reinhold formed an educated Catholic community in Sunnyside. He brought people of like interests and needs together, met with them, prayed with them, taught them, and challenged them. For example, he brought together young couples in mixed marriages, and met with them regularly to discuss the particular challenges that were theirs.[25] He worked with teenagers on faith formation and took them on trips into the wilderness, just

---

[21] *HAR*, 139.

[22] Ibid., 140.

[23] Among these were Assumption College, Windsor, Ontario (1943); Mundelein Seminary, Chicago, Illinois (1943); St. Mary's College, Notre Dame, Indiana (1944); The University of Notre Dame, Notre Dame, Indiana (1944–1949).

[24] *HAR*, 140.

[25] Interview with Mrs. Marian Tanasse of Sunnyside, WA, June 7, 2000.

as other pastors had done in Germany when he was young.[26] When large numbers of Mexican migrant workers began moving into the area, he formed groups of adults and teens among them as well, and involved other parishioners in caring for their physical and spiritual needs. Rather than establish these groups entirely by himself, however, he employed another strategy. First he identified a leader in the community itself, invited that person to use his or her gifts for the community and then empowered the person to bring others together. Thus he developed lifelong leadership in them from which the state of Washington still benefits today.[27]

In 1953, after fifteen years of faithful service, Reinhold resigned as author of *Worship*'s monthly Timely Tracts, although he continued to write for that periodical occasionally. He wanted to direct his increasingly limited energy to those who still needed convincing, and regarded *Worship* readers to be the already convinced. To those who would grieve this loss and write letters trying to entice him to remain he wrote, "Don't write me—write for your diocesan weekly, for secular papers, for *Worship*, in letters to the editor, in short articles and long: but let us all keep going, because if liturgy has taught us one thing it is to feel responsibility and to participate!"[28]

Diagnosed with Parkinson's disease in the mid 1950s, once again plagued by difficulties with the local bishop, and wanting to devote more of his time to writing, Reinhold asked to resign from his parish responsibilities in February 1956. After several months of negotiation, he left Sunnyside on May 28, 1956, with what he thought was the bishop's blessing. Unfortunately some miscommunication led to a dreadful misunderstanding and he was accused of desertion. Thus, in what should have been a time for this good servant to rest from his many labors, to redirect his energy and ministry now challenged by a debilitating disease, Reinhold once again found himself wandering alone on alien soil.

Among Reinhold's papers in the Burns Library is an essay he wrote around 1956.[29] In "The Two Flights" he compares and contrasts his

---

[26] Interview with Roger Garrison, Esq., of Sunnyside, WA, June 7–8, 2000.

[27] Interview with Mr. Jose Resendez of Sunnyside, WA, June 8, 2000.

[28] H. A. Reinhold "Turning Point: Lugano," *Worship* 27 (1953): 557–63; here 563.

[29] See John A. Reinhold, "The Two 'Flights,' 1935 and 1956," Box 15, Folder 47, H. A. Reinhold Papers, John J. Burns Library, Boston College. (The author

escape from the Nazis to his departure from Sunnyside. From the context of the essay one can see that it is an apologia, defending himself against those who had accused him of desertion. Correspondence with Bishop Dougherty and other diocesan officials substantiating his claims is also among his papers.[30] Appended to the manuscript is a letter to "John" advising him not to submit this essay for publication. The letter is signed "Fred" with St. Clement Hall as the return address. Fr. (later Msgr.) Frederick McManus, canonist and liturgical scholar, served as an advisor to Reinhold during these "troubles." I was blessed to have a thirty-year relationship with McManus dating back to my time as an advisor to the bishops' Committee on the Liturgy.[31]

When I interviewed him at the very beginning of my research on Reinhold, McManus immediately related the entire saga of "the troubles." Because Reinhold's autobiography ends in 1956, despite the fact that it was not published until 1968, and no reference to "the troubles" ever appeared in print, until McManus rolled out the sad saga for me, I had no knowledge of it. Although he was not silenced, while Reinhold was being investigated all of his writings had to be cleared by the local bishop before they could be submitted for publication. McManus explained that in that era the sanctions could have been much worse. Reinhold could have been silenced or could have even had his faculties suspended or revoked.

Reinhold initially returned to the greater Boston area, where he had good friends and advisors who offered him hospitality, spiritual and psychological counsel, and medical care. He was in residence in Sacred Heart Parish, Roslindale, in the recently erected diocese of Worcester, where his friend Msgr. Edward Murray was pastor.[32] There Reinhold also enjoyed the patronage and protection of the local

---

on the manuscript is Fr. John A. Reinhold. During a brief period of his life Reinhold Anglicized his first name.)

[30] See "Bishop Dougherty," Box 3, Folder 26; Box 4, Folder 1, H. A. Reinhold Papers, John J. Burns Library, Boston College.

[31] Now named the Committee for Divine Worship, this is one of the standing committees of the United States Conference of Catholic Bishops.

[32] The Diocese of Worcester, carved out of the Archdiocese of Boston, was erected on January 18, 1950. John Wright, an auxiliary bishop in Boston, was named Worcester's first bishop and enthroned on March 7, 1950.

ordinary, Bishop John Wright.[33] Another good friend living in the Boston area, Fr. Thomas J. Carroll,[34] assisted with Reinhold's medical care. Carroll's brother-in-law, Thomas E. Caulfield, MD, was a renowned psychiatrist in the area who continued to care for Reinhold even at a distance until his death.

When Reinhold's condition improved sufficiently he went to live in the Catskill village of Wurtsboro, New York, where he helped the pastor, Fr. Harold Smith, minister to the people of St. Joseph's parish there and neighboring parishes in the area as needed.[35] In 1959, when he was appointed bishop of Pittsburgh, and Reinhold's canonical issues had been resolved, Wright welcomed him to that diocese, where he was incardinated in 1961.

During his remaining years in active ministry Reinhold served on Pittsburgh's liturgical commission and as chaplain to a girls' academy, and he continued to publish articles, reviews, and books. At the same time he continued to be an active member of the Liturgical Conference, attending its annual Liturgical Conferences when he was physically able.

In 1963 Reinhold underwent intricate brain surgery at St. Bartholomew Hospital in New York City. Pioneered by Irving S. Cooper,[36] cryosurgery involved freezing the section of the brain that controlled nerves causing the tremors. According to his Christmas letter of 1964 Reinhold told friends that recovery from surgery took almost a year. Although more surgery on the other side of the brain might have eased or eliminated tremors on the other side of his body, he decided the risk of losing his ability to speak was too great.[37] For as long as he was able Reinhold continued to write pastoral articles for a wide variety of Catholic periodicals despite the continuing advance of Parkin-

[33] According to Fr. Edmond Bliven, it was Msgr. Thomas Tobin, the vicar general of the Portland diocese, who connected Reinhold with Wright (interview, December 19, 2001).

[34] Although better known nationally and internationally for his pioneering rehabilitation work with the blind, Carroll was an active member and leader in the Liturgical Conference from its beginnings in 1940 until his untimely death in 1971.

[35] Interview with Msgr. Dermot Brennan, March 21, 2004.

[36] See Kaushik Das, Deborah L. Benzil, Richard L. Rovit, Raj Murali, and William T. Couldwell, "Irving S. Cooper (1922–1985): A Pioneer in Functional Neurosurgery," *Journal of Neurosurgery* 89 (1998): 865–73.

[37] Interview with Judy and Vincent Lackner, November 1, 2003.

son's disease. By 1966, however, his condition had worsened so much that he moved to the Vincentian Home, a recently expanded residence for the chronically ill sponsored by the Vincentian Sisters of Charity with a separate wing for priests, which is still in operation today.[38]

Reinhold spent Christmas 1967 at Mount Saviour and his dear friend, Fr. Damasus Winzen, the prior of Mount Saviour, reflected on those days in his lengthy tribute to Reinhold in the monastery's newsletter:

> It was a great joy to all of us here at Mount Saviour that during his last visit here . . . he was full of peace and joy. I shall never forget the childlike happiness that radiated from his face when, on Christmas morning, Roselinde Albrecht, who works with Herder, was able to present him with the first copy of his Memoirs. It came as a great surprise to him, somewhat like a rainbow, a sign of peace and reconciliation over his life. One can say that his whole stay with us during those weeks, the end of the old and beginning of the New Year, was a wonderful Finale of his life.[39]

Back in Pittsburgh, while recovering from surgery for an intestinal obstruction, Reinhold died at Mercy Hospital in Pittsburgh on January 26, 1968. At the funeral liturgy, which was celebrated at St. Paul's Cathedral in Pittsburgh, Reinhold's gift to the church was expressed well by the homilist, Fr. William C. Clancy:

> What we celebrate here today and give thanks for is a public life, a public ministry, and a public example—a life, a ministry, and an example that taught many in our generation and will teach many for generations to come. But . . . many of us come also to pay a debt— the greatest of all debts, the debt of faith itself. Because Hans Ansgar Reinhold taught us (some of us when we were very young, some of us when we were older) to see in a way we had not seen before, in a way we had not suspected was possible before we read him or knew him. He taught us to see the very things we celebrate today—the mystery

[38] See Vincentian Home, http://www.vcs.org/html/vincentian_home.html (accessed May 16, 2009).

[39] Damasus Winzen, "In the Memory of Msgr. Wolodimir Pylypetz and Rev. H. A. Reinhold," *Mount Saviour Chronicle* 32 (Pentecost 1968): 2–3; here 3.

and the joy of the church, that is, the mystery and the joy of the resurrection and the glory of Christ Jesus.[40]

His earthly remains lie close to a statue of the Good Shepherd in the oblate cemetery at Mount Saviour in Elmira, New York. We can only hope that his spirit remains with us, urging us to celebrate well the mystery of faith around the table of the Lord and in deeds of justice. Writing about his dear friend, Fr. Emeric Lawrence, OSB, noted, "Father Reinhold never rested in his life. He would not want to rest now. For him life has changed, it has not been taken away. And of one thing I am sure: he knows now, as he may not have known while he was with us, that it has all been enormously worthwhile."[41]

---

[40] William C. Clancy, "In Memoriam: H.A.R.," *Worship* 42, no. 3 (March 1968): 130–33; here 130.

[41] Lawrence, "H. A. R.—Death of a Friend," 688.

Chapter 3

Liturgical Movement as Heritage

THE CHURCH AT PRAYER

Gathered around the table of the Lord to celebrate Eucharist today, we look back fifty years to the convocation of the Second Vatican Council as the beginning of a new era. In 1960 the congregation knelt behind the altar of the Lord in silence, watching the back of a priest who prayed in a language that was not our own, no longer anyone's native tongue. The congregation seemed to be pious, but practice determined that they were also silent and appeared to be passive.[1] "Silent spectators," was the pejorative term used by Pius XI in the apostolic constitution *Divini cultus* (December 20, 1928): "It is most important that when the faithful assist at the sacred ceremonies . . . they should not be merely detached and silent spectators." This concept became a foundational principle of the liturgical movement in the United States.

From today's perspective there were also some peculiarities of that era that are essential to explain if you did not experience them yourself or have forgotten them, because they provide the backdrop for appreciating Reinhold's legacy. Although probably not universal, they were common enough to draw the attention of those who knew better.

Born in 1946, I began attending Our Lady Queen of Martyrs parish elementary school in February 1952. In those days New York City schools enrolled students in February as well as September, a practice that was abolished around 1956. It was expected that we would attend the 9:00 a.m. children's Mass on Sundays, and on Monday morning report not only our church attendance but also whether we had received Holy Communion. "Present, Mass and Communion!" was the intended response. The data was not only recorded by our teachers—all religious sisters in that era—but also noted on our report cards each semester.

---

[1] *Divini cultus*, December 20, 1928, in *Acta Apostolica Sedis* (*AAS*) 21 (1928): 33–41.

Fast regulations at the time of my First Holy Communion in June of 1953 forbade any food or drink after midnight, but these regulations were relaxed the following year to permit water after midnight. The regulations were further relaxed in 1957 to permit food and alcohol up to three hours before, other liquids up to an hour before receiving Holy Communion, and water anytime. Junior legalists, we were also scrupulous clock watchers and anxious that we allow the full hour or three hours to elapse before joining the procession to communion.

You see, it was all about receiving Holy Communion; that was the focus of attention, not celebrating Eucharist as it is today. Holy Communion and Mass were divorced in our consciousness because practice rather than theology made it so. Altar servers of that era have told me that if they were assigned to serve a late morning Mass, they were expected to receive communion at the first morning Mass, and then return home for breakfast before serving their assigned Mass. These altar boys of yesteryear also mentioned that the sisters teaching in the parish school received Communion *before* Mass both on Sundays and weekdays so that they could leave Mass early and attend to their other charges. In fact, Communion was often moved for the sake of convenience. On holy days in large city parish churches the distribution of Holy Communion might begin right after the gospel when additional priests would appear in the sanctuary to accommodate the crowds. That way the distribution of Holy Communion would not delay the Mass. Imagine that—Communion delaying Mass! Yes, by today's ecclesiological standards it is easy for us to see that these practices were in definite need of reform. Not everyone had the luxury of that perspective, however.

Forty Hours Devotion, Benediction, Adoration of the Blessed Sacrament, and other devotional practices seemed to have a higher place in the spiritual life of 1950s Catholics than daily Mass had. It might even be that Sunday Mass only received attention because missing Mass was still viewed as a grave sin. Our parish church was crowded for Miraculous Medal Devotions on Monday evenings and Stations of the Cross on Friday nights during Lent. From my child's-eye view, however, I saw that adults rarely came to Sunday Mass on time and hardly ever received Holy Communion.

To be perfectly honest, even as I moved toward adulthood, I rarely questioned any of these practices. That is just the way it was. Questioning one's practices, however, is critical, because only by doing so do we come to understand motivation and then dig deeper to an appreciation of the underlying theology.

PROBING AT PRACTICE

This story has been told and retold so many times that unfortunately I no longer recall its original source. Nonetheless, I remain grateful to the now-anonymous original teller and the lessons my students and I continue to draw from it.

A young woman recently married was helping her mother prepare the annual Thanksgiving feast. On the menu was a fresh ham, and she noticed that in preparing the meat for the roasting pan, her mother cut off the narrow end of the ham. Eager to learn how to become more adept in the kitchen herself, the young woman asked many questions that day about the process of preparing the traditional family foods.

Expecting that the narrow end of the ham might actually be the most delicious portion, she wondered why it was being discarded and so she asked her mother.

"That's the way my mother taught me," was the mother's response. "I think it has something to do with distributing the juices better, but you'll have to ask your grandmother."

That explanation was even more confusing than the procedure itself, so the young woman waited for her grandmother to arrive hoping she would get a better response, but her grandmother's explanation proved to be no better than her mother's had been. "That's the way my mother taught me to prepare the ham. I never asked why."

Fortunately her great-grandmother was also expected for the feast and no sooner did Grammy have her coat off than the young woman began asking: "Why do you cut off the narrow end of the ham before cooking it?"

"Cut it off!" she exploded. "Why would you do that? That's the most tender part."

The young woman explained how she watched her mother prepare the ham and questioned when she saw her cut off and discard the narrow end. Both her mother and grandmother told her that Grammy was the source of the practice. Then Grammy got a faraway look in her eye and gradually began to smile.

"I think I understand," she chuckled. "Long ago in the old apartment when your grandmother was young I only had a small baking pan, so I probably cut off the small end of the ham to fit the pan. What amazes me is that those two have been discarding all that juicy meat for fifty years. Why didn't they just ask?"

Precisely! Why don't we just ask? Why do we take experience for granted and fail to probe it more directly and intensely?

That is exactly what Reinhold did for his entire life—probe at practice. He did this with neither guile nor timidity. More often than not his directness drew criticism, and by his own admission he realized that he could often be too blunt.[2]

Beginning with his debut sequence in *Orate Fratres*, "More or Less Liturgical,"[3] down to the coda, "Timely Questions," in *The Living Light*,[4] Reinhold began with practice and then skillfully dug deeper to the historical and theological core, teaching readers—students, colleagues, priests, bishops, and parishioners—the way to worship in spirit and truth, and not simply on automatic pilot because it was the way they always did it or, more to the point, thought it was always done.

THE SPRIT OF THE LITURGY

As was mentioned in chapter 1, Reinhold's discovery of Romano Guardini's small book *The Spirit of the Liturgy* in 1919 proved to be a turning point in his life, giving him "not so much new insight into the liturgy as a positive attitude towards Catholic teachings."[5]

> The primary and exclusive aim of the liturgy is not the expression of the individual's reverence and worship for God. It is not even concerned with the awakening, formation, and sanctification of the individual soul as such. Nor does the onus of liturgical action and

[2] Reinhold refers to himself as "blunt and irascible" in "Don Luigi Sturzo: A Memoir," *Commonweal* 55 (November 30, 1951): 193–95; here 195.

[3] See H. A. Reinhold, "More or Less Liturgical [#1]," *Orate Fratres* 13 (February 1939): 152–55; "More or Less Liturgical [#2]," *Orate Fratres* 13 (March 1939): 213–18; "More or Less Liturgical [#3]," *Orate Fratres* 13 (April 1939): 257–63.

[4] H. A. Reinhold, "Timely Questions," *The Living Light* 1, no. 1 (Spring 1964): 130–34; 1, no. 2 (Summer 1964): 162–65; 1, no. 3 (Fall 1964): 142–45; 1, no. 4 (Winter 1965): 134–37; 2, no. 1 (Spring 1965): 142–45; 2, no. 2 (Summer 1965): 142–45; 2, no. 3 (Fall 1965): 122–24; 2, no. 4 (Winter 1966): 118–21; 3, no. 1 (Spring 1966): 82–85; 3, no. 2 (Summer 1966): 121–23. In the bibliography I have listed the topic of each essay parenthetically.

[5] H. A. Reinhold, *H. A. R.: The Autobiography of Father Reinhold* (New York: Herder and Herder, 1968), 38; hereafter cited as *HAR*.

prayer rest with the individual. It does not even rest with the collective groups, composed of numerous individuals, who periodically achieve a limited and intermittent unity in their capacity as the congregation of a church. The liturgical entity consists rather of the united body of the faithful as such—the Church—a body which infinitely outnumbers the mere congregation.[6]

You can almost see the young Hans burning the midnight oil reading and rereading Guardini into the early hours of the morning. What he found there for the first time it would seem was an appreciation for the core principle of liturgy, its essence.

His months as a novice at Maria Laach under the leadership of Abbot Ildefons Herwegen and Prior Albert Hammenstede described earlier, where both the study and the practice of liturgy were daily sustenance, strengthened and expanded his experience of that inner core.[7] At Maria Laach he also began a lifelong relationship with Dom Odo Casel who was both mentor and friend.[8] Along with Reinhold's growing appreciation of Dom Odo Casel's *mysterytheologie*[9] was his grasp of the history of the liturgy as seen through the writings of fathers of the church, particularly the development of the liturgical year. Evidence of all this abounds in Reinhold's subsequent writings, and his first publications were actually as a research assistant for Casel.[10] "When one has been forty years a labourer in the field one cannot avoid soaking up information in the field of one's interest. It helped that I was a life

[6] Romano Guardini, *The Spirit of the Liturgy*, trans. Ada Lane (London: Sheed & Ward, 1930), 5–6.

[7] Maria Laach at that time was the headquarters of the Society for the Promotion of the Science of Liturgy (Verein zur Pflege der Liturgiewissenschaft E. V.), which published ten volumes of *Liturgiegeschichtliche Forschungen* (*Research on the History of the Liturgy*); eleven volumes of *Liturgiegeschichtliche Quellen* (*Source Books for the History of Liturgy*); and *Jahrbuch für Liturgiewissenschaft* (the *Yearbook of Liturgical Studies*). See Gerald Ellard, "'A Spiritual Citadel of the Rhineland': Maria Laach and the Liturgical Movement," *Orate Fratres* 3 (October 6, 1929): 384–88.

[8] See H. A. Reinhold, "Dom Odo Casel," *Orate Fratres* 22 (1948): 366–72.

[9] See L. M. McMahon, "Toward a Theology of Liturgy: Dom Odo Casel and the *Mysterientheorie*," *Studia Liturgica* 3 (1964): 129–54.

[10] HAR letter to Abbot Ildefons Herwegen, January 21, 1927. Archives, Maria Laach Abbey.

long friend of such mines of information as Dom Odo Casel and many more."[11]

Like Reinhold I had a similar turning point in my understanding and appreciation of the liturgy. In the parish elementary school where I sang in the choir beginning in the third grade, my first lessons in the real meaning of liturgy came with the final revision of the Holy Week liturgy in 1955.[12] Not only did the choir learn the new music, but our enlightened choir director also meticulously explained the reason for these changes. Similarly, my mother bought every pamphlet printed on the subject of these reforms, so we were not just observers of the changes, we knew them by heart and lived them deeply in the moment. Mother also imposed another liturgical practice on her daughters. Saturday nights after we had our baths and our hair had been washed and curled in preparation for being our Sunday best, Mother would have us read the Sunday gospel. At the time it seemed like a huge imposition on our free time, which we would have rather spent reading Nancy Drew or some other novel. Now I see just how devout Mother was, and how she unknowingly shaped me into a student of liturgy.

I spent the Vatican II years in college in Ohio, where the emerging council documents instantly became our textbooks. As an English major, I even covered the council for our college paper. I sang in the chapel choir and attended daily Mass, encouraged actually by my roommate's father who thought we should take advantage of the luxury of having the college chapel in our dorm building. When I returned to New York after graduation, however, it was to a parish experience that seemed untouched by the council. This confused me, left me frustrated and longing for the participative liturgies I had left behind in Ohio.

After completing a master's degree in English, I took a graduate course in theology, still wondering if my experience of the liturgy in college had been genuine or just a mirage. That one course in the history of the liturgy changed my life and set me on the trajectory that

---

[11] H. A. Reinhold, "A Liturgical Reformer Sums Up," *New Blackfriars* 46 (1965): 554–61; here 559.

[12] *AAS* 47 (1955): 838–47. The unexpected experimental revisions to the Holy Week liturgy came as a one-year trial in 1951, and extended the following year for another three years. See *AAS* 43 (1951): 130–37; *AAS* 44 (1952): 48–63.

has become my life. Not just a theorist, like Reinhold I have been fortunate to be able to play an active role in the pastoral application of liturgy to varying degrees on international, national, diocesan, and parish levels.

A BACKWARD GLANCE

Depending on one's experience of the liturgical changes that Vatican II encouraged, a backward glance is one of either joyful enthusiasm or disgruntled despair. For some people, the fifty years has been a time of painful grief during which it seemed that everything they associated with Catholicism had either been called into question or had vanished from the only world they had ever known. "When will these changes be done?" they groused. At the same time, others have lived those five decades eagerly responding as the changes gained momentum and became part of the fabric of our lives. They saw the years strip away cultural accretions and affectations that masked the church that Jesus called us to be. Fifty years later we all look back, but we see with different eyes the church and the liturgy we once knew.

In order to gauge accurately how much has already been accomplished, it is important to put the liturgical changes into their historical context.[13] After the council, but prior to the publication of the Roman Missal in 1969, there was a good bit of experimentation with the form and structure of the liturgy—some sanctioned; others not. The morning of Reinhold's funeral at St. Paul's Cathedral in Pittsburgh, there was a discussion about whether the eucharistic prayer should be prayed in Latin or English. Reinhold's priest friends who assembled to celebrate lobbied for the vernacular, which had for so many years been a focus of his work and suffering. Bishop Wright as ordinary and principal celebrant, however, won the day and as a final irony Reinhold's funeral Mass, apart from the readings, was celebrated in Latin.[14]

---

[13] For a complete discussion see Keith F. Pecklers, *The Unread Vision: The Liturgical Movement in the United States of America, 1926–1955* (Collegeville, MN: Liturgical Press, 1998). See also Julia Upton, "Carpe Momentum: Liturgical Studies at the Threshold of the Millennium," in *At the Threshold of the Third Millennium*, ed. Francis A. Eigo, 103–38 (Villanova, PA: Villanova University Press, 1998).

[14] Conversation with Dr. Vincent Lackner, a close friend who served as lector at Reinhold's funeral and was present for this discussion (interview, October 31, 2004).

As mentioned previously, when we look to the roots of the liturgical changes that stem from the Second Vatican Council, we find the Benedictines, with one hardy root reaching back into the nineteenth century to the Benedictine Abbey of Maria Laach in Germany. There the monks, dedicated to the study of the liturgy, concentrated their scholarly pursuits on examining the early sacramentaries and commentaries on liturgical celebrations. As a result, they restored for us an understanding of the way in which our ancestors celebrated the sacramental moments of their lives—the communal celebrations of their encounters with the God of history. Many of the manuscripts with which they worked had been lost to scholars of previous centuries.[15] Consequently, in the twentieth century we had the means to connect with our liturgical heritage in a way that was unavailable to previous generations.[16]

Although some critics would have us believe that those changes in the liturgy were originally instigated by a vocal minority of religious blackguards and malcontents, among the roots instead we find the authority of the papacy. Front and center was Pius X, who early in the twentieth century encouraged both the study of the liturgy and the restoration of its classical form, particularly in his *motu proprio* on sacred music (1903), which actually addressed a far broader subject than just music. He wrote, "Filled as we are with a most ardent desire to see the true Christian spirit flourish in every respect and be preserved by all the faithful, we deem it necessary to provide before aught else for the sanctity and dignity of the temple, in which the faithful assemble for no other object than that of acquiring this spirit from its foremost and indispensable fount, which is the active participation in the most holy mysteries and in the public and solemn prayer of the Church."[17]

---

[15] Two of the earliest documents in the history of the liturgy, for example, were only found to be extant in the nineteenth century. The *Didache* (c. 115), which contains the earliest references to Eucharist and baptism, was discovered in 1873, and the *Apostolic Tradition of Hippolytus*, which gives us the oldest eucharistic anaphora, was not identified as such until 1906.

[16] For a complete history, see Joseph A. Jungmann, *The Early Liturgy* (Notre Dame, IN: University of Notre Dame Press, 1959); Jungmann, *The Mass of the Roman Rite* (New York: Benziger, 1951–55); Theodor Klauser, *A Short History of the Western Liturgy: An Account and Some Reflections*, trans. John Haliburton (London: Oxford, 1969).

[17] Pius X, *Tra le sollecitudini*, November 22, 1903, as found in *Acta Sancta Sedis*, 36 (1904): 329–39; here 331. The Latin text can be found in *AAS* 36 (1904): 387–95.

Worship in Spirit and Truth

In numerous other documents he continued to echo his concern for the proper celebration of the liturgy by the clergy and the active participation of the faithful.[18]

In the crypt beneath the main altar of the abbey church of Maria Laach, Prior Albert Hammenstede regularly celebrated Eucharist with the novices and other young people who came to the abbey for retreat or inquiry into the monastic life. The altar faced the community and the presider engaged the assembly in a Dialogue Mass, developing an experience of "full and active participation" and shaping the liturgy that was to come. Maria Laach was not the only place in Western Europe where such explorations were happening, but for such a small chapel it had a mighty impact on the way we worship today.[19]

When I visited Maria Laach in the summer of 2001 I spent a good bit of time in the crypt, "with all the saints," as I wrote in my journal. "Tourists come in and out, Prufrock-like, perhaps unaware of where they trod. Such a small place to have had such a large role in Liturgical history!"

It was truly a privilege to have Fr. Burkhard Neunheuser to interview and serve as tour guide for two days. We had met several years before during one of his summers at Mount Saviour, but that was little more than a chance meeting. This time I had come to draw on his memory of Reinhold, back to 1922 when they were both novices at Maria Laach. At the time of my visit, Neunheuser was ninety-seven years young, with an amazing amount of energy and stamina.

Although he would disagree with me, Neunheuser's English was quite good, and he spoke lovingly about "Father Ansgar," his time at Maria Laach, and his contribution to the church. Reinhold was older than the other novices, and because he had served in active duty during World War I he was also older in the ways of the world, one might say. That broader experience, Neunheuser believed, made Reinhold more "impatient" and more "dynamic." The novice master also named Reinhold infirmarian, perhaps because of his wartime experience in hospitals.

---

[18] See Godfrey Diekmann, "Lay Participation in the Liturgy of the Church," in *A Symposium on the Life and Work of Pope Pius X* (Washington, DC: Confraternity on Christian Doctrine, 1949), 137–58.

[19] See Burkhard Neunheuser, "Die 'Krypta-Messe' in Maria Laach, Ein Beitrag zur Frühgeschichte der Gemeinschaftemesse," *Liturgie und Monchtum* 28 (1961): 70–82.

During our first interview, Neunheuser and I sat in one of the parlors; the next day, however, he arrived with hearing aids, a cane as well as his walker on wheels, and a plan. Besides regaling me with more stories about Reinhold and the abbey's history, he also took me to what he called the "soul" of the abbey—the library. The time vanished, and our visit ended with noonday prayer. I am sure that it took Neunheuser a month to recover from my visit, but he left me with a treasure much greater than I expected, particularly his conclusion that "Father Ansgar was saved for the United States."

Among the roots of the liturgical changes we also find Pius XII, who, with the publication of *Mediator Dei* in 1947, implicitly acknowledged that the efforts of his predecessor needed to be resumed in order to revitalize the liturgy and to allow it once again to be the work and deed of the praying community of believers.[20]

AMERICAN LITURGICAL MOVEMENT

We can almost precisely date the beginning of the American liturgical movement to 1925 when Virgil Michel, OSB, a monk of Saint John's Abbey in Collegeville, Minnesota, went abroad to continue his studies in philosophy at Sant'Anselmo in Rome. There he came to know Dom Lambert Beauduin, a Benedictine monk of Mont Cesar Abbey, who was teaching ecclesiology and liturgy at Sant'Anselmo. According to Colman Barry, OSB, chronicler of the history of Saint John's Abbey, it was "this Belgian pioneer in the modern liturgical revival . . . [who] stimulated Michel's interest in the renaissance of sacramental, liturgical piety based on a realization of the nature of the Church as the Mystical Body of Christ."[21] It is also interesting to note that Reinhold dedicated one of his last books to Beauduin, "a prophet in his own country and first articulate promoter of a better understanding of Pastoral Liturgy . . . this book is a token of gratitude and a small monument."[22]

---

[20] See Pius XII, *Mediator Dei*, nos. 4–5. See also Frederick McManus, "The Sacred Liturgy: Tradition and Change," in *Remembering the Future: Vatican II and Tomorrow's Liturgical Agenda*, ed. Carl Last, 11–32 (New York: Paulist Press, 1983).

[21] Colman Barry, *Worship and Work: Saint John's Abbey and University, 1856–1980* (Collegeville, MN: Liturgical Press, 1980), 265.

[22] H. A. Reinhold, *The Dynamics of Liturgy* (New York: Macmillan, 1961), ix.

Michel has been called "the first twentieth-century American prophet of the new Catholicism" as one of the few American Catholics who was able to "identify the problems of contemporary Christianity as identical with the problems of contemporary secular society."[23] Barry explained that Michel's letters home to Abbot Alcuin encouraged him to make Saint John's Abbey a center for liturgical study and writing, for "he had caught the vision of the potentialities of worshiping Christians realizing their oneness in the Mystical Body of Christ, actively participating in the liturgical and corporate life of the Church and carrying this spirit over into American society."[24]

Although Virgil Michel died in 1938, for forty years, from 1926 until the Second Vatican Council was called by John XXIII in 1961,[25] the ground for reform was prepared by the work he initiated and by the pioneers he gathered and inspired. His most enduring contribution, still an active force more than seventy-five years after its establishment in 1926, is the journal *Worship*. Originally titled *Orate Fratres*, the periodical's original mission was to serve the liturgical apostolate. Michel gathered a broad and diverse editorial board, which from the beginning was a collaboration of laypeople and religious on both sides of the Atlantic Ocean, most of whom continued to serve for many years.[26] Initially the magazine's masthead identified its mission to serve the "liturgical apostolate," and Michel had very specific ideas regarding the characteristics of this service. For him it was essential to emphasize the corporate nature of the church, to underscore the intrinsic relationship between worship and the daily lives of church

---

[23] R. W. Franklin and Robert L. Spaeth, *Virgil Michel: American Catholic* (Collegeville, MN: Liturgical Press, 1988), 32. See also Paul Marx, *Virgil Michel and the Liturgical Movement* (Collegeville, MN: Liturgical Press, 1957).

[24] Barry, *Worship and Work*, 265.

[25] Although John XXIII announced his intention to call the twenty-first ecumenical council of the Roman Catholic Church upon his installation on January 25, 1959, the council was not actually summoned to Rome until December 25, 1961.

[26] Members of the first advisory board (1926–1927) were: Mr. Donald Attwater, Wales; Rev. William Busch, St. Paul, MN; Rev. Patrick Cummins, OSB, Conception, MO; Rev. Gerald Ellard, SJ, St. Louis, MO; Mother Mary Ellerker, Duluth, MN; Rev. Jeremiah C. Harrington (+ June 5, 1926); Rev. Martin B. Hellriegel, O'Fallon, MO; Rt. Rev. F. G. Holwek (+ Feb. 15, 1927); Rev. Leo F. Miller, Columbus, OH; Rev. James E. O'Mahony, OSF, Ireland; Rev. Richard E. Power, Springfield, MA; Mrs. Justine B. Ward, Washington, DC.

Liturgical Movement as Heritage

members, to draw attention to those alienated from the economic order, and to support the renewal of corporate worship everywhere.[27] Reinhold was added to the editorial board in 1938.

By far the most significant result of Vatican II was the restoration of the liturgy to its formative place as "source and summit" of the Christian life. The council cited "full, conscious, active participation" as the goal to be considered before all others. Although sometimes I wonder about the degree to which members' participation in the Eucharist is "conscious," surely we have achieved a level of full and active participation others could only dream about.

In 1940 Reinhold described in detail his dream Mass, noting with sadness that he would probably never see this come to pass. His hopes and efforts were not disappointed, however, and he did live just long enough to experience the initial liturgical changes recommended by Vatican II.[28]

Having studied Reinhold's complete bibliography it is apparent that there are at least three primary themes of his work that are rooted deeply in his life and ministry from that beginning, and continue to branch out not just in his writing but also through his life and ministry: the spirit of the liturgy, the quest for justice, and the importance of architecture. In the end, however, all three are really about allowing oneself to be shaped by the baptismal commitment. "A Christian who wants to know more about the liturgy and to help his fellow Christians to do likewise is not a liturgist. A Christian who wants to live the life of Christ through more intimate integration of his own life with that of the Church and her sacraments is not a liturgist and by no means a rubricist. He is a Catholic Christian, nothing else."[29] With that in mind we turn to look at each of those themes in more depth.

[27] See the History of *Worship* Magazine, http://www.saintjohnsabbey.org/worship/worship/page1.htm (accessed May 17, 2009).

[28] See H. A. Reinhold, "My Dream Mass," *Orate Fratres* 14 (April 1940): 265–70; "A Variety of Things," *Orate Fratres* 18 (July 1944): 418–22; "Jube D'Asnieres," *Orate Fratres* 21 (October 1947): 513–17.

[29] H. A. Reinhold, "More or Less Liturgical [#3]," 263.

Chapter 4

Spirit of the Liturgy

From the moment he arrived on American soil as an immigrant in 1936, Reinhold was an active member of the local church despite restrictions placed on him by the chancery in the Archdiocese of New York. Since he was not permitted to preach or lecture, Reinhold turned to writing and from 1936 until 1966 regularly published articles and book reviews in various Catholic periodicals: first in *Commonweal* as you will note in the bibliography, soon after in *Orate Fratres*, and finally in a number of other periodicals as they began to appear, notably *Jubilee* and *The Living Light*. These articles spanned the length of his ministry as well as the depth of his spirituality and interests.

Reinhold was at heart an educator, and just as St. Benedict recognized the monastery to be a school for the Lord's service,[1] Reinhold saw that the liturgy was similarly a school for the Lord's service. One could say that on arriving in the United States he laid out his Magna Carta in a three-part article in *Orate Fratres*, which predated his becoming a regular columnist there. In "More or Less Liturgical"[2] he presented this, methodically setting out the curriculum for his school. "There is a coherence between life outside and within us, Christ and the world, our mind and the economy of salvation, our person and the church. When all this invades our consciousness, then we begin to understand and we become liturgical. Life and liturgy have become one. Our new endeavor is to make the two parts more congruent."[3]

Reinhold did not mince words when he laid out the rationale for his approach to education through the liturgy. "All this prompts the grave

---

[1] *Rule of St. Benedict 1980*, ed. Timothy Fry (Collegeville, MN: Liturgical Press, 1981), Prol. 45.

[2] See H. A. Reinhold, "More or Less Liturgical [#1]," *Orate Fratres* 13 (February 1939): 152–55; "More or Less Liturgical [#2]," *Orate Fratres* 13 (March 1939): 213–18; "More or Less Liturgical [#3]," *Orate Fratres* 13 (April 1939): 257–63.

[3] Reinhold, "More or Less Liturgical [#1]," 154–55.

question: What do our good Catholic people and even their priests *really* believe? Our consciousness is limited and narrow. Our interest is prompted by our ego."[4] He continued boldly in much the same way that Peter Steinfels would later do by creating quite a stir in a *New York Times* article about what Catholics do and do not believe regarding Eucharist.[5] Reinhold wrote:

> There are too many Catholics whose Catholicism consists of nothing but peripheral things. Everything in their mind is out of scale. They wander from statue to statue in their church and never think of adoring the Father through His Son. They strive to pile up indulgenced prayers and at the same time lose sight of God's infinite mercy. They use holy water and forget their own baptism. I am afraid we would be shocked if we drew up a chart showing how little of the great truths is really present to the minds of contemporary Catholics, and how many unessential, decorative growths and outgrowths have first place in their minds. Even our catechisms often do not show the true scale and real proportions which the edifice of the *oeconomia salutis*, the economy of salvation, is received through its architect, the Holy Ghost. To use the words of the German poet Angelus Silesius, "we must become essential" as opposed to our present chaotic, peripheral and disorganized religious consciousness. The best means to restore the *kosmos* of our faith is liturgy in its fullness.[6]

USE OF THE MISSAL

When I was growing up in the 1950s everyone carried a Sunday missal to weekly Mass, and those who attended Mass during the week would certainly have been more likely to have a daily missal. When I first began studying the history of the liturgy, it was a surprise for me to learn that this was not always so. Only in 1897 were the laity permitted to have copies of the Mass texts in their own language. Prior to that time all those who would print, read, or even possess vernacular missals were threatened with excommunication. On January 12, 1661, Pope Alexander VII prohibited under penalty of excommunication any printing, reading, or even possession of missals. Moreover, all

[4] H. A. Reinhold, "Faith Is a Kosmos," *Orate Fratres* 14 (January 1940): 122–24; here 123.

[5] See Peter Steinfels, "Future Faith Worries Catholic Leaders," *New York Times* (June 1, 1994), http://www.nytimes.com/1994/06/01/us/future-of-faith-worries-catholic-leaders.html (accessed July 13, 2009).

[6] Reinhold, "Faith Is a Kosmos," 124.

extant copies of the missal were to be surrendered immediately. In *Ad aures nostras* he issued the condemnation: "We therefore by special act and from certain knowledge and after mature deliberation condemn, disapprove, and prohibit for all time, and wish to be regarded as condemned, disapproved, and prohibited the above-mentioned missal in the French language, regardless of the author, no matter where and under what circumstance it may be in the future of whatever rank, order, state of life, dignity, honor and pre-eminence."[7]

As mentioned previously, in early 1944 Reinhold was commissioned to begin writing a series of brief articles for the Los Angeles diocesan newspaper, *The Tidings*. In that series of eighty-three weekly columns, Reinhold was teacher, spiritual director, and champion of the liturgical movement, weaving both history and theology with reflections on the liturgical year, enabling readers to participate more actively in the liturgy. Occasionally there were reasoned pleas for a vernacular liturgy, which were seen by some as unnecessary digressions, but on the whole Reinhold followed a very clear syllabus. The inaugural column, which appeared in the January 28, 1944, issue of *The Tidings* made the series' purpose clear: "To make our worship what Christ intended it to be, 'adoration of the Father in Spirit and Truth,' we have to accompany this forward movement with an inward movement, to let the mind keep pace with our mouth. Then when our hearts concord with our voices, as St. Benedict exhorts they should do, there will be one more thing to do: to reflect on how to connect what we pray and sing with what we do out in the world. Altar and daily life must be one, or else our religious practice becomes an escape, a drug."[8]

Prior to the 1969 alterations in the liturgical calendar, the three Sundays that preceded Ash Wednesday were known respectively as Septuagesima, Sexagesima, and Quinquagesima Sundays. In preparing his readers for a deep, fruitful celebration of the Lenten season, Reinhold gave some historical background for the liturgical gatherings: "Septuagesima Sunday has quite a history and its ancestry goes far back to the Near East. It is generally regarded as a pre-Lenten curtain raiser for this most sacred season of the church. Its present Latin name indicates nothing but the fact that it is the Sunday within

---

[7] Keith F. Pecklers, *Dynamic Equivalence: The Living Language of Christian Worship* (Collegeville, MN: Liturgical Press, 2003), 14.

[8] H. A. Reinhold, "Worship in Spirit and Prayer," *The Tidings* (January 28, 1944): 6.

the seventh decade before the great Pasch."[9] Then he gave instructions on how to approach the season, literally taking his readers to our common altar in Rome:

> Take your missal, and if you own one, your short Breviary, and meditate [on] the texts of these holy books on the eve of Septuagesima. We are gathered around the altar in the beautiful Basilica of St. Lawrence the Martyr outside the walls of Rome, or in what is left of it.
>
> In Rome there is already spring in the air. The chaste and plain beauty of the basilica in honor of the youthful martyr suggests beginning and newness. There are indications that we have now discovered the real beginning of the church year in this Sunday and its old texts.[10]

CYCLES OF LITURGICAL YEAR

Reinhold had an alternate perspective on the beginning of the liturgical year as well as the number of cycles occurring in the liturgical year. This perspective was derived from his association and familiarity with the work of Dom Odo Casel. Reinhold advanced this theory in his own writings sometimes at length as we shall see later. When he believed strongly in a scholarly or political point, Reinhold was tenacious. In this series, however, he gently encouraged the reader to consider his alternate view. "Let us, for one year assume that the Church year does not begin with Advent, but with this day [Septuagesima Sunday]. We will see that our method makes sense, more sense than the customary assumption. We cannot here give a scientific reasoning for this unusual assumption. But is not all liturgical prayer nowadays unusual? Are we not going through a phase of discovery of our own hidden riches?"[11]

In most of these columns, Reinhold also made references to the Scripture readings for each of the Sundays. Because today we use a vastly revised liturgical calendar and lectionary, in this study I will add the scriptural references as well as prayer texts although they were not included in the articles.[12] Reinhold obviously presumed that his readers were following along in their missals.

---

[9] Reinhold, "Septuagesima Sunday," *The Tidings* (February 4, 1944): 6.

[10] Ibid., 6.

[11] Ibid., 6.

[12] In that era there was only one other reading in addition to the gospel pericope assigned for each Sunday, and only one cycle of readings. The current three-year cycle of three readings went into effect in 1969.

What do we find in these texts[13] to nourish our mind and to stir our deepest emotions? Great Things! An appeal to build in ourselves and in the world the Kingdom of Heaven, to work and till the fields of the Spirit.

Our Lord and St. Paul call us to start again, however advanced the hour of our life may be. It will be a hard fight, we will have to become real athletes of Christ, forgoing many things in order to win.

And between these admonitions and the great initial summons of a new beginning there sounds the eternal dialogue between groaning, weak and sinful man and the God of mercy, the Lord of our faith and trust, in the songs with which the Church accompanies the readings, the prayers and the processions of the great sacramental mystery. Take your missal and savor the richness of thought and sentiment of this Sunday.[14]

Reinhold began the following week's column with a reflection on St. Paul. Although I was not yet born at the time these columns were published, even the following decade when I was in elementary school reading Scripture was not encouraged at all. From today's perspective we might say that in that era many Roman Catholics were still suffering from a deep Counter-Reformation reluctance to delve into the Bible lest they fall victim to the temptation of interpreting the text for themselves, which was considered to be a Protestant predilection. Quite the opposite, Reinhold encouraged the reader not just to reflect on the week's texts, but to delve further into the Scriptures and apply them to daily life.

St. Paul appeals to people of our age perhaps more than any other apostle. Above all he has written more than any one of them, St. John perhaps excepted. In all his writings his own strong and very human personality shines through, his labors for the gospel, his arguments with stubborn disciples, his defense against intrigue and calumny. He is an apostle and saint of flesh and blood, vigorous, warm hearted, broad minded and bent on essentials. His training as a rabbi is plainly visible, but no one has, like Paul, shed all legalism and fought his way through to a pure religion of charity and the Spirit.

With this great apostle in mind we have to open our missal today, when we prepare our Mass by a short meditation on its texts. By the way, this meditation, or if the word sounds a bit too ponderous, let us call it, this preview, is absolutely necessary for an understanding of the liturgy of the day.

[13] 1 Cor 9:24-27; 10:1-5; Matt 22:1-16.
[14] Reinhold, "Septuagesima Sunday," 6.

Spirit of the Liturgy

The word-compositions of our old Masses are so delicately balanced and intertwined that we cannot just rush to church, grab a missal and then try to keep up with the priest at the altar. We may be able to do the latter once we are familiar with the prayers of the ordinary of the Mass and once we have overcome the initial missal trouble of turning leaves and not getting mixed up. But what good is this to our soul?[15]

PREPARING THE SOUL

As was mentioned earlier, at times rather than writing as a teacher, Reinhold came across more as a wise spiritual director — cognizant of the local Sunday parish experience and transparent enough to share the workings of his own soul. Notice again the reference to worship in spirit and truth, which continued to be the core of this work as well as his life's ministry. Here we also hear the overtones of sarcasm, which, as we shall later see, often characterized his tenure as *Orate Fratres*'s timely tractor. "To be able to keep up with the rather rapid recitation of the priest in the shorter Latin text is a physical achievement, a sort of sport or hobby. But where does the spirit and the truth and the worship come in, unless we are prepared? Later, after a few years, all the Masses will be so familiar that a few words of the Introit bring back the mind picture of its whole composition, just as we recognize Beethoven's victory symphony from its first four notes."[16] There we definitely find the overly optimistic Reinhold at work, in contrast to the self-revealing realist in the following passage. "But even then we face a difficulty: boredom—unless we now preview our Mass which we know so well to find new angles and aspects, to let it grow as our life and personality grows."[17]

Again Reinhold reminded readers of the stational liturgy in Rome. "In our minds we are gathered on this Sunday around the high altar of St. Paul's basilica in Rome, our station church. Here rest his remains. In this Mass he comes to life and speaks to us in his epistle, the great epic of his apostolic labors.[18] Let us remember that we made a new start last Sunday."[19]

"Here is an appeal to work for the kingdom of God like Paul. . . . This epistle is but the apostle's response to Christ's own appeal in

---

[15] Reinhold, "Sexagesima Sunday," *The Tidings* (February 11, 1944): 6.
[16] Ibid., 6.
[17] Ibid., 6.
[18] See 1 Cor 9:24-27; 10:1-5.
[19] Reinhold, "Sexagesima Sunday," 6.

Worship in Spirit and Truth

the gospel of the day, the similitude of the sower. Paul's fruit was hundred-fold—we will be lucky if ours will be three- or ten-fold. It will—if we keep it in a 'good and perfect heart and bring forth fruit in patience.' Yes patience—patience also with ourselves."[20]

Reinhold demonstrated how each element of the liturgy builds: "The choir parts of this Mass, introit,[21] gradual[22]/tract,[23] offertory[24] and communion[25] antiphon, fit easily into this main theme. Their note is the same mood as last Sunday, an almost somber earnestness, a despair of human powers but a deep faith in God."[26]

In summary he concluded, "This Sunday . . . is a new theme or motif in the great symphony of the opening Holy Year of the Church and of our own soul; it challenges and warns, it is humble and yet full of trust! We will therefore take up our task 'not putting trust in anything that we do ourselves,' but as Paul taught us saved by Him, 'who shows forth His wonderful mercies': The Lord (Offertory)."[27]

The following week the title of Reinhold's column changed to "Worship in Spirit and Truth" and remained so for the rest of the series. He continued in his role as spiritual director, preparing his readers to "enter the great annual retreat . . . this annual purging of our human personality of those things that have crept in during the course of the year."[28] He also recommended the custom to selecting a good Life of Christ or a saint's biography for daily spiritual reading during the Lenten season. "If none of these things are on your program, you may just as well shelve your missal. It opens its deeper meaning only to a mind that worships in its spirit and its truth!"[29]

ANNUAL RETREAT

When it came to the final pre-Lenten Sunday Reinhold reminded his readers that we "enter the great annual retreat of the church which

---

[20] Ibid., 6.
[21] Ps 43:23-26.
[22] Ps 82:19, 14.
[23] Ps 59:4, 6.
[24] Ps 16:5, 6-7.
[25] Ps 47:4.
[26] Reinhold, "Sexagesima Sunday," 6.
[27] Ibid., 6.
[28] Reinhold, The Tidings (February 18, 1944): 6.
[29] Ibid., 6.

serves us to renew our baptismal vows on Easter and, with these vows, the fervent spirit of baptism, which is the death of the old Adam and resurrection in and with Christ of the new Man." In language that sounds more characteristically contemporary, he continued: "Our program will be this annual purging of our human personality of those things that have crept in during the course of the year. Holy Saturday Communion should find us renewed, if we follow the Church and go again through her catechumenate."[30] Keep in mind that although since 1975 the church has benefited from the restored catechumenate so active in most parishes today, in Reinhold's day his use of the term was purely metaphorical.

It is also important to remember that Lent was the only time of the year in which the church offered a daily cycle of Mass texts. During the rest of the year there were only separate readings assigned for feasts; at other Masses (ferial Masses) the readings of the previous Sunday were repeated. This offered Reinhold a much greater opportunity to comment not only on the daily texts but also on the station churches.[31] With this as backdrop he made further recommendations for his readers' annual retreat. "Daily Mass, if possible, or if not at least daily reading of the Mass texts at home; a modicum of fasting even if there is a general dispensation due to the war, again if we can do so; alms-giving which can easily be substituted by work for the Red Cross, for your pastor, for the poor, by donating of blood plasma; and, of course, no movies, even if it hurts."[32] Repeating a recommendation he made previously, Reinhold again suggested, as he did the previous week, choosing a good life of Christ or saint's biography because "It opens its deeper meaning only to a mind that worships in its spirit and its truth!"[33]

The next passage will give you a feel for how Reinhold accompanied and led his readers through the season of Lent and throughout the liturgical year:

[30] Ibid., 6.

[31] From as early as the third century Christians in Rome marked the Lenten journey by visiting a different church in the city each morning for prayer. The daily missal to which Reinhold refers in his columns lists the appropriate station church for each day of the season. See John F. Baldovin, *The Urban Character of Christian Worship: The Origins, Development, and Meaning of Stational Liturgy* (Rome: Pont. Institutum Studiorum Orientalium, 1987), 36.

[32] Reinhold, *The Tidings* (February 18, 1944): 6.

[33] Ibid., 6.

Sunday—the city of Rome and we with her are gathered around the tomb of St. Peter to participate in its Mass. The grand opening is the psalm of trust, Ps. 30.[34] Sung by the choir and meditated by ourselves word after word it will fill us with new faith and confidence in our Father's guidance. The epistle[35] is the high canticle of charity of St. Paul, something to be memorized and savored—and lived: "We see now through a glass in a dark manner, but then face to face." The beatific vision is described as the univocal end of a road which starts with our charity on earth. All other things will vanish and be transformed, but charity will bring us from clarity to greater clarity until it is fulfilled by the unveiled gaze of love of our Heavenly Father.[36]

Reinhold continued connecting the remaining readings and prayers to his readers' everyday lives. The gospel,[37] for example, related what he refers to as the "touching story of the blind man who cried while busybodies tried to silence him: 'Jesus son of David, have mercy on me.'" Reinhold advised, "You and I are the blind man in the crowd, blind in many ways, but faith will heal us, if we continue to cry. Thus minded, we approach the communion table, asking 'Lord that I may see,' and then the communion verse, taken from the 77th psalm, will be the response of our soul: 'and the Lord gave them their desire; they were not defrauded of that which they craved,' to see, to become more and more seeing, until we see face to face. Thus epistle and gospel are beautifully implemented in communion. This Lent will 'enlighten' our spiritual eyes."[38]

Turning his attention next to preparing for Ash Wednesday, Reinhold recommended that "besides receiving the ashes and making your definite and firm program for your annual forty days retreat from ordinary life, read your missal, especially those three beautiful responsories which are to be sung during the distribution of the ashes.[39] What a language! The Mass is celebrated in one of the oldest churches in Rome, the sanctuary of the Dominican order on the

---

[34] "In Thee, O Lord, have I hoped, let me never be confounded: deliver me in thy justice, and save me" (*St. Andrew Daily Missal* [*SADM*], ed. Dom Gaspar Lefebvre [St. Paul, MN: E. M. Lohmann Company, 1940], 258).

[35] See 1 Cor 13:1-13.

[36] Reinhold, *The Tidings* (February 18, 1944): 6.

[37] See Luke 18:31-43.

[38] Reinhold, *The Tidings* (February 18, 1944): 6.

[39] See Joel 2:13; 2:17; Ps 78.

brow of the Aventine Hill.[40] It teaches us how to fast, first in Joel's, the prophet's words giving hope even to the most confirmed sinners."[41]

The station church for the First Sunday of Lent is St. John Lateran, the "mother" of all Roman churches. Reinhold commented, "We can write over the gate of this week the one word: Decision. You cannot help feeling its necessity, when you read St. Paul's stirring words in the Epistle[42] which again lead up to the even greater climax of the Gospel:[43] Christ's own retreat and temptations."[44]

He proceeded to demonstrate how one meditates with the texts, the monastic practice of *lectio* at work, although without making specific reference to it. "Decisions for and against are actions which frighten us common and stumbling Christians. It is truly an admirable psychology that the Church in this grandiose and simple Mass should take up one verse of the Gospel ['He hath given His angels charge over Thee, and in their hands shall they bear Thee up, lest perhaps Thou dash Thy foot against a stone,'[45]], a quotation of the Compline Psalm 90, and unfold its quieting, trusting words in unending singing: the Introit, Gradual, Tract, Offertory and Communion are all taken from it, and, to say the truth, it accompanies us all through Lent. The devil quotes it dishonestly and by distortion when he tempts Christ."[46] Reinhold did not include a complete analysis, however, but encouraged his readers to experience the "joy of discovery" on their own.

CELEBRATING THE PASCH

After accompanying his readers throughout the intensive spiritual retreat that is Lent, Reinhold observed, "It is regrettable that most of our people nowadays who are so zealous and faithful in their observance of the Lenten regulations and who come almost daily to Mass during that period, do not know that the great Easter Week after the

---

[40] Santa Sabina. Throughout the season of Lent Reinhold continued to draw attention to the station churches, at least by name, often including background information as well.

[41] Reinhold, *The Tidings* (February 18, 1944): 6.

[42] 2 Cor 6:1-10.

[43] Matt 6:1-11.

[44] Reinhold, *The Tidings* (February 18, 1944): 6.

[45] *SADM*, 292.

[46] Reinhold, *The Tidings* (February 25, 1944): 7.

day of Resurrection is of equal liturgical importance."[47] He playfully referred to the octave as "seven days of merriment," and the great fifty days as the "honeymoon of the Spirit." Sixty years later, not much has changed, but we will leave those issues for discussion in chapter 7.

Reinhold pressed on with his critique, however, demonstrating again his characteristic bluntness. "One often wonders how it happened that our spiritual sensibilities became so blunted and dulled that we almost seem to have forgotten that there are moods and thoughts to every Mass which invite us to conform. It is surprising to see how often pious people . . . do things which definitely indicate that they are not in the least attuned to the mystical life of their church, but stay . . . so enclosed in their own individuality that they don't feel like paying any attention to the goings on in the realm of sacramental life around themselves."[48]

The following year he made a similar critique: "Far too little is made of the beauty of the week after Easter. The overwhelming drama of Holy Week has taken up so much of us that we seem to be unable to stand any more celebration. Anyway, modern man seems to be unable to conceive of religion as anything radiant, triumphant and victorious. The sad, the gloomy and the tearful have the day in so many versions of Christian piety."[49]

Explicating some of the symbols of the paschal season, Reinhold gave an extended reflection on holy water, an inadequate term in his opinion. "What is its original meaning? It replaces the CANTHARUS, a running fountain in the entrance court of the churches of the early centuries, set up for the lustration of the faithful and pilgrims: to wash their faces, hands and often their weary, dusty feet. It received a blessing to bring it into the neighborhood of the spiritual things: to baptism, to baptismal water."[50]

He then invited readers to make some connections: "Is it not easy to see then, what this running spring of clear blessed water signifies? 'Like the hart panteth after fountains of water so my soul panteth after thee, O God. My soul has thirsted for the living God.' It symbolizes, then, the cleansing, reviving power of God in baptism. It is there to help us renew our baptism. Before we enter we 'baptize' ourselves

47 Reinhold, *The Tidings* (April 7, 1944): 7.
48 Reinhold, *The Tidings* (April 28, 1944): 6.
49 Reinhold, *The Tidings* (April 6, 1945): 10.
50 Reinhold, *The Tidings* (April 28, 1944): 6.

again, invoking the Father and the Son and the Holy Spirit, in whom we were re-born, with sorrow for our sins, with renewal of our baptismal vows to appear justified and with ready hearts in the temple of the Living God."

Reinhold did not stop there, but rather proceeded to point out the limitations of those who use holy water without any intention, or with different intentions. He questioned, for example, why people would bless themselves with holy water before going to High Mass during which the priest blesses the congregation with holy water. Similarly he questioned those who bless themselves with holy water when leaving a church. The possibility of multivalent symbols seemed to elude him, at least in his writings. There are so many instances like that when I sincerely want to have a conversation with him. Granted, even if he were still living, we would be bridging more than sixty years during which both practice and spirituality have developed, but he could not have known how liturgical practice would develop over time or the degree to which people would be shaped by participating in worship more actively.

CELEBRATING THE ASCENSION

Reinhold's exuberance in discussing the feast of the Ascension is indicative of the importance liturgical celebrations in general held for him. Often he included references to the hymns, texts, and prayers of the day's Office, expecting that at least some of his readers were using their breviaries as well as their missals daily: "The music of Ascension Day, not only of the Mass, but the Hymns and Antiphons of the sacred Office are of unique beauty, especially the Vesper Hymn and the 'I shall not leave you as orphans' of the Magnificat. The whole Mass is one shout of triumph, victory and joy."[51]

Reinhold's entire reflection on the Ascension made me wonder what his reaction would be to our current situation in the United States in which some dioceses celebrate the Ascension as a moveable feast forty days after Easter, while others transfer it to the following Sunday. Maybe we can get a hint from his observation:

> There is no reason, at least no sufficient one, why this great Mass should not be celebrated with all its solemn splendor in our churches, at our altars. The fact that many people go to work and our churches

[51] Reinhold, *The Tidings* (May 12, 1944): 6.

have to take cognizance of this fact is no excuse at all for us. There are always people who can come, too young and too old for work, but willing to represent the others and to celebrate. The children can sing. There are places where the solemn Mass of this day is held at 6 a.m. Why not? Will not the worker go to work with a bit of the splendor of this feast reflected in his soul if we let him begin this great Holy Day with the triumphant Master? What an uplift![52]

Although some might consider Reinhold's comments to be overly optimistic or too simplistic, I appreciate the fact that in every instance he imagined and encouraged the very best in liturgical celebrations, worship in spirit and truth. Liturgy is work, so why not work for the best. "The liturgy of the church is on a higher and therefore more difficult and exacting level. It demands thinking attention. It is not soothing and relaxing like so many popular devotions. It is keen and glowing."[53]

LITURGY AND DEVOTIONS

Another recurrent theme in Reinhold's *Tidings* series was reconciling the relationship between liturgy and devotions. Although I was not born until the year after the series concluded, during my childhood I recall some puzzling inconsistencies. Our parish church was filled with adults on Monday evenings for the Miraculous Medal Novena exercises, but those same people were noticeably absent from the Communion procession on Sunday morning. Although the fast laws might have had something to do with it, I do not think that tells the entire story.

Reinhold wrote, "For years and years scholars and priests have waged a single-handed fight for a more correct attitude in our devotional life—to no avail. It seems that we prefer the time of minor resistance: if the people like it, let them have it. The consequence is sensational sentimentalism, unfocused attitudes and a general mood of laissez-faire in all things that concern our prayer life."[54] Taking his place in line of scholars and priests, he continued by reflecting on the texts of that week: "We can only understand the text of the Mass for the eighth Sunday after Pentecost, especially the profound

---

[52] Ibid., 6.
[53] Reinhold, *The Tidings* (July 7, 1944): 6.
[54] Reinhold, *The Tidings* (July 21, 1944): 6.

Postcommunion,[55] when and if we stop acting as if at Mass the end and aim of our worship were the Blessed Sacrament. It is not the end and purpose, but the means through which we worship God. If we would only read the Secret[56] and Postcommunion of this Mass in the light of these remarks, we would notice how definitely the Church treats the 'Sacra Mysteria' as a means to an end, and not as the end."[57]

Ever the teacher, at every opportunity Reinhold emphasized the importance of liturgy over devotion: "Conformity with Christ is first achieved in a mystical, immediate and real way in the sacraments. This way is beyond our experience: we do not perceive it with our senses, nor can our mind fathom and rationalize it."[58] Similarly, ever the artist he also criticized the cheap and sentimental in ecclesiastical décor: "Truth smothered with the fake splendor of spurious architecture, cheap plaster statues out of commercially run ecclesiastical hardware stores, truth scorned with unfitting hymns and prayers is truth defaced and offended. . . . Before we do this and that and the other new thing, before we try new gadgets, new approaches and new methods, why do we not first try to celebrate our liturgy decently."[59]

In another column he recommended:

> If we did nothing this Sunday (4th after Easter) but concentrate on its collect,[60] its secret prayer[61] and its post communion,[62] the instruction

---

[55] "May this heavenly mystery, O Lord, heal us both in soul and in body; and may we ever feel within us the power of the sacrament we celebrate" (*SADM*, 825).

[56] "Receive, we beseech Thee, O Lord, the gifts of thy bounty which we bring to Thee, and by the power of Thy grace, may these holy mysteries sanctify our lives in this world and bring us to the joys of eternity" (*SADM*, 825).

[57] Reinhold, *The Tidings* (July 21, 1944): 6.

[58] Reinhold, *The Tidings* (September 8, 1944): 6.

[59] Reinhold, *The Tidings* (September 15, 1944): 7.

[60] "O God, who makest the minds of the faithful to be of one will, grant to thy people to love that which Thou commandest and desire that which Thou dost promise; that so, among the changing things of this world, our hearts may be set where true joys are to be found" (*SADM*, 665).

[61] "O God, who by the sacred communion of this sacrifice hast made us partakers of the one supreme divine nature: grant, we beseech Thee, that as we know thy truth, so we may follow it by a worthy life" (*SADM*, 667).

[62] "Assist us, O Lord our God, that by these gifts which we have received in faith, we may be purified from vice and delivered from all dangers" (*SADM*, 667).

and uplifting emotion derived from those three prayers would suffice to carry us over the whole following week, apart from the immediate effect Holy Communion has on us after we have duly participated in the divine sacrifice. . . . So many people do not see any fruit from frequent communion just because they have detached it from the sacrifice, and have made it into a private devotion—a sort of mystical "Thou and I" affair, forgetting what St. Thomas, the Fathers, the liturgy and the Gospel say about this banquet.[63]

Reinhold referred to readers' letters, which proved his thesis that "People, who have taken their missal to Church to participate more intimately in the 'great and terrible mystery' of the blessed passion, resurrection, ascension of our Lord, find themselves completely frustrated and unable to follow the Mass. All kinds of private devotions have taken its place, and while the sacred texts are performed at terrific speed, and the course of the Mass completely upset through willful changes, these people lose courage."[64]

SPIRITUAL DIRECTION

Occasionally Reinhold gave his readers an assignment, or a suggestion for how they can derive more from liturgical celebrations or seasons. For example, he suggested that they compare all of the introits from the eighteenth to the twenty-fourth Sundays after Pentecost and then the Third Sunday of Advent, remarking that "There is a certain delicate mood of peace: salvation, forgiveness; hope and trust in them which, together with their psalms, binds them into one."[65]

A few weeks later he again explained his approach to the liturgical year, seeing in it two cycles rather than one. You may recall that this was mentioned earlier in this chapter, when we saw the beginning of the series when Reinhold asked his readers to suspend their disbelief, if you will, that the liturgical year could begin at some other point than the First Sunday of Advent. From his perspective the year had two cycles: the first beginning with Septuagesima Sunday and continuing until the seventeenth Sunday after Pentecost; the second

---

[63] Reinhold, *The Tidings* (April 27, 1945): 10.
[64] Reinhold, *The Tidings* (May 4, 1945): 10.
[65] Reinhold, *The Tidings* (October 6, 1944): 6.

beginning with the eighteenth Sunday after Pentecost concluding with Candlemas, which in that era concluded the Christmas season.[66]

Reinhold's focus remained consistent, always encouraging the proper disposition for worship and countering criticism with education and reflection:

> One or the other reformer has voiced his criticism of a popular mentality of Catholics. It was said that Catholics, though theoretically orthodox and with the right doctrine in the books, are practically straying in Judaism; i.e., relying on their own efforts and trying to build up a credit account to present to God, thus forgetting the fundamental truth of Christianity that all our merits and good works are free gifts of divine grace; that we cannot stand before God's tribunal with claims or achievements to be justified. If anybody uses his missal with thought, understanding and heart, he can never fall into this practical error. The language is particularly univocal, clear and forceful in this respect. Of course, those to whom these prayers are like dead and magic formulas, or who inebriate themselves by their beautiful sound, will never detect anything but what they look for. But that is just what we are after: to transcend the surface values and to worship in spirit and truth.[67]

When I think of the clamor and distractions of our own day, I wonder what Reinhold would have to say to us if this is how he encouraged people of his era. "The quiet, noble and restrained ways of prayer have to be learned again by a generation of people who get their emotional stimulus from Hollywood and its counterparts."[68] What would he ever make of cell phones ringing in the middle of the eucharistic prayer? Perhaps it would simply be a perceptive reminder: "The liturgy is nothing undetached. It is close to life. It has its ascetic and social philosophy, and the liturgy itself, if integrated into our lives, is a safe spiritual guide, at least as safe as any spiritual director could be. It heals the prevalent legalism of so many faithful, and is poison to smugness, naturalism and other deadly vermin that undermine the life of grace, even when outward appearances look all right."[69]

[66] See Reinhold, *The Tidings* (October 20, 1944): 6. See also "Incarnation and Parousia," *Commonweal* 35 (December 19, 1941): 214–16; "How Many Cycles Has the Liturgical Year?" *Orate Fratres* 17 (January 1943): 102–10.

[67] Reinhold, *The Tidings* (November 10, 1944): 7.

[68] Reinhold, *The Tidings* (November 17, 1944): 7.

[69] Reinhold, *The Tidings* (January 26, 1945): 7.

Opening up the treasures of liturgical history, he encouraged his readers to develop a deeper liturgical spirituality:

> We do not walk up to the altar bearing gifts, as our ancestors did in beautiful visibility of their sacrificing lives: and even the processional (the offertory) has been curtailed to one-third of its words and a hundredth of its fullness by an impatient, self-centered and drab generation that dig themselves cisterns beside the living wells.
>
> Imagine the joyful procession in which you walk and sing, bearing your gifts and yourself: 'O God, my God, to Thee do I watch at break of day, and in Thy name I raise my hands—Alleluia. For thee my soul thirsteth and yet more my body that I may see Thy power and Thy glory, and in Thy name I raise my hands—Alleluia. In solemn lands of sunrise I try to fathom Thee, and thou has become my helper, and I shout with joy under the cover of Thy mighty wings and in Thy name I raise my hands—Alleluia.'[70]

In reflecting on the liturgy of Trinity Sunday, Reinhold advised "See how beautifully the word of charity is taken up by the Sunday epistle[71] and gospel.[72] For the next 17 Sundays this supreme law of the Kingdom of Christ is particularly stressed."[73] Then he reflected on the introit as one might during *lectio*, "See also the way the introit takes up these thoughts. 'Lord, I hope in Thy mercy (for the future); my heart is joyful in Thee as my Saviour (come to me anew in the paschal mysteries).' This is set against a psalm of human fear and anguish,[74] as inspired by the gray everyday treadmill of our lives."[75] And again he advised, "Follow the Sunday Masses. Meditate [on] their texts before and through Mass. Sing them. Enter into the gentle, forward-bearing stream of spirituality of the Bride of Christ."[76]

In another column, this for the fourth Sunday after Pentecost, he reflected on another prayer: "The secret has a truly amazing word: 'Compel to Thee our wills even if they are rebellious.' There is not

---

[70] Reinhold, *The Tidings* (April 13, 1945): 10.

[71] 1 John 4:8-21.

[72] Luke 6:36-42.

[73] Reinhold, *The Tidings* (May 25, 1945): 10. Notice that Reinhold has subtly referred again to his theory regarding two cycles in the liturgical year.

[74] Ps 12:6.

[75] Reinhold, *The Tidings* (May 25, 1945): 10.

[76] Ibid.

a person with an honest mind who would not join in this prayer over the bread and wine ready to be consecrated. For a discouraged heart—cf. St Peter's disappointed words in today's gospel![77]—this is the language of love. 'Force us back to thee, even when we rebel: take our freedom, only save us.' We should memorize these words for hours of despondency and temptation." [78] Although the Latin verb in the prayer is *compélle*, it is rendered into English as "draw," which hardly has the energy in it that Reinhold arouses. Comparing Reinhold's reflection to the English text[79] rendered in its day again we see how he functioned as a spiritual director for his readers. Although our Lectionary and prayer texts are very different today, there is much we can find in the method of Reinhold's reflections that will help us worship in spirit and truth. "To worship in Spirit and Truth has a profound meaning. It may mean to celebrate the Church's holy days and seasons in oneness with God through His son and in His Spirit. It may also mean that our own worshiping should progress over mere outward celebrating into our own innermost heart and mind—the obvious meaning of the words in the answer Christ gave the Samaritan woman at the well of Sichar."[80]

A QUESTION OF LANGUAGE

It all began unraveling as the summer of 1945 began, and within six weeks Reinhold was suddenly terminated as author of the weekly *Tidings* series. It all turned on a question of language—the English language, or "the vernacular" as it was sometimes snarled by its opponents. Reinhold honestly believed that he had authorities as high as Pius XII for allies. He noted a "change in tenor" in the pope's introduction to the newly revised Psalter, which had been published in March of that year. The only way in which Reinhold could conceive that "a better intellectual participation of the clergy in the worship of the Church" was possible was if the liturgy was in the vernacular.[81] From that point on Reinhold made repeated pleas for the vernacular

---

[77] Luke 5:1-11 relates the story of the great catch: "Go away from me, Lord, for I am a sinful man" (Luke 5:8).

[78] Reinhold, *The Tidings* (June 15, 1945): 10.

[79] "We beseech Thee, O Lord, be pleased to accept these our offerings; and in Thy mercy draw our rebellious wills unto Thee" (*SADM*, 803).

[80] Reinhold, *The Tidings* (June 29, 1945): 10.

[81] Reinhold, *The Tidings* (July 6, 1945): 14.

in *The Tidings*, which I have no doubt led to his termination, although correspondence with the editor does not so indicate.

It is probably no coincidence that the following month's Timely Tract in *Orate Fratres* sounds distinctly like an apologia. "I had intended to write this . . . on the vernacular in the liturgy, because several critics have in recent months attacked (and distorted) the arguments I have cited in favor of the vernacular."[82] Those arguments had nothing to do with being avant-garde, but everything to do with living the gospel and thirsting for justice, which is where we now turn our attention.

---

[82] H. A. Reinhold, "Open Wounds of the Mystical Body," *Orate Fratres* 19 (September 1945): 462–66; here 462.

Chapter 5

Quest for Justice

> We must be burning with a thirst for justice, for our neighbor, for our country and for mankind. Otherwise our alms create bitterness and are only a balm on our own sore souls.[1]

WORSHIP SEASONS JUSTICE

As was mentioned previously Reinhold's interest in the vernacular was inextricably linked with his concern for social justice. Prior to the Second World War, "in Al Smith's day," Reinhold observed, "Catholic Action was equated with sending one's children to Catholic Schools."[2] He believed that only with the Scripture texts in the vernacular would it be possible for the laity to be shaped for mission effectively. Only in that way would they see the connection between word and mission. This also links back to his experience as a member of the Benedictine community of Maria Laach, first as a novice and then as an oblate. As his colleague in the American liturgical movement Gerald Ellard wrote, "The monks of Maria Laach are fully persuaded that a fuller participation by Catholics in the Liturgical life of the Church will throw light on most of our modern religious and social problems."[3]

From his earliest days as a chaplain for the Franciscan sisters in Niendorf, as was discussed in chapter 1, Reinhold also took on responsibility for ministering to the migrant farmworkers who lived in the area, and he carried this pastoral concern with him into his ministry to seamen. Not content simply to provide the seamen with shelter and sacraments, Reinhold felt obligated to raise their consciousness to the social inequities that surrounded them and held them bound.

[1] H. A. Reinhold, "Worship in Spirit and Truth," *The Tidings* (February 18, 1944): 6, referring to the liturgy of the Friday after Ash Wednesday (Isa 58:1-9).

[2] John G. Deedy Jr. "Restless Ambassador of Christ," *Jubilee* 8 (November 1961): 7–11; here 10.

[3] Gerald Ellard, "'A Spiritual Citadel of the Rhineland': Maria Laach and the Liturgical Movement," *Orate Fratres* 3 (October 6, 1929): 384–88; here 386.

The homilist at his funeral noted, "Reinhold suffered over the plight of migrant workers. He suffered for the Jews. He suffered for the refugees. And this was not a mere intellectual suffering. This man was deeply troubled by the sufferings of man. No matter how wisely in any particular event, he involved himself always in causes which gave some practical expression to his concerns. He knew that Jesus Christ must be sought out and served in his brothers, in his lonely and suffering brothers, throughout all human history."[4]

Reinhold was particularly interested in the work of Dorothy Day and Peter Maurin. He was one of *The Catholic Worker*'s earliest subscribers and he visited the Catholic Worker house in Manhattan during his early visits to the United States.[5] Some of his earliest writings examined the movement's contribution to the church,[6] and when he later settled into working with the seaman's apostolate in Seattle, Washington, he helped to establish a Catholic Worker house in Seattle.[7] As one of Dorothy Day's friends and collaborators wrote:

> Father Reinhold never ceased, in the midst of his strenuous liturgical research and long and painful illness, to be concerned with the poor, the underprivileged and oppressed. This rare combination of a strict, sophisticated scholar and an extraordinarily sensitive humanist, did not represent two parallel, but essentially different spheres. It was made possible because the two spheres were inspired by a common love: the love of truth. For in Father Reinhold's mind, liturgy, properly interpreted and understood, was the reflection of Divine Truth,

[4] William Clancy, "In Memoriam: H.A.R.," *Worship* 42, no. 3 (March 1968): 130–33; here 133. See also *Time's Covenant: The Essays and Sermons of William Clancy*, ed. Eugene Green (Pittsburgh: University of Pittsburgh Press, 1987), 135–39.

[5] Reinhold made several trips to New York between 1932 and 1935 courtesy of the steamship lines. See Dorothy Day, "On Pilgrimage—March 1968," *The Catholic Worker* (March 1968): 2.

[6] See H. A. Reinhold, "Jungkatholische Bewegung allerwegen," *Schweizer Rundschau* 32 (1935): 727–32; "Catholic Worker Movement in America," *Blackfriars* 19 (September 1938): 635–50; "House of God and House of Hospitality," *Orate Fratres* 14 (December 1939): 77–78.

[7] See Robert Ellsberg, ed., *The Duty of Delight: The Diaries of Dorothy Day* (Milwaukee, WI: Marquette University Press, 2008), 52.

expressed in symbols. And the defense of man's dignity and rights is nothing else but this truth put into action.[8]

In one of Reinhold's early Timely Tracts we see these two attributes in action. He cultivated in his readers an understanding of the broader patterns of liturgical practice in Europe and regularly made the connection between liturgy and justice clear. For him that connection was a mandate.

Cardinal Faulhaber[9] in 1934 introduced in Munich the "charity offertory." The faithful brought to the altar—I hear it is now being done in many German churches—whatever they wanted to give to the poor: money, clothes, food and books. There it was accepted by the priests and the servers and deposited in the sanctuary during the service. It participated in the liturgical offertory and consecration. The old blessing over *"haec omnia"* before the little elevation somehow regained its original meaning. This was and is being practised several times during the year.

The Cardinal has given us a great example. Two humble lay people [Peter Maurin and Dorothy Day] and their followers and friends right here in this country give us another one. Can't we combine the two? For the true revival of liturgical piety and its re-integration into Christian lives I know no better way than this *"missio"* of neighborly love. If the floods of living water, descending from the altar into the parish, spilled over into a house for pilgrims (whom we call hoboes) and guests, for wanderers and the poor, would that not be a sermon from the roofs and housetops? A rectory basement, an old school, a barn will do for a beginning.

The great beneficiaries will not be the poor, but the priests, the parish and those who work for the poor. Those who have seen the Catholic Worker places in Mott Street or on Blue Island Avenue know how much these are in need of light and joy and the beauty of Christ's

---

[8] Helene Iswolsky, "Farewell to Father Reinhold—Friend and Teacher," *The Catholic Worker* (March 1968): 8. Iswolsky's complete tribute is found here in appendix C.

[9] Michael Cardinal von Faulhaber served as bishop of Munich for thirty-five years, from 1917 until his death in 1952. Reinhold regarded him as a true spiritual leader, helping the faithful to make wise judgments in the shadow of mounting atrocities of the German state. See letter from Reinhold to Abbot Herwegen and Dr. Barion, February 24, 1934 (Archives, Benediktinerabtei Maria Laach).

"mysteries." How it would change the lives of our parishioners if they had to enter the church past the church hospices![10]

ENDURING SADNESS

That he was not able to get ecclesial leaders to see and act on the awful truth about the atrocities of the Nazi regime haunted Reinhold until the end of his life. As we saw in chapter 1 it was speaking that truth that got him expelled not just from his life's work but ultimately from the homeland he had served loyally almost to the point of death in the First World War. Exiled in the United States he still kept trying to speak the truth, engaging in serious research among refugees and attempting to bring their plight to the attention of both ecclesial and government officials.[11]

Underlying all of these efforts was the conviction that if members of the Catholic community were worshiping God in their own language, they would be closer to worshiping in spirit and truth—living the gospel and raising up the poor.

Nowhere was Reinhold's enduring sadness more evident than in his review of Margaret Bourke-White's book *"Dear Fatherland, Rest Quietly": A Report on the Collapse of Hitler's "Thousand Years."*[12] Renowned photojournalist for *Life* magazine from its beginning in 1936, Bourke-White was the first woman war correspondent permitted to work in combat zones during World War II, and one of the first photographers to enter and document the death camps. *"Dear Fatherland, Rest Quietly"* is her intense description of that experience, and the photographs alone capture the horror of it all. Reinhold commented: "The book is vivid, warm and almost fascinating, although its success is going to be hampered by the fact that it is about a year too late for its own purposes. I hope it will be read by the many people who are already beginning to forget what it was really like when our armies entered the vanquished enemy's land after bursting open that iron

[10] H. A. Reinhold, "House of God and House of Hospitality," *Orate Fratres* 14 (December 1939): 77–78; here 77.

[11] See Collection #023B (papers of the National Catholic Welfare Conference Bureau of Immigration New York Port Office for the 1920s through the 1970s), Box 137, File 3835(b), which contains correspondence from H. A. Reinhold from October 1936 to April 1941. Center for Migration Studies, Staten Island, NY.

[12] See H. A. Reinhold, Review of *"Dear Fatherland, Rest Quietly"* by Margaret Bourke-White, *Commonweal* 45 (January 10, 1947): 327–28.

curtain."[13] What must it have been like for him to read that book, published ten years after he was banished from his dear fatherland, a living witness to the human tragedy he had so valiantly tried to prevent?

There is another ironic yet poignant connection between Reinhold and Bourke-White: both were diagnosed with Parkinson's disease in 1956. Bourke-White describes her diagnosis vividly in her 1963 autobiography, *Portrait of Myself*: "Parkinsonism is a strange malady. It works its way into all paths of life, into all that is graceful and human and outgiving in our lives, and poisons it all."[14] In January of 1959 Bourke-White underwent experimental brain surgery, known then as cryosurgery, pioneered by Dr. Irving S. Cooper.[15] With the patient fully awake during surgery, the skull was opened, the brain was exposed and the nerves that controlled the tremors were first identified and then destroyed by freezing. The following year this surgery was reenacted and televised in an *NBC Sunday Showcase*,[16] which I recall seeing as a child. Also under the care of Cooper, Reinhold underwent this same surgery in 1962, and as with Bourke-White the tremors on one side of his body ceased immediately. Recovery was long and arduous, as he described in a letter to friends:

> On December 4th I entered St. Barnabas Hospital in the Bronx to have my chemo-thalamectomy, which you probably saw on TV or read in articles, especially Margaret Bourke-White's. I will spare you the unpleasant details . . . but the operation was a 95% success. The moment the needle and its below zero temperature reached the thalamus of my brain, I felt that I was cured . . . but the recovery period is longer than I expected. . . . The remaining symptoms (tremor of the right hand, numbness of my fingertips and the sole of my right foot) have not grown worse and are easy to bear.[17]

[13] Ibid., 327.

[14] Margaret Bourke-White, *Portrait of Myself* (New York: Simon & Schuster, 1963), 364.

[15] See Kaushik Das, Deborah L. Benzil, Richard L. Rovit, Raj Murali, and William T. Couldwell, "Irving S. Cooper (1922–1985): A Pioneer in Functional Neurosurgery," *Journal of Neurosurgery* 89 (1998): 865–73; Stanley Stellar, "Reminiscences on Stereotactic Neurosurgery," *Neurosurgery* 57 (August 2005): 347–53.

[16] See "Case History," *Time*, January 11, 1961, http://www.time.com/time/magazine/article/0,9171,894643,00.html (accessed May 11, 2009).

[17] Several of Reinhold's friends gave me copies of this letter, which is dated February 1, 1963.

In the letter he anticipated having the same surgery on the right thala-
mus in May or June of 1963, which would ease or end the symptoms
on his left side. He subsequently decided against further surgery because he did not want to risk losing his ability to speak as Margaret
Bourke-White did following surgery on the other side of her brain.[18]
Reinhold obviously believed that he needed his voice to continue his
ministry until this insidious disease laid final claim to him.

VERNACULAR SOCIETY

Collaboration proved to be both strength and strategy for those
involved in the liturgical movement on both sides of the Atlantic.
Employing that same strategy, and involving much of the same popu-
lation, those in the liturgical movement who were interested in in-
corporating more extensive use of the vernacular in worship began
meeting together during the annual meetings of the Liturgical Conference and eventually formed their own organization, following the
approach that was taking place in England with the formation of the
English Liturgy Society.[19]

Founded in 1946, initially as an interest group within the Liturgical
Conference, the Vernacular Society (originally named the St. Jerome
Society) had as its stated purpose "to study, in accordance with the
teachings of the Catholic Church and with due regard of ecclesiastical authority, the possibilities of a greater use in parishes of English
in the public prayers, the rites and ceremonies and the administration
of the sacraments, to the greater glory of God and the sanctification
of souls."[20] What began with a small network of five individuals[21]
within five years had 837 active members.[22]

Reinhold's principle concern was that because people had become
religiously inarticulate, they failed to see the connection between lit-

[18] Interview with Judy Lackner, October 31, 2004.

[19] Later renamed the Vernacular Society of Great Britain, this society was
formed on July 22, 1943, inspired by Fr. S. J. Gosling, a parish priest of Alton,
Stoke-on-Trent. See Mark Turnham Elvins, *Towards a People's Liturgy: The Importance of Language* (Leominster: Gracewing, 1994), 59.

[20] Masthead of *Amen*, the official newsletter of the Vernacular Society, Vernacular Society Records, CVER 5, Archives of the University of Notre Dame.

[21] See Keith F. Pecklers, *Dynamic Equivalence: The Living Language of Christian
Worship* (Collegeville, MN: Liturgical Press, 2003), 42–77; here 42.

[22] *Amen* 6 (October 1, 1951): 4.

urgy and life. "Their prayer life, once rich and all-embracing, is now reduced to a set of half a dozen formulas. They can't speak to God unless they recite and repeat Our Fathers and Hail Marys. God is the 'great bureaucrat' to whom you submit your applications, which appear the more urgent the longer they are. You must use forms stabilized by tradition and custom. You don't sing hymns and psalms to God, nor do you use the language of your own heart. We have become religiously inarticulate . . . our person and the church."[23] You can see how he does not mince words, which endeared him to some but drew the ire of others.

LINKING TO JUSTICE

Rather than being shaped by a liturgy that was linguistically inaccessible, Reinhold believed that people were being shaped more by the devotional life of the church. Although in itself there is nothing wrong with devotional practices, when they supplant the liturgy they leave the community diminished because people have not heard the Scriptures proclaimed or been given the full range of opportunity to worship in spirit and truth. Although Reinhold made this distinction repeatedly, often only half of his message was heard—the half that seemed to call devotions into question.

> Still another shrinkage and impoverishment can be observed: the language of most of our devotions has become poor because of overstatement, superlatives, and the tendency to be effusive and gushy. Its province has narrow boundaries of feeling, narrower boundaries of reason, and no cosmic character at all. Most of our devotions speak the language and think the thoughts of the eighteenth century. Almost all of our hymns are on the sentimental side.
>
> Why is this so? Because we are disoriented. Religion has unwittingly been dislocated. It is not so much bad will, lack of interest or intentional disregard. It started long ago. The sphere of the supernatural has been shriveling in our minds and, since acting always follows being, it shrank in our practical lives too.[24]

[23] H. A. Reinhold, "More or Less Liturgical [#1]," *Orate Fratres* 13 (February 1939): 152–55; here 155.

[24] H. A. Reinhold, "Thunderstorm Religion," *Orate Fratres* 16 (1942): 33–36; here 33–34.

Quest for Justice

Reinhold had a hypothesis regarding the reason for this shriveling:

> Our low Masses last thirty minutes with announcements and Com-
> munions. Their attendance is mostly guaranteed by the penalty of
> mortal sin. The only visible activity during these Masses is that of the
> well dressed young ushers parading at least twice down the aisles and
> tossing baskets full of envelopes and coins into foolproof contraptions.
> The spoken and audible world is the card party and the seat collection
> talked up. Do these glamorous rites as a performance convey what
> they contain? Even if the people try to catch up with the celebrant in
> their missals—quite a hard task in most cases—they will under the
> most favorable conditions perform a good meditation. What is so
> Catholic about that? Don't Protestants, Jews and Muslems [sic] medi-
> tate and pray? Where is the soul-stirring "actio"?[25]

Yes, soul-stirring *actio* was Reinhold's enduring concern, and he
firmly believed that *actio* would invade the consciousness of those who
were truly liturgical,[26] and for them liturgy and life, worship and justice, would become one, manifesting true congruence.[27] The true test
for liturgical spirit would be "if those who stand up for it at the same
time serve the poor in houses of hospitality, help organize parish coop-
eratives, lead in labor movements, or come from such practical profes-
sions as doctors, nurses, housewives, teachers and priests. As long as
we see fruits with the flavor of the gospels in the very parishes which
stress liturgy, we need not worry. The worry comes from the other
side. In this country, with its primarily practical outlook and its lack of
contemplation, we are far more apt to become victims of a certain religious vulgarism, if I may say so, than to be misled by highbrows."[28]

His answer was simple: "Here is the plan; to become more and more
transformed into Christ and to receive the power of His death and resurrection to save and sanctify the world."[29] Even *Time* magazine saw

[25] H. A. Reinhold, "That Interesting Fiction: The American Standard of Living," *Orate Fratres* 14 (July 1940): 409–12; here 411.

[26] Reinhold, "More or Less Liturgical [#1]," 155.

[27] Ibid.

[28] H. A. Reinhold, "Popular Christianity," *Orate Fratres* 14 (February 1940):
169–72; here 169–70.

[29] H. A. Reinhold, "Christian Formation through the Liturgy," *The Wanderer*
(June 19, 1941): 5ff.

wisdom in what he advocated, quoting him in its August 27, 1951, issue's Words of the Week:[30]

> Live an ordered, respectable life, not without discipline and sacrifice, and the reward is peace! But is that the peace Jesus speaks of? Or is it a smug peace anticipating the hereafter? . . .
>
> Our way, if we are fully Christian in intention, is to . . . be patient and courageous, not in ourselves, but in Him. To face, not halfway, not turning back, but to face toward the year 1952. Not to divide the world into the elect who . . . have the answers . . . and the sots who are foolish enough not to be so sure. To know that Fascist and Communist, capitalist and socialist, Hindu and American, leaders and masses, are all in the same boat—the earth. That 2000 years ago Jesus started something that did not reach its climax in the thirteenth century, that did not go wrong in the sixteenth century, and that must face what is true in nuclear physics and psychoanalysis, as it tried to face the Arab threat with hylomorphism and Aristotelian dialectics.
>
> The greatest sin of our age is impatience and its child is the short cut—in politics, in economics—and in Reno. Whether we bring salvation depends on our endurance and the readiness to accept the fact that we are cross-bearing pilgrims.[31]

CONTEMPLATIVE PRESENCE:
FOR THE SAKE OF THE WORLD

Mere physical presence at Mass alone, even accompanied with reception of Holy Communion, Reinhold taught, "would not automatically integrate Christ into us." Rather, he taught that "we must leave our own little world of preferences, emotions, likes and dislikes" and surrender them at Mass, "the *tremendum mysterium*." He reasoned that "our task has become greater than ever in history. We face a fiercer and more brutal world than our forefathers. While they were threatened by iron and fire, prison and tyrants, we face evil in the disguise of humanitarian secularism, calculated and reasoned out, complete systems of secular, inner-worldly, anti-supernatural redemption. The anti-Christ has become mature." Therefore, "with every fiber of our being, not only emotion, not only reason, not only will but with our whole

---

[30] "Words of the Week," *Time*, August 27, 1951, http://www.time.com/time/magazine/article/0,9171,815267,00.html (accessed May 14, 2009).

[31] H. A. Reinhold, "The Christian in the World," *Orate Fratres* 25 (August 1951): 405–11; here 411.

Quest for Justice

being we have to throw ourselves into His arms and expose our souls to the influx of His power." Only if we do this, "if we open our ears to His message of joy, if we rise above ourselves and merge with Him in our surrender to the Father in the act of consecration, if we really con-celebrate, participate in the sacrifice-banquet and let the center of his life be the center of our own person: then we will function in the Body that alone can save the world."[32]

---

[32] Reinhold, "Christian Formation through the Liturgy," 5ff.

Chapter 6

Building on Faith

> The real tradition of the church, of course, is not a matter of architecture or style at all, but of the evolution of the human spirit under the inspiration of faith.[1]

A SENSE OF PLACE

From Reinhold's autobiography we learn that while he was still quite young his parents, probably unwittingly, were nurturing in him an interest in liturgy and architecture. As was mentioned earlier, his father's favorite pastime with him was to visit Protestant churches on Sunday afternoons, while his mother loved the baroque architecture of southern Germany.[2] Since both of my parents had similar interests and took my sister and me to Mass at a different church most summer Sundays, I understand how a sensitivity to space and place is nurtured.

As was mentioned in chapter 1, shortly after its establishment, Reinhold's bishop sent him to Rome to continue his archaeological study at the Pontifical Institute for Christian Archaeology. The institute's purpose is the "study of the remains of ecclesial life down the centuries"[3] and although Reinhold's impatience with his studies was probably due to his extensive previous knowledge of the subject, he used the opportunity of studying in Rome to absorb all he could by firsthand experience of the city's churches and culture. What are likely his notes from this period are extant in the Reinhold Papers at

---

[1] H. A. Reinhold, "Thoughts on Church Planning," *Orate Fratres* 23 (October 1949): 509–14; here 509.

[2] H. A. Reinhold, *H. A. R.: The Autobiography of Father Reinhold* (New York: Herder and Herder, 1968), 11; hereafter *HAR*.

[3] John Paul II "Message to Archbishop Zenon Grocholewski, Grand Chancellor of the Pontifical Institute of Christian Archaeology," December 11, 2000, http://www.vatican.va/holy_father/john_paul_ii/speeches/2000/oct-dec/documents/hf_jp-ii_spe_20001212_grocholewski_en.html (accessed May 6, 2009).

the Burns Library,[4] but even more significant are the many references to his visits to Roman churches that continued to appear in essays throughout his writing career.

REVOLUTION IN CHURCH ARCHITECTURE

Even a cursory glance at Reinhold's extensive bibliography found at the end of this book will demonstrate that not only did his earliest writings concern church architecture but the subject continued to fascinate him throughout his life. An architect who captured his imagination early was Rudolf Schwarz (1897–1960), who among other significant ecclesiastical projects collaborated with Romano Guardini on the chapel at Burg Rothenfels.[5] It was the simplicity of Schwarz's designs and their lighting that had the greatest enduring impact on Reinhold's own approach to architecture:

> One of the major interests lies in the altar, its liturgical position and its adornment. The chapel at Rothenfels and its large halls furnish a very interesting and inspiring topic for discussing the lighting of our churches. Rudolf Schwarz, who with his friend, Emil Steffmann, is the most radical and revolutionary leader in this architectural movement and whose first church, Corpus Christi at Aachen, caused a storm of protest in Germany, claims that the technical possibilities of modern lighting should be utilized for churches. I have myself celebrated and seen many a Mass in these empty and simple churches, and I can only say that nowhere except in the catacombs did I feel in such a way the reality of our holy Liturgy—and is that not the meaning of a church?[6]

[4] See "Basiliche," Box 14, Folder 6, H. A. Reinhold Papers, John J. Burns Library, Boston College, which seems to be Reinhold's notes from his studies at the Pontifical Institute in Rome, taken in Italian and accompanied by his own drawings and commentary in German.

[5] See H. A. Reinhold, "The Architecture of Rudolf Schwarz," *Architectural Forum* 52 (January 1939): 22–27. See also Rudolf Schwarz, *The Church Incarnate: The Sacred Function of Christian Architecture*, trans. Cynthia Harris (Chicago: Henry Regnery Co., 1958); and John W. Dixon Jr., "The Iconic Architecture of Rudolph Schwarz: An Essay on Architectural and Theological Method," http://www.unc.edu/~jwdixon/articles/schwarz.html (accessed January 20, 2009).

[6] H. A. Reinhold, "A Revolution in Church Architecture," *Liturgical Arts* 6 (1938): 123–33; here 125.

Today Schwarz's *The Church Incarnate* would be classified as a theological reflection on architecture in general and ecclesiastical architecture in particular. From reading it, one can hypothesize that Reinhold absorbed more from Schwarz than an appreciation of his architectural style. Schwarz could also be the source for Reinhold's theological approach to architecture. The original German edition of Schwarz's book[7] was in Reinhold's library and his annotations lead one to see what is considered worthy of note. For example, Schwarz wrote:

> This then is our task:
> To build churches out of that reality which we experience and verify every day; to take this our own reality so seriously and to recognize it to be so holy that it may be able to enter in before God. To renew the old teachings concerning sacred work by trying to recognize the body, even as it is real to us today, as creature and as revelation, and by trying to render it so; to reinstitute the body in its dignity and to do our work so well that this body may prove to be "sacred body." And beyond all this to guard ourselves against repeating the old words when for us no living content is connected with them.[8]

This is by no means to say that Reinhold agreed with all of Schwarz's positions. Quite the opposite! Reinhold was very clear about which architectural elements he considered to be central and which were peripheral. Similarly he was adamant about some elements of the basic plan for a church and held fast to them despite criticism. For example, he thought that pews imprisoned the congregation and it would be preferable ecclesially, therefore, for them to be seated on low stools, as one would see today at St. Gervais in Paris: "Pews . . . the nightmare of architects, because they obliterate the architectural lines of all churches, make them look fussy, pretty and bottomless. I think they are even part of the reason why our people don't sing. Give me nice little lightweight stools."[9] It would do Reinhold's heart good to see those small, lightweight stools at St. Gervais packed

---

[7] See Rudolf Schwarz, *Vom Bau der Kirche* (Würzburg: Werkbund-Verlag, 1938).

[8] Schwarz, *The Church Incarnate*, 11. See http://www.archive.org/stream/churchincarnateto10224mbp/churchincarnateto10224mbp_djvu.txt (accessed May 6, 2009).

[9] Reinhold, "Thoughts on Church Planning," 514. See also H. A. Reinhold, "Jube D'Asnieres," *Orate Fratres* 21 (October 1947): 513–17.

with people old and young, not just for Eucharist but also for Evening Prayer. They come from their business offices or ministries and spend time in contemplative silence before the services begin, and then return to the streets to take up the business of their lives. Now under the leadership of the Monastic Community of Jerusalem,[10] the community at St. Gervais, both monastic and lay, have found a rhythm of prayer and service that draws and forms others much as Reinhold dreamed.

SPEAKING OF LITURGICAL ARCHITECTURE

Reinhold's most sustained effort with regard to liturgical architecture was the summer course he originated in the University of Notre Dame's Liturgy Program[11] and taught there from 1947 to 1954. His notes from the course, which can be found in archives at the University of Notre Dame,[12] were subsequently edited and published by the University of Notre Dame Press as *Speaking of Liturgical Architecture*. In this monograph Reinhold traced the history and development of liturgical architecture and made bold statements regarding his position on specific elements. These he reiterated in other writings with remarkable consistency: baptistery, sanctuary, nave, devotional furnishings, location of the choir, seating, lighting, and circulation.

A solution that appealed to him, although not in perfect alignment with all he proposed, was given in *Speaking of Liturgical Architecture* as shown in figure 3.

An even better illustration of this solution can be found in St. Joseph's Church in Sunnyside, Washington, which was constructed under Reinhold's direction by Seattle architect T. F. Hargis Jr. and was dedicated in 1950. Adé Bethune visited Reinhold's church in 1954 and described it in the *Catholic Art Quarterly*:

[10] Founded at St. Gervais in Paris in 1975 by Fr. Pierre-Marie Delfieux, chaplain at the Sorbonne University, the Monastic Community of Jerusalem now also has foundations in Vézelay, Strasbourg, Mont-Saint-Michel, Brussels, Florence, Montreal, and Rome. See Communities of Jerusalem, Who We Are, http://jerusalem.cef.fr/jerusalem/en/en_21tous.html (accessed May 5, 2009).

[11] See Michael Mathis, "The Notre Dame Liturgy Program," *Liturgical Arts* 16 (1947–1948): 3–7, which describes the program and Reinhold's role in it.

[12] See H. A. Reinhold, "Liturgical Places" in Michael A. Mathis Papers, CMTH 17/22, archives of the University of Notre Dame.

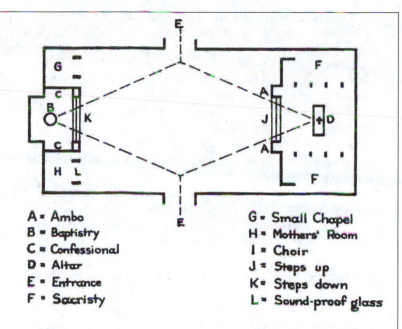

A = Ambo
B = Baptistry
C = Confessional
D = Altar
E = Entrance
F = Sacristy

G = Small Chapel
H = Mothers' Room
I = Choir
J = Steps up
K = Steps down
L = Sound-proof glass

Entering the church from the sides[1] would, with one glance, reveal the twofold foci of the church, baptism and eucharist. It would also give better circulation, as the church would empty itself in two streams flowing in opposite directions. It would make for cross-ventilation. It would have the added advantage of bringing the congregation, on entering, to the center of the church, and it would counteract the obnoxious tendency of staying away from the front pews. The sneaking in during services would be less easy--it would make for attendance on time.[2]

Figure 3

What strikes you first about St. Joseph's Church is the walled garden, and the façade with neither door nor window in its solid red brick wall. Immediately, you find yourself in the presence of mystery and silence. You know and you feel that you will leave the street and its traffic behind you to penetrate through the garden into another world.

When Father Reinhold showed me the building, we entered through the doorway of the old outgrown church (fig. 4). This has now been made into the parish hall. A surprise was awaiting me. My guide opened a door at the side of the hall, and we found ourselves above a sunny square vestibule. A curved flight of stairs took us down into it, to face a large square double-door. This is the entrance to the church.

Building on Faith

It is dignified and beautiful; and it is entirely hidden from the street. As you enter it you are thrown directly into the middle of the church. Lovers of the last pews must go to as much trouble here as if they were struggling for first places. Nor can latecomers come in unnoticed! It is a wonderful surprise to enter a church which is a bright, roomy, square enclosure illuminated only from above by two rows of windows right under the roof. To the left, at the east, is the sanctuary and to the right, at the west wall, the baptistery.

The baptistery is a semi-circular space two steps down from the floor and separated by an iron grill. It is beautiful. There is no mistaking the font as one of the cardinal points of the building, and it is as fully open to view to the community as is the Altar which faces it at the opposite end of the church. This was the first time I saw the Font centered on the same axis as the Altar. It was just what I had wanted to see but had visualized so far only in the form of plans.[13]

Later in the essay Bethune describes other sections of the church as well:

And now I would like to describe the sanctuary in St. Joseph's Church in Sunnyside. Here the sanctuary as well as the nave is square. A smaller square, built to the east of the nave, the sanctuary is also taller and brighter. The light in it is wonderful—clear but not blinding. It comes from an unseen row of ten windows in the west, high above the nave, so that no one, neither celebrant, nor preacher nor congregation, has to face glaring panes of glass. Apparently this is also how the sanctuary of New Mexico's old adobe church is illuminated. And without question, it seems to me one of the very best solutions to that problem. Certainly the light in the sanctuary should come from above and it should come from higher up than the nave, i.e., the sanctuary should be the highest spot of the church, and the light should illuminate but not glare in anyone's face. Such considerations, both for the dignity of the rites and for the comfort of the human beings who are using the building, are a part of good architecture and lessons which more architects could follow.

Unlike good children, the choir of St. Joseph's parish is heard but not seen. No swivel-head can even hope to catch a glimpse of the singers; there is no choir-loft in the rear. The singers are established instead, at the side of the sanctuary but hidden from both congregation and

---

[13] Adé Bethune, "Font and Altar: Footnotes on Sacred Architecture," *The Catholic Art Quarterly* 15 (Pentecost 1954): 88–105; here 93.

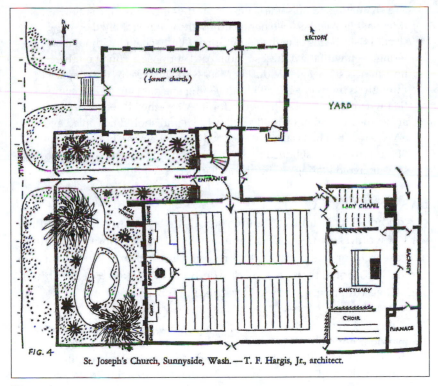

FIG. 4

St. Joseph's Church, Sunnyside, Wash. — T. F. Hargis, Jr., architect.

Figure 4

priest by vertical wooden louvers. They even have their own private entrance so that they may leave or arrive without disturbing anyone.

To the left of the sanctuary there is, what seems to me, the most unusually excellent feature of this building and one which I heartily recommend to every architect in the country. In fact, I think Father Reinhold should receive an award from the Catholic Mothers of America for this outstanding contribution to the Catholic life in our time.

Mothers with babies are welcome to St. Joseph's Church in Sunnyside. They are not told to stay home if they cannot prevent their infants from howling *during* the ceremonies. Neither are they banished to that gloomy institution going under the worse name of "cry room." Not so at St. Joseph's! Father Reinhold planned a gracious Lady chapel to the side of the sanctuary. It has its own Altar where he says Mass for his small week-day congregation. And it has a large plate glass window looking directly upon the main Altar in the sanctuary. What could be more natural than to have this the place for mothers and their babies, right under the patronage of Our Lady of Guadalupe? Here is motherhood exalted and given the place of honor instead of being segregated as a shameful and noisome state. Yet, at the same time, the suffered little ones are neither seen nor heard by the congregation; they may scream their heads of in their soundproof Lady chapel without interfering even with the dullest sermon. And suppose a young mother finds it necessary to leave during Mass—she just leaves the chapel through its own side-door without feeling she has caused any commotion whatever; no one is the wiser for it. Altogether, it seems as good an arrangement that I would say it is ideal and should be copied everywhere. The chief difficulty in such an arrangement, however, is one of illumination. A subdued light must be carefully planned from above so as to avoid glaring on the inside plate glass window.[14]

LASTING LEGACY

And how has Reinhold's church stood the test of time? Exceedingly well, it would seem. As I mentioned earlier, I visited Sunnyside during my research for this project. More recently I sent Kerry Turley, the deacon at St. Joseph's there, a copy of Adé Bethune's sketch of the church and asked him to assess the difference. He wrote:

> As for the church today, the walled garden and the façade with neither door nor window in its solid red brick wall is still there. In 1963 the school was built, the convent was added to the church and the parish hall was divided into a chapel and a dining/living room for the sisters. You may recall that this is the chapel where daily Mass is held. The curved flight of stairs is no longer there and the church restrooms are in that area now. Next to the restrooms is a new area called the gathering room, where we vest and gather the liturgical ministers before Mass.
>
> The baptistery was removed years ago (I never heard a good reason why) and a section of the semi-circular of wrought iron is now behind the altar. The confessionals were moved up front near the furnace room and pews now reach to the rear of the church and the choir room is now the Blessed Sacrament room. The room Father Reinhold called the Lady Chapel is still where it was.[15]

In addition Turley updated the Bethune sketch (fig. 5) to provide a clearer picture of this lasting legacy.

---

[14] Ibid., 101–2.
[15] Kerry Turley, e-mail message to author, March 10, 2009.

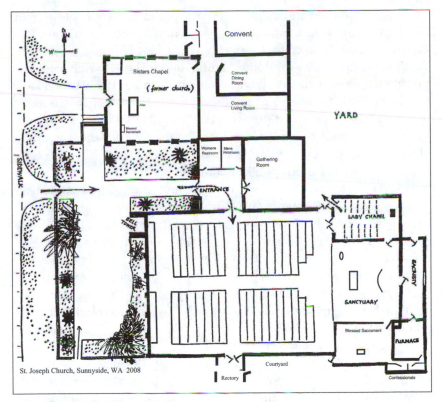

Figure 5. Used with permission.

EPISCOPAL DIRECTIVES ON CHURCH BUILDING

Even before *Mediator Dei*[16] was issued by Pope Pius XII on November 20, 1947, a "rather acrimonious controversy" in Germany prompted him to urge that the German hierarchy set up a liturgical commission to establish strategy and tactics for moving liturgical concerns forward wisely. According to Reinhold its results were gratifying and they produced "collections of excellent hymns eliminating all of the traditional trash which grows like weeds wherever musical principles and theology yield to emotionalism and a philosophy of success; several well graded forms of dialogue Mass with different degrees of participation and clear principles of selectiveness; plain and easy

---

[16] See http://www.vatican.va/holy_father/pius_xii/encyclicals/documents/hf_p-xii_enc_20111947_mediator-dei_en.html (accessed May 6, 2009).

rules for the amount and manner of participation of the people at high Mass and their posture during the sacred rites."[17] The commission's final document, "Directives for the Shaping of the House of God from the Spirit of the Liturgy of Rome," edited by Fr. Theodor Klauser, then president of Bonn University, was issued in 1949. An English translation by Fr. William Busch was published in the December 1949 issue of *Orate Fratres*.[18] Reinhold's essay "An Epochal Document on Church Building" summarized and commented on their work, seeing in this "lucid, reverent, and rational document" a cause for rejoicing.[19]

For ten years in various publications and educational settings Reinhold had been teaching the very principles and conclusions outlined in this document. The clarity and consistency of this document had to have been warmly affirming for him to read. At the same time it stoked within him the "desire that some similar document may help the American clergy and architects in their planning, to end the present chaos and to finish forever the state of affairs where dozens of controverted rubrics are upheld with fierce zeal by opponents while there seems to be no general principle according to which we could judge."[20] Although there were recommendations published by various dioceses in the United States, there were no country-wide guidelines issued until the publication of *Environment and Art in Catholic Worship*, published by the United States Conference of Catholic Bishops in 1978, almost thirty years after the German document and ten years after Reinhold's death.[21]

HOW TO LOOK AT LITURGICAL ARCHITECTURE

In a 1958 article, Reinhold posed a series of questions, along with the inevitable commentary we have come to expect, which would enable a parishioner to assess the degree to which his or her own parish church met the ideals of contemporary liturgical architecture. Of

[17] H. A. Reinhold, "An Epochal Document on Church Building," *Liturgical Arts* 18 (February 1950): 29–30.

[18] See William Busch, trans., "Directives for the Building of a Church," *Orate Fratres* 24 (December 1949): 3–12.

[19] Reinhold, "Epochal Document," 30.

[20] Ibid.

[21] In 2000 the United States Conference of Catholic Bishops published Built of Living Stones: Art, Architecture, and Worship, which "builds on and replaces" the previous document. See http://www.usccb.org/liturgy/livingstones.shtml#6 (accessed May 7, 2009).

course we are reading them more than fifty years later and in a liturgical context quite far removed from what Reinhold knew or expected, perhaps even beyond what he as a consummate dreamer could have imagined. Still the questions themselves are valid and as with so much of his writing, give us a way to understand and appreciate our own houses of worship. They are presented here in the same order in which he posed them in the article, although in some instances I have revised them for a consistent intention. In the original the questions were posed in both the present tense and the future tense, making it a bit confusing to determine whether Reinhold's intention was to address current structures or future ones. I surmise that he meant both, and so present the questions in the present tense:

1. Is the church "in its inspiration representative of the apostolic and consecrating spirit, which is the church's spirit at all times?"[22] The question as well as the issue behind it was Reinhold's core concern regarding "worship in spirit and truth." Unlike the other questions posed in the article, he provided no embellishment to this first essential question.

2. "Is it truly organized: are its parts organically distinct? Does it show by its structure inside and out that it is meant for the meeting of the . . . Body of Christ and the celebration of His mysteries? Is the main body of the church truly 'an upper room' free of distracting accessories? Are baptistery and confessionals coordinated? Have smaller, more intimate chapels been provided for individual devotions?"[23] Today Reinhold would probably be speaking in particular of a separate chapel for the reservation of the Blessed Sacrament, but his attention to the need for devotional space in its proper order is important, since he was often criticized for denigrating the need for devotions or for a devotional life. He never denigrated them, but rather recommended proportionality—that they not supplant the centrality of the Eucharist.[24]

3. "Apart from its liturgical functions," how does the church "serve as a monument to faith, as part of the city and of the landscape: how

[22] H. A. Reinhold, "Art, Architecture and the Christian: Some Notes on How to Look at Churches Past and Present," *Jubilee* 5 (April 1958): 17–20; here 19. An edited version of this essay can also be found in Reinhold's *The Dynamics of Liturgy* (New York: Macmillan, 1961), 84–92.

[23] Reinhold, "Art, Architecture and the Christian," 19.

[24] See H. A. Reinhold, "Meaning and Necessity of 'Devotions,'" *Proceedings of the National Liturgical Week* (1940): 169–76.

does it fit with the surrounding architecture; is the building appropriate to its particular site, and does it realistically reflect the economic and social conditions of the parishioners? Have local building materials been put to skillful use?"[25]

Reinhold's concerns here were clearly not just architectural. In 2004 St. Thomas More Church was dedicated on our campus of St. John's University in New York. In the course of preparing for its construction, after interviewing six architectural firms, each of which had built fine churches, the building committee selected the firm of Martin A. DeSapio, AIA. That firm had designed several churches in our region of the country, some of which we visited. Each of the churches impressed us with its fidelity to the principles of the Second Vatican Council and in particular because each looked as though it truly belonged to its neighborhood. Although they shared certain basic principles, they were far from being clones of each other. That factor in particular led us to believe that the architects would collaborate with us on the project and not arrive at the first meeting with a complete design of how our church should look. The collaboration proved to be rich and rewarding, and it is difficult to imagine that our church was not always the centerpiece of our campus.[26] Even though we have a central-plan church, I think that Reinhold himself would honor the result.

To be honest, I have spent a long time pondering his vehemence that the altar not be placed in the center of the church. He wrote about it in various articles and actually named himself an apostle against the practice, carrying on a "single-handed fight against central, cruciform churches."[27] "It would not be right to place the altar in the center of the church because the priest could never face the whole congregation either in prayer or sermon; like a bull ring or a boxing arena, such an arrangement would tend to create merely spectators, not participants. (In this sense, the circular floor-plan with the altar in the middle is quite opposed to the spirit of the liturgy.)"[28] In my mind we have had several discussions about this and I think I come out on the winning end for several reasons.

[25] Reinhold, "Art, Architecture and the Christian," 19–20.

[26] See Julia Upton, "A Church for the University: St. Thomas More," *Church* (Winter 2005): c10–c13.

[27] H. A. Reinhold, "Leads from Germany," *Orate Fratres* 23 (September 1949): 462–67; here 462.

[28] Reinhold, "Art, Architecture and the Christian," 19.

Worship in Spirit and Truth

The chapel at Mount Saviour, where Reinhold spent so many retreats, is a central-plan church with the altar in the center. Although Reinhold wrote about his experiences there several times, there is never any reference of criticism regarding the placement of the altar there. Perhaps worshiping with the extended community in that holy place gradually began to reshape his understanding and to resolve some of the problems he anticipated with an altar in the center of the worship space. Furthermore, it is important to keep in mind that all of Reinhold's critique is based on a pre–Vatican II approach to liturgy. As we saw earlier, he certainly had a "dream Mass" in mind as far back as 1940, but close as they were there was still a wide gulf between dream and reality. Even after having lived with the post–Vatican II liturgy for close to forty years, it was difficult for me to estimate how powerfully the altar in the center of our worship space would reshape the community.

4. "Does something about the building say its purpose is a supernatural one? Is it built in a style that is not outlandish, foreign, or pseudo-traditional?"[29] "Ultimately, we deal with the unutterably, invisible and spaceless. We would be better off if our frailty permitted us to do without all representation, but that would be the harshness of historical iconoclasm, condemned as an exaggeration."[30]

5. "Is the church 'uncluttered'? Does it emphasize space, leaving room for the eye to see the essential?"[31] Elsewhere he explained that "the floor plan must provide for the fullest possible participation in worship. The altar should face the congregation and be clearly visible. Any second altar should be in a small chapel out of sight of the congregation, so that it will not detract from the liturgy at the main altar."[32]

6. "Does the church show a truly Christian spirit of poverty? (A dignified poverty, not shoddiness or destitution.)"[33] "Poverty is not the same as cheapness, shoddiness, bad taste or ugliness."[34] Today

[29] Ibid., 20.

[30] H. A. Reinhold, "Liturgy, Architecture and the Arts," *The Irish Ecclesiastical Record* 95 (May 1961): 299–305; here 301.

[31] Reinhold, "Art, Architecture and the Christian," 20.

[32] H. A. Reinhold, "Liturgy and Church Architecture," *Good Work* 24 (Fall 1961): 112–18; here 116.

[33] Reinhold, "Art, Architecture and the Christian," 20.

[34] Reinhold, "Liturgy, Architecture and the Arts," 302.

Reinhold might very well also add a concern for sustainability to the question posed. "In its new area of life the church becomes progressively less extensive and more intensive . . . the spare, slender, light and open rather than the ponderous, ornate and cavelike darkness of the past are now the outward symptoms of a radical change."[35]

7. "What about size? . . . The small and intimate congregation still remains the ideal. In a mass civilization any further concentration of the crowd is dangerous, especially in the spiritual field. The crowds flowing through our large, double-story churches in and out of hourly Masses have become amorphous, anonymous, impersonal, religiously asphyxiated, starving from unnatural and unnourishing mass spiritual feeding. And this should not be."[36] And on that emphatic note Reinhold ended his extended reflection on how to assess a house of worship.

IN GOOD COMPANY

Throughout his years of ministry Reinhold collaborated with artists and architects. One of the earliest, mentioned previously, was Peter Anson (1898–1975), who Reinhold first came to know through his relationship to the International Council of the Apostleship of the Sea (Apostolatus Maris). Anson's exquisitely detailed description of Reinhold's ministry in Bremerhaven[37] takes the reader with him inside the *Seemansheim*, making you feel as if you are right there in the room with them. It is probably his skill as an artist that enabled him to give such vivid descriptions. Anson's books are all richly illustrated, and in addition he spent two years studying at the Architectural Association School of Architecture[38] in London. When he was preparing his illustrated book *Churches: Their Plan and Furnishing*, which was dedicated to Reinhold, Anson also invited Reinhold to "Americanize"

[35] Reinhold, "Art, Architecture and the Christian," 20.

[36] Ibid.

[37] See Peter F. Anson, *Harbour Head: Maritime Memories* (London: John Gifford Limited, 1944), 175–82.

[38] Established in 1847, the Architectural Association describes itself as "Britain's oldest and most vital school of architecture, an institution whose independence of thought and operation have been fought for by the generations of students, tutors and staff who have passed through its doors" (http://www .aaschool.ac.uk/Default.aspx?section=school&page=aa%20history&sst=1 [accessed May 10, 2009]).

the book.[39] Commenting on the task, Reinhold wrote that the book's "outstanding feature is the fact that Peter Anson represents the liturgical wing of art, architecture, and rubrics. I had little to add and less to change, and when I did so, the initials H.A.R. warn the reader of it."[40] So, scattered throughout the book are detailed notations by way of analysis or commentary, sometimes supporting the author, but occasionally offering a word of gentle dissent.

Another important friend, colleague, and collaborator was Arthur Graham Carey (1892–1983), a descendant of John Jacob Astor and one of the founders of the Catholic Art Association. They probably got to know each other during 1937, the year Reinhold taught at Portsmouth. Among Reinhold's papers at the Burns Library, there is extensive correspondence between the two, and it is obvious that their relationship was particularly close. Reinhold baptized the Careys' children, was anticipated to serve as chaplain to their community in Benson, Vermont, and had arrangements to be buried there.[41] Carey's Church of Christ the Sun of Justice in Benson was described in Adé Bethune's article "Font and Altar" referenced earlier in this chapter.

Reinhold's advice on liturgical buildings and renovations was continually sought by parishes and dioceses around the country, but the crowning recognition for him had to have been receiving the Elbert M. Conover Award in October 1966. Established in 1953 by the Church Architecture Guild of America, this award is given periodically to non-architects in recognition of their significant contributions to religious architecture. In addition to being a nonarchitect, those given the award must "demonstrate a passion for and dedication to quality worship and sacred spaces; foster spiritual values; and promote a cross-denominational community focused on religious arts and architecture."[42] Reinhold was the fifth person to receive the award, which is still being given today, surely a well-deserved personal triumph.

[39] See Peter F. Anson, *Churches: Their Plan and Furnishings* (Milwaukee, WI: Bruce, 1948).

[40] H. A. Reinhold, "Editor's Note," in ibid., vii.

[41] See "Graham Carey," Box 3/3, H. A. Reinhold Papers, Burns Library, Boston College.

[42] Elbert M. Conover Memorial Award, http://www.aia.org/practicing/groups/kc/AIAB079827 (accessed May 15, 2009).

Chapter 7

Called to the Same Hope

> Just as night and day flow gently into one another, and as the four
> seasons develop imperceptibly, the Liturgy is something live, growing
> and organic. There is never anything frantic, hasty, theatrical in the Lit-
> urgy. The Roman spirit is one of virile moderation and majesty.[1]

SUMMING UP

Writing toward the end of his life and still concerned about liturgical celebrations, Fr. Reinhold reflected that he and his colleagues in
the liturgical movement always maintained that an "internal reform"
would follow naturally if things were left to develop. Nonetheless,
he left us with more seasoned advice, "We cannot pin our hopes of a
'follow-through' on another miracle. What we now need is hard work
and intelligence (and, above all, prayer),"[2] by which he surely meant
praying the liturgy as it is intended to be prayed. That is no small
agenda, and even though he gave that advice forty years ago, the
needs of the church are even clearer now, after having been left to develop for several decades. Liturgy, as the word itself implies, requires
work. Sometimes I think that when we pray for peace, we expect that
it will be like some "happily ever after" we were deluded into expecting from childhood fairy tales. Peace takes work! The same is true
with marriage. It is unrealistic to expect that the bliss experienced on
one's wedding day will magically remain permanent. For some reason
humans expect that we will live into a time of permanent equilibrium
this side of the grave. As St. Paul observed in his letter to the Philippi-
ans, if we are to continue living the liturgy, this will mean "productive
toil" for us.

---

[1] H. A. Reinhold, "Incarnation and Parousia," *Commonweal* 35 (December
19, 1941): 214–16; here 215. An edited version of this essay can also be found in
Reinhold's *The Dynamics of Liturgy* (New York: Macmillan, 1961), 62–67.

[2] H. A. Reinhold, "A Liturgical Reformer Sums Up," *New Blackfriars* 46
(1965): 554–61; here 554.

Elsewhere I have described Reinhold as an architect of the liturgical movement in America,[3] and I still believe that metaphor and double entendre is appropriate, because he not only designed how the objectives of the liturgical movement could be achieved in the United States, he also contributed more writings on liturgical architecture than anyone else in that era. Someone else, however, identified him as the "spiritual director of the Liturgical Movement,"[4] and after having read and analyzed everything Reinhold published during his illustrious career, as well as a considerable amount of his private correspondence, I find that description to be even more apt.

This chapter will focus on what one might call Reinhold's last liturgical will and testament. As such it will naturally draw on all of his writings, but will be most attentive to the echoes of his last work. For example, the inaugural issue of *The Living Light*, a major catechetical journal still published quarterly in the United States out of the Catholic University of America, included a column by Reinhold titled Timely Questions. The column continued for two years, from Spring 1964 until Summer 1966 when it abruptly ended, probably because of Reinhold's declining health, although I did find one additional manuscript for the series that was never published. The topics he discusses in these ten columns give us added insight into his thinking.

Another summative work is Reinhold's 1961 volume *The Dynamics of Liturgy*. This is almost entirely a collection of essays published elsewhere over the course of his career, although, apart from a list of not quite accurate copyright dates, only one of the original sources is specifically referenced in the text. The sources of the original essays, as best as I have been able to determine, are listed in appendix D. Some appear in *Dynamics* in their original state, some were edited lightly for the collection, and a few were substantially altered. Taken together they stand as a kind of liturgical manifesto.

[3] See Julia Upton, RSM, "H. A. Reinhold: Architect of the Liturgical Movement in America," *Benedict in the World: Portraits of Monastic Oblates*, ed. Linda Kulzer and Roberta Bondi (Collegeville, MN: Liturgical Press, 2002), 187–99.

[4] See editor's note to H. A. Reinhold, "The Silence and Singleness of Prayer," *The Current: A Review of Catholicism and Contemporary Culture* 1 (May 1961): 61–64; here 61.

Nathan Mitchell recalled the work of Paul Ricoeur, who noted nearly fifty years ago that we live in an "age of forgetting the signs of the sacred."[5] Mitchell wrote:

> Ritual does more than "remember" or "repeat" or "celebrate" a reality; it rewrites—redefines—that reality. Ritual engagement is thus a critical tool in that circular process of accessing symbols which demands that we "understand by believing and believe by understanding." . . . If women and men today are to access the great symbols of Christian tradition, what they need is not "liturgical correctness" . . . or even "better aesthetics, but a *hermeneutics of ritual engagement*."[6]

Although he did not use that term, Reinhold would certainly concur with the underlying spirit of that approach to liturgy today, and one could say that in his writings about liturgy he illustrated a hermeneutic of ritual engagement.

After interviewing Reinhold just about on the eve of opening session of Vatican II, John Deedy wrote, "Father Reinhold recommends 'patience and perseverance' and breathes a prayer that the Second Vatican Council will make perfectly clear the place which the liturgy must enjoy in the life of Catholics. If such comes, he is convinced that 'the liturgy will be installed in its rightful place, and the people's full participation in it will be achieved in a generation or two.'"[7]

Here we are a generation or two later reflecting on what has been achieved. With apologies to Karl Barth, elsewhere I have categorized these as "the already, the not yet, and the not quite."[8] Reinhold would be so pleased with the "already," challenged by the "not yet," and frustrated by the "not quite." Before listening to his advice on how to respond to the "not yet" or the "not quite," however, it is important to remind ourselves how far we have already come since Vatican II—

[5] See Paul Ricoeur "The Symbol: Food for Thought," *Philosophy Today* 4:3-4 (1960): 196–207; here 203.

[6] Nathan Mitchell, "Liturgical Correctness," The Amen Corner, *Worship* 71 (January 1997): 62–71; here 68–69. See also Timothy Radcliffe, *Why Go to Church? The Drama of the Eucharist* (New York: Continuum, 2008).

[7] John G. Deedy Jr., "Restless Ambassador of Christ," *Jubilee* 8 (November 1961): 7–11; here 8.

[8] See Julia Upton, "The Eucharistic Assembly: Standing in Your Presence to Serve," *Monastic Liturgy Forum Newsletter* 13 (Autumn 2001): 4–12.

Called to the Same Hope

how the church today differs from the church in which Reinhold worshiped even toward the end of his life.

ALTERED STATES OF ECCLESIAL CONSCIOUSNESS

In the years since Vatican II we have gradually entered an "altered state of ecclesial consciousness." There is less of that Counter-Reformation siege mentality that I recall so vividly from my youth and with which so many of my generation were raised. As was true of Reinhold's parents, mine also liked to visit various types of churches, but each time we entered a Protestant church I became fearful, concerned that I was doing something illicit and as a result something terrible might happen to me. Neither of my parents could understand my reluctance and reticence, but then they were more worldly wise people not subjected to the scare tactics I experienced in the parish elementary school. Once I remember attending the wedding of a family friend at a Congregational Church. As a family we had been very involved in all of the preparations and my mother had sewn much of the bride's trousseau. Nonetheless, such stern warnings from the nuns about not even appearing to participate in a non-Catholic service thundered so loudly in my head that I could barely experience the joy and beauty of the occasion. "The times they are a-changin',"[9] we began singing, and eventually we lived into those times of change in the church as well as in the rest of American society.

Today Roman Catholics more readily recognize themselves as Christians than they did a generation or two ago. Ecumenical services and institutes have helped to create circles of conversation among various religious groups, and religious education programs have begun to develop at least a rudimentary understanding and appreciation of other religious traditions. Evangelization programs and initiation processes are increasingly central to the life of the typical Roman Catholic parish today.

When I teach liturgy at the university and in diocesan liturgical formation programs I always begin with the Greek root for the term "liturgy," defining it as "work of the people." I have followed that explanation with the question, "Who is doing the work?" Forty years ago when I first began teaching, a timid answer would inevitably come back: "The priest?" Now the answer is more resounding: "We

[9] Composed by Bob Dylan in 1961, "The Times They Are A-Changin'" is the title song of his 1964 album.

Worship in Spirit and Truth

all do!" Yes, as Reinhold anticipated, the assembly has gradually been reshaped through several decades of celebrating the Eucharist, and not simply "hearing Mass" as we used to say in the pre-council years.[10]

The basic symbols have changed. Fifty years ago, apart from getting married, a woman entered the sanctuary only to change the altar linens or scrub the floor. Now sanctuaries are filled with laypeople—male and female. Taking their rightful place as members of the community, they proclaim the Scriptures, serve at the altar, and assist in the distribution of Holy Communion. Special ministers of Holy Communion even make regular communion calls at homes of the sick. Laypeople also serve as catechists, directors of religious education, parish administrators—in almost all areas of pastoral life that do not require ordination.

A WARM AND LIVING LOVE OF THE SCRIPTURES

Another goal achieved as a result of Vatican II has been fostering "a warm and lively appreciation of sacred scripture,"[11] which is reflected in Catholic communities today. Because my mother was unable to explain to me why I could not go to the Episcopal Sunday School along with all my Protestant preschool friends, I was privileged to join them, with the blessing of the rector. That "warming and living love" for Bible stories and lessons was fostered in me at a young age, but it was gradually replaced by confusion when I began attending Catholic elementary school. There I was warned against reading the Bible because I might not "get it right" and could fall into what seemed to be treated as a crime—interpreting Scripture personally.

Scripture study began as a kind of a curiosity in the Roman Catholic community in the mid-1960s, if you are old enough to recall. There was the discovery of the Dead Sea Scrolls,[12] which made front-page news in the years immediately preceding the council. This led some

---

[10] See Frank C. Senn, *The People's Work: A Social History of the Liturgy* (Minneapolis: Fortress Press, 2006).

[11] ". . . in order to achieve the restoration, progress, and adaptation of the sacred liturgy it is essential to promote that warm and lively appreciation of sacred scripture to which the venerable tradition of both eastern and western rites gives testimony" (*Sacrosanctum Concilium*, 24).

[12] This term refers to the series of manuscript finds in Palestine near the Dead Sea beginning in 1947 and continuing to 1961. See Daniel Harrington, "What's New(s) About the Dead Sea Scrolls," *CrossCurrents* 44 (Winter

Catholics to dip into the Scriptures as a current events item. Study groups began forming in the years after the council, as more and more Catholics wanted to understand the context for Scripture texts they now heard proclaimed in the vernacular at Mass. Keep in mind that in the pre–Vatican II liturgy there was only one cycle of Sunday readings, which consisted of two readings: one from an epistle, the other from a gospel. Except for special feasts and the seasons of Lent and Advent there were no readings assigned to weekdays. The Sunday readings were simply repeated at regular weekday (ferial) Masses. As a result, at Sunday Mass prior to the publication of the revised Lectionary in 1969, Roman Catholics heard no readings from the Old Testament and only 17 percent of the New Testament.[13] Gradually Bible vigils began to replace Benediction as Roman Catholics became more at home with the Word.

It is no wonder then that scriptural images now lace the assembly's prayers, songs, and speech. Parishioners turn to the pages of Scripture more regularly for comfort, inspiration, and challenge. The Word now nourishes us in a way we could not have imagined a generation or two ago. It is a great blessing!

SOCIAL ACTION: THE MISSING LINK?

The "right" questions to ask about liturgical celebrations are not those that deal exclusively with liturgical correctness, but more properly those that assess how the community's sense of corporate mission is strengthened as a result of being immersed in mystery—of breaking open the word and breaking bread around the common table. North Americans seem to have lost their sense of the sacramental character of life and of the body—both the human form and the *mystici corporis*. Too often Eucharist is discussed almost exclusively in terms of what happens to the bread and wine, how relevant the homily is, whether or not the prayers are inclusive or the celebrant is dynamic. The first Christians focused instead on what happened to the people who shared the bread and wine in memory of Christ. We have two

---

1994–95): 463–76. (See http://www.crosscurrents.org/deadsea.htm [accessed April 13, 2009].)

[13] This included 33 percent of Matthew, 16 percent of Luke, 28 percent of John, and 5 percent of Mark. See Martin Connell, *Guide to the Revised Lectionary* (Chicago: Liturgy Training Publications, 1998) for a list of texts in the 1969 Lectionary that were not in the previous one, the Missal of Pius V (1570).

thousand years of stories about people whose lives have been transformed by their experiences around the Christian family table. Some are celebrated as saints, but others were ordinary citizens who were able to do extraordinary things because their faith in themselves, in God, and in the community was strengthened at Eucharist. Those are the stories that communities must remember to repeat.

"To participate in the meal is to enact that vision, to surrender oneself to its value, meaning and truth,"[14] Nathan Mitchell wrote. In coming to the eucharistic meal we testify to our common belief that it is the Lord Jesus who sustains and nourishes us, and we pledge we will likewise sustain and nourish one another with the bread that is our lives. That is our pledge to humanity. In his address to the forty-first International Eucharistic Congress in Philadelphia in 1976, Fr. Pedro Arrupe reminded us that "if there is hunger anywhere in the world, then our celebration of the Eucharist is somehow incomplete everywhere in the world."[15]

Living just over the edge of the third millennium, we have come to expect easy answers and quick solutions to questions and problems we barely have time to frame. Technology is moving at such a numbing pace that before we can even master the latest piece of electronic equipment it is obsolete. Often it seems that people do not want to be engaged by mystery, but entertained in spite of it.

Once upon a time people used to fast before coming to worship. Although I am not recommending a return to what had often become "mindless" practices of the past, there is something to be said for coming to the banquet table hungry—not just fasting from food, but hungering for God both physically and spiritually. Physical hunger that reminds us ultimately of our deep spiritual hunger for communion with each other and with God can be a powerful religious experience. What are we to do? What would Reinhold say? He would urge us to come to the table hungering for God alone, knowing that the Lord of the harvest, who provided manna for our ancestors in faith, and who

[14] Nathan Mitchell, *Eucharist as Sacrament of Initiation* (Chicago: Liturgy Training Publications, 1994), 76.

[15] Pedro Arrupe, "The Hunger for Bread . . . ," Address to the Forty-first International Eucharistic Congress, Philadelphia, 1976. See also Julia Upton, "Liturgy/Eucharist/World," in *Contemporary Spirituality: Responding to the Divine Initiative*, ed. Francis A. Eigo (Villanova, PA: Villanova University Press, 1983), 115–35.

Called to the Same Hope

multiplied loaves and fishes literally and figuratively from generation to generation, will again come to feed us in this banquet which draws us together in faith and gives us meaning.

LESSONS FOR A LIFETIME

As was mentioned earlier there are some elements of liturgical life and worship, what I call the "not quite" and the "not yet," that need some further development because the message has not been received or implemented fully. In addition, because liturgy is a living reality, it will always require attention so that the community can deepen its experience of the Lord and its service to the world. Using Reinhold's words and ideas, I will develop these more throughout the rest of this chapter, but here are the seven lessons that from my perspective are most important for us to learn if we are to enable our communities to worship in spirit and truth:

- Begin with the basics.

- Foster active participation.

- Collaborate!

- Read broadly and deeply.

- Make room for mystagogy.

- Shape a space for worship and devotion.

- Run while you have the light.

BEGIN WITH THE BASICS

In 1943 Reinhold published a monograph, *Our Parish: House of God and Gate of Heaven*,[16] commissioned as a "discussion aid" by the Confraternity of Christian Doctrine. It could be seen as a primer for the series of articles in the Los Angeles *Tidings*, which was discussed extensively in chapter 4. *Our Parish* opens with a discussion of the importance of examining the parish itself—its geographical setting—and then moves on to looking at the church building and finally to the central place of the altar. Reinhold never presumed that his readers

---

[16] H. A. Reinhold, *Our Parish: House of God and Gate of Heaven* (New York: Paulist, 1943).

Worship in Spirit and Truth

recalled the basics, so like a good teacher he always found a way to review key points of the discussion by returning to essentials.

As one who "championed the cause of liturgical worship at a time when liturgical reformers were looked upon with suspicion or written off as pious cranks," Reinhold was "classified as *avant garde* and lumped, sometimes disdainfully, among the liberals." In the field of liturgy, however, he can only be regarded accurately as a conservative. "True conservatism preserves the essentials," he stated, "but is quite willing to shear off wild growth. True progress does not ride roughshod over what is good and mature. As true conservatives . . . we wish to see a popularly understandable worship which retains its traditions intact for the future generations of Christians. This often is poorly understood by those who take a negative stand."[17]

In 1958 the first of his books was published, *The American Parish and the Roman Liturgy*. In the introduction he set out its schema, which illustrates the lesson at hand. There is a "need for universal meditation on what has already been done and a proper understanding of it. Next, there is the necessity of appreciation of the trend of historical, doctrinal, and liturgical affairs. . . . Finally . . . there must be a discussion of things desirable and a searching for what yet ought to come."[18] The book was reviewed broadly and very well received.[19]

Here we are two generations later still in need of a return to basics both for presiders and congregations. Unfortunately, the liturgical changes after Vatican II were not uniformly implemented with the guiding hand of those skilled in education. The changes also did not come in one full sweep. In fact since 1964 we have experienced waves of change as each of the sacramental celebrations were revived and revised. Some were ripples of change, while others seemed more like tsunamis. All, I believe, could have benefited from better implementation, and as we look ahead to a revised Roman Missal we have

[17] Deedy, "Restless Ambassador," 7.

[18] H. A. Reinhold, *The American Parish and the Roman Liturgy: An Essay in Seven Chapters* (New York: Macmillan, 1958), vii.

[19] For some examples see Gerald Ellard, *Critic* 16 (May 1958): 45; William Petrek, *Commonweal* 67 (March 28, 1958): 664–65; Alexander Schmemann, *St. Vladimir's Seminary Quarterly* 2 (Spring 1958): 49–50; Gerard Sloyan, *Catholic Educational Review* 57 (March 1959): 207–9; Leo Trese, *Worship* 32 (June 1958): 379–80; Bishop John Wright, *America* 98 (February 1958): 516.

another opportunity to return to basics as a first step in implementation. Reinhold would urge us to do so boldly.

FOSTER ACTIVE PARTICIPATION

If we needed one command to sum up Reinhold's desire for the liturgy it would be "Participate!" Nothing, Deedy wrote, distressed Reinhold more than "an inactive and silenced laity, particularly at the most supreme and sublime of liturgical services—the Mass." In that interview Reinhold himself said, "The tragedy is that over the centuries the function of the layman was reduced to the point where he became a mere spectator at a half-hour 'show' and a hurried 'show' at that." Although Reinhold recognized that Pius XII's encyclical *Mediator Dei* did much to alter the situation, he did not think that "the barriers to intelligent, full participation" would be completely removed until at least parts of the Mass were in the vernacular.[20]

What does active participation look like? Unfortunately, in many Catholic parishes active participation is measured by the degree to which members of the congregation sing the hymns. Praying together and singing together are not unimportant, but they are far from the full measure of participation, "True liturgical participation must have social and political consequences,"[21] wrote Mark Searle, and no one would have supported that more than Reinhold.

"The liturgy in its most dynamic form calls the whole man to serve. The average Christian must undergo a change that is noticeable to the onlooker: you can't Sunday after Sunday participate in the life-giving mysteries of Christ's death and Resurrection without becoming more and more conscious of your brothers and sisters taking part in the same mysteries."[22] Active participation in the liturgy, therefore, would result in active participation in society—especially serving the poor and most vulnerable. "Our conscience should be alerted and the impact of this neighbor-relation should be tremendous. It should hurt us deeply if we are not living the mysteries which we profess to believe.

[20] Deedy, "Restless Ambassador," 8.

[21] Mark Searle, *Called to Participate: Theological, Ritual, and Social Perspectives*, ed. Barbara Searle and Anne Y. Koester (Collegeville, MN: Liturgical Press, 2006), 44.

[22] H. A. Reinhold, "The Societal Implications of a Dynamic Liturgy," Manuscript in Subject Files A–K, Box 15, Folder 38, H. A. Reinhold Papers, John J. Burns Library, Boston College.

Worship in Spirit and Truth

To participate in the Holy Banquet and not to recognize our deepest social obligation should bother our conscience."[23]

Toward the end of his life, Reinhold became more involved in ecumenism as well,[24] which for him was a consequence of his active participation in the liturgy and the liturgical movement. "If the layman, fully aware of his responsibility, becomes an active participant in the Church's worship," Reinhold observed, "his mind naturally will display a deeper understanding of his role in the mission of the Church. From this will flow a keener sympathy for the separated churches because of his own deeper understanding of the Word of God. He will be filled with greater sympathy for those of the Eastern churches, because they worship the same way in their own liturgy. He will also be more centered in God than when he was apt to yield to a temptation of mechanical outward worship as a mere spectator."[25] At his funeral the homilist observed, "Reinhold had a passion for unity. He hated nationalism and he longed for an international order. But, even more to our point, he longed for the unity of those who believe in Jesus Christ, who share his hope because they are marked already with his sign. For ecumenism as for the liturgy, Father Reinhold was a mighty prophet."[26]

COLLABORATE

Reinhold collaborated his entire life, as we saw in so many instances in the first part of this book, and he would urge us to do likewise. Writing during Vatican II, Reinhold gave reference to another mode of collaboration.[27] Not long after he became pastor of St. Joseph Parish in Sunnyside, Washington, he paid a courtesy visit to the local ministerial association. The ministers there were shocked to have a Catholic priest

[23] Ibid.

[24] See H. A. Reinhold, "In These Ecumenic Times," *The Lamp* 61 (November 1963): 10–11; "Liturgy and Ecumenism," in *Dialogue for Reunion: The Catholic Premises*, ed. Leonard Swidler, 38–53 (New York: Herder and Herder, 1962); "Liturgy and Reunion," *Commonweal* 75 (January 5, 1962): 379–82; "The One Church, A Challenge to Us as Catholics," *Proceedings of the North American Liturgical Week* (1960): 106–12.

[25] Deedy, "Restless Ambassador," 11.

[26] William Clancy, "In Memoriam: H.A.R.," *Worship* 42, no. 3 (March 1968): 130–33; here 133. See also *Time's Covenant: The Essays and Sermons of William Clancy*, ed. Eugene Green (Pittsburgh: University of Pittsburgh Press, 1987), 135–39.

[27] Reinhold, "In These Ecumenic Times," 10–11, 22, 24.

join them and looked upon him with "latent suspicion." After all, it was 1948, long before ecumenism came to be in vogue, even a clarion call of John XXIII. Reinhold continued to meet with his colleagues, although they did not drop their guard.

Reinhold's involvement in the Liturgical Conference,[28] from its very inception in 1940 to virtually the last day of his active ministerial life in 1965, is the most sustained example of his urge to collaborate. For much of that time he served as a member of the conference's board of directors, and he gave presentations at most of the annual Liturgical Weeks. Appendixes to the early volumes of the conference's *Proceedings* give precise details on attendance, listing the number of priests, sisters, and laity in attendance by state. During his years of ministry in the state of Washington, often only one priest from the state is listed in attendance. The one exception was the 1947 Liturgical Week, which took place in Portland, Oregon, and not surprisingly attracted many more people from the Northwest. It included an art exhibit organized by Reinhold.[29]

From 1938 until 1956 Reinhold also served as a member of the editorial board of *Orate Fratres*, and there were many other instances in which he partnered with others to achieve his aims and he taught others to do so as well. From his perspective, Reinhold considered that his role in forming the Vernacular Society was his "only real contribution to the American liturgical movement."[30] Although a minor player, Reinhold was also active in the Rural Life Conference[31] during his time as pastor in Sunnyside, moved particularly by the needs of migrant workers in the area.

During my interviews in Sunnyside I also learned more about how Reinhold fostered leadership among the young. He would identify those with leadership qualities and then give them increasing responsibilities. Long before there was ever discussion about base ecclesial

[28] See Lawrence J. Madden, "The Liturgical Conference of the U.S.A.: Its Origin and Development: 1940–1968" (doctoral diss., Universität Trier, 1969). During much of this time Reinhold also served as a member of the board.

[29] See H. A. Reinhold, "Work of the People," *Commonweal* 46 (September 26, 1947): 571–73.

[30] H. A. Reinhold, *H. A. R.: The Autobiography of Father Reinhold* (New York: Herder and Herder, 1968), 140–41.

[31] See Michael J. Woods, "The Intersection of the National Catholic Rural Life Conference and the American Liturgical Movement, 1920–1960" (doctoral diss., Catholic University of America, 2008).

communities, Reinhold was forming them in rural Washington among teenagers and adults alike. We can learn from that, especially with regard to our youth, the future of the church.

They are a hands-on generation that responds best relationally. Too often they have been raised by television sets and on video games. They are what I have elsewhere called a generation of refugees—victims of a war against the human spirit. They are as much refugees in search of a homeland for the soul as any of the refugees who trooped to our shores in the past century.[32] It is my belief that by engaging them in discussion on substantive issues and in direct service that lifts the burdens of others, we will be able to provide an appropriate homeland or heartland for this millennial generation for whom violence and consumerism have become a way of life. One of the deep joys of working with this age group year after year is that they help me to retrieve remnants of my own idealism and remind me what energy there was in thinking that I could help change the world.

> Then I myself will gather the remnant of my flock out of all the lands where I have driven them, and I will bring them back to their fold, and they shall be fruitful and multiply. I will raise up shepherds over them who will shepherd them, and they shall not fear any longer, or be dismayed, nor shall any be missing, says the LORD. (Jer 23:3-6)

As Reinhold did, we might consider ourselves appointed as shepherds and invite young adults to engage in ecclesial work even if they are not in the pews. They are vibrant, intelligent young adults who think deeply about social justice issues. If I were privileged to be pastor of a parish today, I would ask my parishioners to give me the names of young adults who are not active members of the church or not necessarily even members of the church. I would telephone them myself and invite them to participate in a specific activity in which the parish regularly engages: homeless shelter, after-school program, senior citizens' luncheons, whatever it may be. Neil Howe and William Strauss's research tells us that millennials are "doers. Their attitudes and use of time reflect this."[33] Later I would invite them to dinner

---

[32] See Julia Upton, "A Generation of Refugees," *The Catholic World* 238 (September/October 1995): 204–11.

[33] Neil Howe and William Strauss, *Millennials Rising: The Next Great Generation* (New York: Vintage/Random House, 2000), 168.

Called to the Same Hope

and engage them in conversation over what they think we could be doing or ought to be doing together to make our corner of the earth a more just and peaceful place for people to live and work in harmony. Parishioners might consider suggesting this to pastors or trying it out themselves.

When I was a much younger and deeply disillusioned young Catholic, a pastor reached out to me and invited me to join the parish liturgy committee. His simple invitation changed my life and shaped my future. The prophet Isaiah urges us to broaden the tent:

> Enlarge the site of your tent,
>   and let the curtains of your habitations be stretched out;
> do not hold back; lengthen your cords
>   and strengthen your stakes.
> For you will spread out to the right and to the left,
>   and your descendants will possess the nations
>   and will settle the desolate towns. (Isa 54:2-3)

READ BROADLY AND DEEPLY

Just about everyone I interviewed in the course of my research made some reference to the huge number of magazines and journals found on Reinhold's desk and coffee table. As mentioned previously, at the end of his life Reinhold donated his entire library to Mount Saviour Monastery in Elmira, New York. After eliminating duplicates, the acquisition consists of 1,182 separate volumes, spanning several centuries with some dating back into the early seventeenth century to those published in 1966, the year of the donation. Although most are in English, many are in other languages as well. Writing about his longtime friend shortly after his death, Fr. Damasus Winzen, OSB, the prior of Mount Saviour, wrote, "The constant widening of his horizons remained one of his main preoccupations all through life. His library shows the vast range of his interests. We find in it books on politics and social sciences, which always held a prominent place in his interest and studies. There is a magnificent collection of books on Christian art, on theology, on poetry, on literature, and especially, of course, on liturgical subjects."[34]

Both the breadth and the depth of his reading are even more evidenced, however, in his writings. Just about every one of his Timely

---

[34] Damasus Winzen, "In the Memory of Msgr. Wolodimir Pylypetz and Rev. H. A. Reinhold," *Mount Saviour Chronicle* 32 (Pentecost 1968): 2–3; here 3.

Tracts in *Orate Fratres* makes some reference to a book he had recently read, and several of his *Commonweal* essays could more properly be classified as extended book reviews. In addition, to date I have found over seventy of Reinhold's book reviews, several of which review more than one book. His intellect was insatiable, and so should ours be if we are to continue to make liturgy a living and life-giving reality in our own day, connecting table and marketplace.

MAKE ROOM FOR MYSTAGOGY

When the rites of Christian initiation were revised in the 1970s, I feared two things: that translators would find a more "relevant" word than "mystagogy" and that the last stage in the process would be entirely eclipsed. While we have survived the first hurdle and the word "mystagogy" remains in our texts if not in our hearts, I am not so sure that we yet understand the spiritual significance of the last stage. Mystagogy is far beyond the pale of our cultural horizon and moving even farther away at a lightning pace.

Today most of what present themselves as the mysteries of life are thought to be explained by science. For inquirers, catechumens and candidates the mysteries of faith are similarly presented and discussed during the time of the months or years of preparation. In the third century when Theodore of Mopsuestia and St. John Chrysostom were preaching, however, it was not until after initiation had been completed that the mysteries were pondered.[35] Elsewhere I have described it as similar to a "honeymoon" for the new members of the community.[36] More regular practice of reflecting on the mysteries of faith in general would surely enliven preaching in the community, enable us to live more balanced lives, to celebrate our beliefs more robustly, and to hand on the faith to our children and our children's children.

"Without humility we cannot discuss religious problems," Reinhold wrote. "Our intellectual strainings in other fields are bound to affect our faith. We are obliged in conscience to match what we find in our innermost hearts with the insights that history and philosophy,

[35] See Enrico Mazza, *Mystagogy: A Theology of Liturgy in the Patristic Age* (Collegeville, MN: Liturgical Press, 1989).

[36] See Julia Upton, *A Church for the Next Generation: Sacraments in Transition* (Collegeville, MN: Liturgical Press, 1990), 37, 45–46; Upton, *Becoming A Catholic Christian: A Pilgrim's Guide to the Rite of Christian Initiation of Adults* (Washington, DC: Pastoral Press, 1993), 77–81.

Called to the Same Hope

literature and the sciences have given us. This meditative enrichment demands silence, integrity, and care. It can be pursued in the climate of the liturgy."[37]

Although he might not have known it at the time, T. S. Eliot was speaking of mystagogy when he wrote in "The Dry Salvages":

> We had the experience but missed the meaning
> and approach to the meaning restores the experience
> in a different form.[38]

Mystagogy requires leisure and a measure of courage, but if one is totally absorbed with more superficial concerns, one never has the leisure necessary to worship God alone or to plumb the depths of mystery who is God. To quote the poet William Wordsworth, "for this, for everything we are out of tune. It moves us not."[39]

One can see from most of his writings how Reinhold immersed himself in the mysteries of faith and life, but on his deathbed he gave even more eloquent witness to how he had been absorbed in and formed by the liturgy. Fr. Raymond Utz, ordained in 1963, helped to care for Reinhold in his declining years, particularly in his last illness at Mercy Hospital in Pittsburgh, and was with him when he died. To the end Reinhold held forcefully to his theology of the sacrament of the sick as the last sacrament and an anointing for glory[40] and refused to be anointed until death seemed immanent. Utz described the format of Reinhold's last confession as an extended version of the Good Friday intercessions. "Fr. Reinhold would mention a name or situation and describe it in some detail, and then have me pray about the person or situation framed by what he had said. This went on for about thirty minutes the day before he died."[41] From Utz's description, it was evident that in his dying days Reinhold had spent time reflecting on the mysteries of his life and turned them all to prayer.

---

[37] H. A. Reinhold, "The Silence and Singleness of Prayer," *The Current: A Review of Catholicism and Contemporary Culture* 1 (May 1961): 61–64; here 64.

[38] T. S. Eliot, "The Dry Salvages," in *Four Quartets* (New York: Harcourt Brace Jovanovich, 1971), 39.

[39] William Wordsworth, "The World Is Too Much With Us" (c. 1802).

[40] See H. A. Reinhold, "Eternal Glory: Sacrament and Treatment of Death in the Christian Tradition," *Commonweal* 35 (November 7, 1941): 66–69.

[41] Interview with Rev. Raymond Utz, January 12, 2007.

"We are concerned with the people, the people of the 20th Century, the people here in America," Reinhold stated in the interview with Deedy. "We see the starvation diet of their spirituality shrinking further as time goes on, while radio, press and motion pictures expose them continuously to the impact of sensation, thrill and emotional upheaval."[42] If that is what he was thinking forty years ago, imagine what he would say to us today.

SHAPE A SPACE FOR WORSHIP AND DEVOTION

In order to weave mystagogy into the fabric of our lives, we need to shape in and for ourselves a space for devotion as well as for worship. We discussed shaping a space for worship extensively in the previous chapter, but it is also important to discuss the place of devotion today. Once again, we need to remind ourselves of what liturgical life was like in the era when Reinhold was writing. He died before the current Roman Missal was promulgated (1969), so for his entire ministry the Mass was in Latin while devotions such as the rosary, novenas, and Benediction were in the vernacular. As we saw in chapter 4, the use of vernacular missals in the United States did not begin to develop until the mid-1940s and then people used them more to follow along with the priest at Mass than to nurture spirituality outside of Mass.

From my youth I recall that crowds of people attended Miraculous Medal Novena exercises on Monday evenings in the 1950s. "Novenas are accidental to the life of the church," Reinhold commented, but because they "give the congregation a part to do . . . speak to the heart . . . and are full of action and response, they have the appeal and popularity which should belong primarily to the Mass."[43] Although he was often accused of being against devotions, quite to the contrary Reinhold supported them strongly, in their proper place.

"One day," Reinhold wrote, "we shall have the great experience of realizing what we are doing, and tears of gratitude will flow for our having been chosen to take part in the great praise offered to God through Christ by the whole family of the Church."[44] Here we are, having lived into that great day, better able to worship in spirit and truth. This does not, however, eliminate our need for devotional time.

[42] Deedy, "Restless Ambassador," 8.

[43] Ibid., 9.

[44] H. A. Reinhold, "Timely Questions [Active Participation]," *The Living Light* 1, no. 1 (Spring 1964): 130–34; here 132.

Quite the contrary! "When Mass is being celebrated, let us enter into its spirit and give ourselves wholly to this sacrifice and banquet. We should find another time—for private devotions, for going into our room, closing the door and letting our Father in heaven alone see our heart."[45] In the last forty years, I suggest, we have even greater need for that private time, because our society has changed exponentially.

One of the most intriguing books I have ever read is titled *The Silent Pulse: A Search for the Perfect Rhythm That Exists in Each of Us*. In it, biologist George Leonard develops the thesis that the entire universe has a single pulse, sharing the same heartbeat. Using scientific data he demonstrates that after an hour or so a group of people in the same room will begin to show evidence that their hearts are beating with the same pulse. We experience this phenomenon metaphorically, label it "synchrony," and regard it with surprise. Leonard has studied the phenomenon with the discipline of a scientist and sees it as the right order of things, the "silent pulse of perfect rhythm."[46]

In my youth our culture kept Sunday holy unto the Lord. Stores—even pharmacies—were closed; we wore Sunday clothes and indulged in the Sunday pleasures of visiting, family dinners, and relaxation. What has happened to all our lost sabbaths? Have we mortgaged our opportunity to beat with a divine pulse?

"Time," the historian Edward Thompson observes, "is now currency; it is not passed but spent."[47] People are all so busy they no longer have time to relax—to sabbath, if you will. And what are they so busy doing? Studies across the United States have shown that people there spend more time shopping than people anywhere else. Not only do they spend a higher fraction of the money they earn, but with the explosion of consumer debt, they are now spending what they haven't earned.[48]

---

45 Ibid., 132–33.

46 George Leonard, *The Silent Pulse: A Search for the Perfect Rhythm That Exists in Each of Us* (New York: E. P. Dutton, 1978), 132. See also Russell G. Foster and Leon Kreitzman, *Rhythms of Life: The Biological Clocks that Control the Daily Lives of Every Living Thing* (New Haven, CT: Yale University Press, 2004).

47 Edward P. Thompson, "Time, Work-Discipline, and Industrial Capitalism," *Past and Present* 38 (December 1967): 56–97; here 61.

48 Juliet B. Schor, *The Overworked American: The Unexpected Decline of Leisure* (New York: Basic Books, 1991), 3. See also Schor, *Born to Buy: The Commercialized Child and the New Consumer Culture* (New York: Scribner, 2005).

In an article titled "Making Sense of Soul and Sabbath: Brain Processes and the Making of Meaning," James B. Ashbrook advances two interconnected speculations: that sabbathing is found in the brain's biorhythms; and that the essential structure of our unique individuality requires sabbathing for its coherent vitality. "Because we are creatures whose essence involves the making of meaning, the biorhythms of sabbathing and remembering are the means by which soul makes its story viable."[49]

In the essay, Ashbrook recounts a wonderful anecdote that reportedly took place in Africa during the last century. He tells of a caravan of traders that had been pushing their porters hard. Eventually, the porters stopped, and nothing would get them going again. When the traders demanded to know what was wrong, the Africans explained: "We have been traveling so long and so fast that we need to wait for our souls to catch up with our bodies." While Ashbrook calls jet lag "an empirical equivalent" of "waiting for our souls to catch up with our bodies,"[50] in the first decade of the twenty-first century I think that our souls are still on the losing end. We need to shape a space for both worship and devotion—the time and space needed for our souls to catch up with our bodies.

RUN WHILE YOU HAVE THE LIGHT

Echoing John 12:35, the Prologue to the Rule of St. Benedict urges, "Run while you have the light of life, that the darkness of death may not overtake you." By now it is probably an understatement to say that no one ran faster and farther than Reinhold during his lifetime. His bibliography alone gives eloquent testimony to it, as does the broad spectrum of his ministry on both sides of the Atlantic and both coasts of the United States.

Reflecting on his ten-year association with Reinhold in 1949, the editor of *Orate Fratres* observed that the experience "never included a dull month . . . nor . . . the editorial anguish of waiting for an overdue manuscript. No matter how busy with organizing a seamen's club at Seattle, with the details of parochial work at Sunnyside and its missions, with lecturing throughout the country, or with writing of books

[49] James B. Ashbrook, "Making Sense of Soul and Sabbath: Brain Processes and the Making of Meaning," *Zygon: Journal of Religion and Science* 27, no. 1 (March 1992): 31–49; here 32–33.
[50] Ibid., 32.

and other articles, he never let *O.F.* down. Better yet, he never let *O.F.* readers down. However brief, his Tract always managed a vigorous push in the right direction. H.A.R.'s Tract might disturb, but it would not be ignored." Yes, Reinhold ran while he had the light of life: he roamed freely; everything was grist for his mill; and nothing of human relevance escaped his attention. With his vivid, earthy style of writing, laced with concrete images, he drove home abstract principles.[51] The editor went so far as to conjecture that without Reinhold the magazine might have had a struggle to continue existence.

Readers echoed, describing Reinhold as "a firebrand, a whirlwind, a cyclone. And like the cyclone he has at the center a great calm wherein his readers too, can find a quiet, firm anchor in Christ."[52] Another response to the testimonial included the observation that Reinhold "has fought many a good battle by himself, and it is time we gathered around him instead of behind him." Further noting that Reinhold always presented a total picture of the church, that writer continued, "In an era that constantly tries to do violence to the Church by the shrinking process of pietism or sectarianism or secularism, it is hard to think of any greater service he could render."[53] Frank O'Malley, then professor of English at the University of Notre Dame and managing editor of *The Review of Politics* wrote that Reinhold was a "tyger . . . our dear tyger, our tender thaumaturge."[54]

Reflecting on his death, the *Bulletin of the Liturgical Conference* noted that Reinhold "happily had lived long enough to see the church he loved begin (just begin) to come alive, and his ideas, his openness, his appreciation of all things were young until the end. He was afflicted by none of the bitterness which oldsters who were one-time pioneers sometimes exhibit in the face of progress. Perhaps because he remained a pioneer."[55] Reinhold lived just long enough to see most of his dreams for the church come true. Perhaps the most poignant, given all that he suffered for the sake of a vernacular liturgy, was seeing Pope Paul VI celebrate Mass in English on his trip to the United States in October of 1965. "Instead of a solemn pontifical Mass, Paul chose to

---

[51] Godfrey Diekmann, *Orate Fratres* 23 (April 1949): 275–77; here 276.

[52] Sara B. O'Neill, "To the Editor," *Orate Fratres* 23 (May 1949): 326.

[53] James O'Gara in ibid., 326–27.

[54] Frank O'Malley, "To the Editor," *Orate Fratres* 23 (September 1949): 477.

[55] "John A. Reinhold: 'Suddenly a Bang and an Awakening,'" *Liturgy: Bulletin of the Liturgical Conference* 13 (March 1968): 2–4; here 3.

recite a simple Low Mass, to which the congregation responded rousingly in English. In keeping with the liturgical reforms of the Vatican Council, lessons were read by laymen, and twelve children—the only ones to receive Communion from the Pope that day—brought the bread and wine to the altar to be consecrated."[56] The moment was not lost on Reinhold, who wrote that "perhaps the greatest thing which has happened to us 'liturgical promoters' was the fact that the Holy Father celebrated the mass in the 'new' style with English . . . being the language of the liturgy. The English language came out of the mouth of the reigning Pope on a solemn liturgical occasion."[57]

Reinhold ran and he urged others to do likewise when he retired as a regular columnist for *Worship*. "Don't write me—write for your diocesan weekly, for secular papers, for *Worship*, in letters to the editor, in short articles and long: but let us all keep going, because if liturgy has taught us one thing it is—to feel responsibility and to participate!"[58] Fifteen years later, Godfrey Diekmann wrote something similar that still echoes today: "What we need badly today are a few more H. A. R.s internationally as well as locally, to take up his mantle in the thorny task of pastoral implementation, in preserving 'style' without stifling the demands of life."[59]

[56] "The Pilgrim," *Time*, October 15, 1965, http://www.time.com/time/magazine/article/0,9171,834512-4,00.html (accessed May 10, 2009).

[57] H. A. Reinhold, "Timely Questions [Vernacular]," *The Living Light* 2 (Winter 1965): 118–20; here 118.

[58] H. A. Reinhold "Turning Point: Lugano," *Worship* 27 (1953) 557–63; here 563.

[59] Godfrey Diekmann, "In Memory of H.A.R.," *Worship* 42 (March 1968): 177–79; here 178.

Called to the Same Hope

Finale

Sickness before death is a very appropriate thing and I think those who don't have it miss one of God's mercies.[1]

In "The Catholic Establishment," *Commonweal* associate editor John Leo compiled a short list of influential Catholic publications and writers whose "chief business . . . is the shaping and publicizing of the issues that will dominate American Catholic life." Leo described them as "liberal, progressive, largely urban, suspicious of institutions, antiwar . . . and concerned mainly with intramural Catholic problems."[2] Father Reinhold is not listed among them, but rather along with Dorothy Day as two who have graduated from member to "establishment hero."[3]

No one could have been more surprised to read that than Reinhold himself. Dorothy Day lived long enough to see herself become a revered elder in our midst, but Reinhold was both physically and psychologically challenged by the ravages of Parkinson's disease for more than a decade. Moreover, in that decade he was also challenged by the ravages of misunderstanding and persecution, which left him a displaced cleric, *persona non grata*, for more than five years after his departure from Sunnyside in 1956 until his eventual incardination in Pittsburgh in 1961. Even after that many continued to regard him with suspicion.

As was mentioned in chapter 2, when I began my research into Reinhold's life, the first person I interviewed was Msgr. Frederick McManus, then still a giant in the liturgical movement, longtime consultant to the United States Conference of Catholic Bishops' Committee on the Liturgy (now the Committee on Divine Worship), and one of Reinhold's closest friends. As soon as I mentioned Reinhold's name, however, Fred immediately delved into a detailed recitation

---

[1] Flannery O'Connor, *The Habit of Being: Letters of Flannery O'Connor*, ed. Sally Fitzgerald (New York: Farrar, Straus and Giroux, 1979), 163.

[2] John Leo, "The Catholic Establishment," *The Critic* 25 (December 1966–January 1967): 24–29; here 25.

[3] Ibid., 27.

and analysis of that sad chapter of his life. At the time I knew only the sketch Reinhold himself provided in his autobiography, so Fred's vehemence shocked me. Apart from a brief epilogue, the autobiography ends with his departure from Sunnyside in May of 1956, almost twelve years before he died.

As I continued my research and met more of Reinhold's friends and colleagues, however, many urged me to tell the whole story, to provide the details they knew to be true, to correct the record so to speak. Because those five difficult years remained shrouded in secrecy, they believed erroneous assumptions had been made that damaged Reinhold's reputation and consequently blurred the enormity of his contribution to the liturgical movement in America. Out of respect for them and for Reinhold himself, I have decided to add this finale, which elaborates more on those difficult years I briefly mentioned in chapter 2. Although the details do not add more to our understanding of Reinhold's contribution to liturgy as a discipline, they help us to see the full measure of the man, what he suffered, and how he endured. That in itself is a valuable lesson. Since Reinhold's life and ministry were focused on worship in spirit and truth, perhaps my research will help to reveal a bit more of the truth of the man.

Early in 1951 Reinhold began discussions with the bishop of the Seattle diocese, asking for a smaller parish where he could devote more of his waning energy to writing. On June 22, 1951, he specifically asked to be transferred to the then-vacant parish in Chelan, one hundred miles north of Sunnyside. His request was summarily dismissed by the chancellor. However, when the erection of the Yakima diocese was announced the following day, Reinhold was elated finally to be out from under the control of Bishop Thomas Connolly and his chancellor, Msgr. Joseph P. Dougherty.

The "beginning of the end," as Reinhold put it, began almost immediately. Shortly after the Diocese of Yakima was erected, formed from portions of the Dioceses of Seattle and Spokane, Joseph Patrick Dougherty, the very person who seemed to have persecuted Reinhold the most, was named bishop.[4] As chancellor of Seattle, Dougherty was in a position of influence with the ordinary, and Reinhold was sure that over the years his confidence had been betrayed, particularly while he was quarantined during World War II. According to

---

[4] Dougherty served as vice-chancellor from 1934 to 1942; and chancellor from 1942 until he was named bishop in 1951.

Reinhold, Dougherty was "the man who had found it necessary regularly to report on my activities to Bishop Shaughnessy; and Bishop Connolly, when we met, thought it fit in the presence of a lay parishioner of mine to call me 'a half-baked liturgist and crackpot at that.'"[5] Today we might argue that Reinhold was naïve to confide in the chancellor who had so long given him difficulties, but Reinhold was obedient and followed ecclesiastical protocol as he understood it.

After five years of strained relations and in ill health, in February 1956 Reinhold wrote to Bishop Dougherty and asked to resign as pastor. Finding himself "3000 miles from the centers of learning and . . . foremost connections," Reinhold's plan was to attend the International Liturgical Congress in Assisi and then settle back in the East as chaplain at Graham Carey's settlement in Benson, Vermont. Instead the bishop appointed a vicar coadjutor, who effectively deprived Reinhold of most of his functions as pastor, "to restore order to the parish."[6]

In response, Reinhold sought the counsel of Msgr. Thomas Tobin, vicar general of the Archdiocese of Portland. Prior to Diocese of Seattle's elevation in 1951, the Archdiocese of Portland had been Seattle's metropolitan see, so it is not surprising that Reinhold would have turned to its vicar general for advice and assistance as he had done previously with similar matters. It is also likely that they collaborated on some of the justice issues discussed here in chapter 5 since Tobin was "renowned for his commitment to labor and other progressive causes . . . and sponsored an annual labor school and invited labor leaders and managers to study Catholic social teaching and dialogue about current issues in the workplace."[7] On Tobin's recommendation, Reinhold "requested from the bishop of Yakima a leave of absence from the diocese effective immediately—April 21, 1956."

To Reinhold's surprise, he received a gracious letter in answer: "the bishop would grant me a leave of absence, but to relieve me of any worry he would also accept my resignation from the parish if I so desired to offer it. He added that if I wished ever to return to the diocese he would see that I was given a position elsewhere." Although

[5] H. A. Reinhold, *H. A. R.: The Autobiography of Father Reinhold* (New York: Herder and Herder, 1968), 143; hereafter cited as *HAR*.

[6] H. A. Reinhold to Graham Carey, February 11, 1956, Box 3, Folder 3, H. A. Reinhold Papers, John J. Burns Library, Boston College.

[7] Msgr. Chuck Lienert, "Priests Have Taken Up Labor Cause," *Catholic Sentinel* (August 19, 2008).

Finale

Reinhold eventually intended to resign from the diocese, he did not want to do so until he was properly situated in another diocese. "On May 1st the parishioners gave me a memorable farewell party and a large purse."[8] All of this is corroborated by correspondence found in the Reinhold Papers at the Burns Library.

Reinhold's registered letter to Bishop Dougherty included a series of forwarding addresses as he traveled through Seattle, Washington; Portland, Oregon; Ryegate, Montana; and Yankton, South Dakota before heading south to St. Louis, Missouri. When he arrived there on June 7 he received a registered letter with a reply card, which had been forwarded from Sunnyside. "This letter was a well-aimed blow: I was accused of deserting my parish and being absent without leave. Unless I resigned at once or returned within five days [time that had already elapsed], I would be suspended."[9]

Tobin advised Reinhold to resign over the phone "before the bishop started brooding and making out 'funny' documents, and to submit my trouble to the [Apostolic] Delegate in order to put the brakes on the Yakima Chancery."[10] Reinhold tried to call Bishop Dougherty immediately, but the chancellor told him that the bishop was out of town and refused to tell him how he could be reached. The chancellor also refused to accept or help Reinhold with his resignation. Therefore, Reinhold wrote out his resignation and in a separate letter tried to convince the bishop that he had acted in good faith, taking the bishop's letter of May 21 at face value.

Reinhold's next stop was Notre Dame, where he waited several days to hear from Dougherty. When no response came, he traveled to Washington DC where he called on the Apostolic Delegate to present his case as Tobin had recommended. He then traveled on to Burlington, Vermont, to stay with Graham Carey, as originally planned.

[8] *HAR*, 147.

[9] John A. Reinhold, "The Two 'Flights,' 1935 and 1956," Box 15, Folder 27, H. A. Reinhold Papers, John J. Burns Library, Boston College, 28. Msgr. Frederick McManus explained to me that during this difficult period, Reinhold wanted to be called "John" instead of "Hans." From 1957 to 1959, for example, Reinhold was listed as John A. Reinhold on the board of directors of the Liturgical Conference. Although not consistent, during that period he also signed some of his correspondence as "John."

[10] Ibid., 28.

Carey and Reinhold visited with the bishop of Burlington to request permission for Reinhold to reside as a chaplain in Benson, Vermont, with faculties in his diocese. Ryan agreed to this with the proviso that the arrangement was approved by Dougherty. Ryan also recommended that Reinhold take some time in this new situation before requesting incardination in Burlington. Following the interview, Reinhold traveled to Mount Saviour in Elmira, New York, for retreat.

Upon returning to Benson, Reinhold learned that instead of approving the arrangements in Burlington, Dougherty had written to Ryan saying that in spite of Reinhold's resignation, he was absent without permission and intimated that he might even be leading a double life. This seemingly hopeless turn of events plunged Reinhold into utter despair, and in that condition he went to St. Joseph's Abbey in Spencer, Massachusetts.

Fr. Thomas Carroll, longtime colleague, advisor, and friend took Reinhold under his care for the remainder of his life. A leader in the Archdiocese of Boston, Carroll was a renowned national expert in the care of the blind, having worked extensively with World War II veterans suffering from blindness and neurological impairments.[11] He arranged for Reinhold to be placed under the care of his brother-in-law, Thomas E. Caulfield, MD, a well-known psychiatrist. Hospitalized for a time at Bournewood Hospital, Reinhold soon took up residence in Sacred Heart Rectory in Roslindale to be close to his doctors. Msgr. Edward Murray, pastor at that time, was a good match for Reinhold. It is said that Murray built bridges between Boston's religious communities, was credited with playing a key behind-the-scenes role at the Second Vatican Council, reached out to Protestants, Jews, and other religious traditions in hopes of achieving greater interfaith understanding, and was a true patron of the arts. Although Reinhold was not able to attend the Assisi Congress because of these circumstances, he was able to report on it in *Commonweal*.[12]

Bishop John J. Wright—a Boston priest, former auxiliary bishop of Boston, and at that time ordinary of the Diocese of Worcester—took

[11] Tuck Tinsley, "Father Thomas Carroll: A Leader and a Legend," Lecture at the Carroll Luncheon, Blinded Veterans Association Convention, Reno, Nevada, August 13, 2004, http://www.aph.org/hall_fame/bios/bva_speech .html (accessed May 2, 2009).

[12] See H. A. Reinhold, "The Lesson of Assisi," *Commonweal* 65 (October 5, 1956): 7–10.

Finale

Reinhold under his special care, encouraging him to continue writing. Wright even sent an emissary to Yakima and Portland to assist with Reinhold's situation there, but to no avail.[13] Wright's letters to Reinhold are wonderfully pastoral, while Reinhold's in response show the depths of his depression: "Even though I eat and drink and sleep 'the book,' there are still enough free moments in which to brood over the unresolved questions that follow me around like dark clouds overhead. Though they are far away, I can't ignore them."[14] In a letter to Helen Mann from that period, Reinhold said that he had experienced similar depressions in 1923 and 1935, "but this time it got me good." When his depression lightened by early fall, Reinhold traveled to New York City to spend some time with his good friends there.

The following summer, Reinhold moved to St. Joseph's Church in Wurtsboro to assist the pastor, Fr. E. Harold Smith, who had been an associate at Corpus Christi Parish when Reinhold was in residence there from 1943–44. When he informed Bishop Wright of this opportunity, Wright responded, "If it is agreeable to the diocesan authorities there that you have the faculties of the diocese and keep up parish activities, so much the better. I would not feel free to offer you so great an advantage here in view of the fact that my efforts to secure permission to do so did not receive an affirmative response. It greatly pleases me that the other diocese has felt free to go ahead without asking any permission."[15] Archival correspondence demonstrates that Dougherty continued to write and lobby other bishops to have Reinhold discredited. A July 2, 1958, letter written for Dougherty by Vice-Chancellor John A. Eher to Michael Mathis thanks him for replacing Reinhold on the program at the University of Notre Dame.[16]

Little of the correspondence or references to medical concerns ever mention Reinhold's Parkinson's disease, yet it is very evident from his handwriting alone that his physical condition was deteriorating from the disease. Today it is recognized that depression is a common sequela of Parkinson's disease, which "typically involves unstoppable

[13] See "Wright I," Box 10, Folder 16, H. A. Reinhold Papers, John J. Burns Library, Boston College.

[14] H. A. Reinhold letter to Bishop John Wright, November 29, 1956, in "Wright I."

[15] Bishop John Wright to H. A. Reinhold, June 27, 1957, in "Wright I."

[16] CMTH [Michael Mathis Manuscripts] 17.16, "Rev. H. A. Reinhold," Archives, University of Notre Dame.

feelings of hopelessness, helplessness, and diminished self-worth . . . which some believe results from disruption of neurotransmitter systems in the brain."[17] In a round-robin letter to all his friends, written from Wurtsboro in January 1959, Reinhold gave an extensive update on his health and ministry, made possible by the Manns who provided him with a Dictaphone and someone to transcribe his correspondence. Indicating that his right hand was worse, he explained that "periodically, and especially when I am under strain, it begins to shake so violently that I cannot even hit the keys on my electric typewriter which I bought two years ago to enable me to correspond with the outside world as my longhand writing was illegible."[18]

He explained that he had been living in Wurtsboro, "a pleasant exile," for more than eighteen months through the kindness of Cardinal Spellman. "Father Smith is understanding, witty, and a learned and wise man. We have many things in common and there is a great deal of communication of minds between us." But there was still no resolution to his difficulties with the bishop of Yakima, who still required that Reinhold spend a month in penance at New Melleray Abbey in Dubuque, Iowa. "I can see no good in my trip to New Melleray, except that I can say I went to the limit and showed my willingness to do my own part. I strongly resent being 'punished' like a schoolboy who misbehaved at an age when others receive their best parish and other recognitions—not that I want any, but it is the contrast . . . I am being put to by a tyrannical and vindictive man."[19] Caulfield was concerned that in Iowa, far from the support of physicians and friends, Reinhold's depression might surface again. There was certainly evidence of that growing concern as he closed that letter to Helen Mann: "Thus the forces that have harassed me since 1938 are winning their final victory over me on the outside and I go down in visible defeat: I wonder what it all means in the light of eternity? First Hitler, now JPD and his serfs: why does everything I ever do fail?"

A week later, however, he sent Mann a postcard of the refectory at New Melleray, written in a very shaky hand, signed "Father Anscar,

[17] William J. Weiner, Lisa Shulman, and Anthony E. Lang, *Parkinson's Disease: A Complete Guide for Patients and Families* (Baltimore: Johns Hopkins University Press, 2001), 75.

[18] H. A. Reinhold to "My Friends Across the Globe," January 1959, Box 8, Folder 4, H. A. Reinhold Papers, John J. Burns Library, Boston College.

[19] H. A. Reinhold to Helen Mann, January 1, 1959.

Finale

Obl. St. Mariae ad Lacum." It concludes, "There is great peace here!" and from his autobiography we know that there he dictated his memoirs, making good use of the month's experience. Beyond that Cistercian abbey, however, storm clouds continued to gather.

While Reinhold was at New Melleray, Carroll wrote to Damasus Winzen at Mount Saviour, asking if he would request that the Abbot of Maria Laach write to Bishop Dougherty on Reinhold's behalf: "Members of the hierarchy in this country have been able to do nothing with reasonable requests to Bishop Dougherty, and I doubt that any more attention will be paid to the Abbot of Maria Laach," but Carroll thought it worth the try. He admitted that it was a "diplomatic move" that Dougherty would likely refuse, but "his unreasonable refusal will be another factor if it becomes necessary to bring this case to a tribunal in Rome."[20]

By January 1959 Wright had been appointed bishop of Pittsburgh, and he promised Reinhold a place there once his canonical status had been regularized. Reinhold wrote, "I often think of my future in Pittsburgh or near Pittsburgh. There is so far no news from Yakima. They are probably brooding over a nasty reply to my offer to see several doctors of their choosing. They usually take three to four months and then catch me by surprise."[21] Reinhold also indicated in that letter that he was still shaking badly, not able to do much and tired easily. The situation had not been resolved by the summer either, as he wrote to Helen Mann, "I don't do very much, not even in my own field. I haven't even the go to dictate the rest of my autobiography. It all seems such an effort and so futile."[22]

Reinhold moved to Pittsburgh that fall and served as pro tem chaplain to the sisters at St. Eudes Institute, a boarding school for girls. A buoyancy returned to his writing almost immediately. "Bishop Wright spoke to the priests today—marvelous—it is amazing to find a Bishop of his breadth of mind—of his wit and of his acumen. Sisters are good, the house is pleasant, my room is quiet and peaceful and I should have all the time to work on my books."[23] As he adapted to his new surroundings, Bishop Wright increased Reinhold's responsibilities, "It

[20] Thomas Carroll to Damasus Winzen, February 5, 1959, Box 2, Folder 3, Thomas Carroll Papers, John J. Burns Library, Boston College.

[21] H. A. Reinhold to Bishop John J. Wright, April 13, 1959, in "Wright I."

[22] H. A. Reinhold to Helen Mann, July 7, 1959.

[23] H. A. Reinhold to Helen Mann, October 2, 1959.

occurs to me that not only are you well enough to try a little increased responsibility, but may well profit, spiritually and therapeutically, from a change at this time."[24]

In January of 1961 Reinhold traveled back to Yakima to meet with Bishop Dougherty. The event was covered in the January 13, 1961, issue of the diocesan newspaper, *Our Times*. It noted that "Father H. A. Reinhold, former pastor of St. Joseph's Parish in Sunnyside, returned to Yakima last weekend to visit the Most Rev. Joseph P. Dougherty, Bishop of Yakima, prior to assuming an assignment in the Diocese of Pittsburgh." Noting that he had been in ill health since the spring of 1956, the brief article noted that the new assignment would give Reinhold "an opportunity to devote himself to writing for which he has exceptional talent." The article included a picture of both Dougherty and Reinhold in front of a print of the *Madonna Enthroned with Angels and Prophets* by Giovanni Cimabue, a gift from Reinhold for the bishop's residence. A picture taken of Reinhold in Dougherty's residence during that visit radiates relief.

The long-awaited letter of excardination followed shortly thereafter. In response to a letter from Wright dated January 26, 1961, Dougherty wrote, "Please know how grateful I am for your so charitably agreeing to Father's incardination in the Diocese of Pittsburgh pursuant to my excardinating him for a just cause from the Diocese of Yakima at his request. I shall prepare the prescribed testimonial and excardination documents, which will be sent to Your Excellency at an early date. The present letter certifies my intention to excardinate Father Reinhold perpetually and absolutely in accordance with his petition and Your Excellency's agreement to incardinate him."[25] On March 10, 1961, Reinhold was incardinated in Pittsburgh, softly ending that sad chapter in Reinhold's life.[26]

Godfrey Diekmann observed that "this liturgical prophet had the happiness of seeing most of his aims, long the object of suspicion and the occasion of personal harassment, officially sanctioned by highest church authority. What we need badly today are a few more H. A. R.'s

---

[24] Bishop John J. Wright to H. A. Reinhold, January 12, 1960, "Wright I."

[25] Bishop Joseph P. Dougherty to Bishop John J. Wright, February 8, 1961, Box 4/1 "Bishop Dougherty," Reinhold Papers, John J. Burns Library, Boston College.

[26] Dougherty attended Reinhold's funeral in January 1968, resigned as bishop of Yakima on February 5, 1969, and was named auxiliary bishop of the Archdiocese of Los Angeles the same day. He died the following year.

Finale

internationally as well as locally, to take up his mantle in the thorny task of pastoral implementation, in preserving 'style' without stifling the demands of life."[27] "He was the first really 'free' and open Catholic and priest I ever met," Tom Barry of The Sower Press wrote. "That was in 1935 or 36—he was living at the Leo House . . . and his troubles with the New York Chancery had just begun. He was a kind of Knight with no armor—a gentleman by birth and grace of God—and a man terrifically brave and unafraid . . . yet wise and compassionate and loving."[28]

Far beyond the pale of all that suffering, now knowing precisely "what it all means in the light of eternity," I like to think that Father Reinhold is feasting at the heavenly banquet and would want to join us in singing "Hope of Abraham and Sarah,"[29] a hymn by Ruth Duck that so poetically summarizes and celebrates his wonderful ministry to the church of his generation and beyond.

Hope of Abraham and Sarah,
friend of Hagar, God of Ruth,
you desire that ev'ry people
worship you in spirit, truth.
Meet us in our sacred places,
mosque and synagogue and church.
Show us paths of understanding;
bless us in our common search.

Root us in our own tradition,
faith our forbears handed down.
Grow us in your grace and knowledge;
plant our feet on solid ground.
Cultivate the seeds of sharing
in this world of many creeds.
Keep us open, wise in learning,
bearing fruit in loving deeds.

Hope of Abraham and Sarah,
sov'reign God whom we adore,

[27] Godfrey Diekmann, "In Memory of H.A.R.," *Worship* 42, no. 3 (March 1968): 177–79; here 178.

[28] Tom Barry to Br. Peter of Mount Saviour, February 7, 1968.

[29] Ruth Duck, "Hope of Abraham and Sarah," copyright © 2005 by GIA Publications, Inc., 7404 S. Mason Ave., Chicago, IL 60638. www.giamusic.com. 800.442.1358. All rights reserved. Used by permission.

Worship in Spirit and Truth

form in us your new creation
free of violence, hate, and war.
So may Torah, cross, and crescent,
each a sign of life made new,
point us t'ward your love and justice,
earth at peace and one in you.

Finale

Appendix A			
Rev. H. A. Reinhold—Chronology			
1897	09	06	Born in Hamburg, Germany; father = Bernard
1914–1918			Military service with the German army
1917	05		Seriously wounded in France (right leg smashed)
1917	10		Applied to interpreter school; passed; assigned to a unit in Chalet
1918	Sp/Sum		Studied in Freiburg
1919			Found Guardini's *Spirit of the Liturgy*
1920–1921			Studied at the Jesuit Seminary, Innsbruck
1921	09		Studied briefly at seminary in Bressanone
1922	04–09		Entered the novitiate at Maria Laach Abbey
1922	10–12		Served as assistant purser aboard the SS *Hamburg* en route from Hamburg to Java, Indonesia
1923	Spring		Enrolled, University of Münster where Johannes Quasten was a classmate
1924	06	11	Became an oblate of Maria Laach
1925	12	18	Ordained for diocese of Osnabrück; assigned to Niendorf, a "resort town on the Baltic Sea"
1925	12	19	Sang first mass at Ursuline Convent in Osnabrück
1928	Summer		Selected to go to Rome to resume archeological studies at the Pontifical Institute of Archaeology
1929			Appointed bishop's secretary to the seaman's apostolate
1930			Founded the German branch of the International Council on the Apostolate of the Sea
1931	Spring		Established the first Catholic Seamen's Home in Germany in Bremerhaven

1932	11	08	Made the first of five trips to New York and was in Times Square the night FDR was elected to his first term
1933	01	30	Hitler named Chancellor of the Republic
1933	01	31	Transferred to Hamburg
1934	06	30	Hitler's purge of former comrades, Night of the Long Knives, during which Reinhold was summoned before them
1934			International Seaman's Apostolate Annual Convention held in Hamburg
1935	04	30	Required by five Gestapo agents to leave his work
1935	07	10	Resided in London for three months before becoming an assistant in Interlaken, Switzerland
1936	08	20	Entered the United States on SS *America* and initially resided at The Leo House on W. 23rd St. in New York City
1936			Attended seamen's rally at Madison Square Garden
1936	08	27	Requested faculties from Msgr. James Francis McIntyre, chancellor of the Archdiocese of New York
1936			Invited by George Schuster to write for *Commonweal*
1936	10		Resided at St. Margaret's in Middle Village, New York, and studied at Columbia
1937	09	20	Teaching post at Portsmouth Priory, during which time he discovered Harvard's Widener Library
1938			Two weeks with his mother; she returned to Germany
1938	07		Sailed on *Ile-de-France* for Paris
1938	10		Invited by Gerald Shaughnessy, bishop of Seattle, to serve as port chaplain in Seattle
1938			Began writing for *Orate Fratres*
1938	10	15	Arrived in Seattle—*not* expected at cathedral

1938	11		Bishop Shaughnessy decided to "try him out" in the cathedral parish before assigning Reinhold to the seaman's apostolate
1939	03		Began tenure as *Orate Fratres*'s Timely Tractor
1939	07		Associate editor *Orate Fratres*
1940	10	21–25	Chicago: First National Catholic Liturgical Week
1940			Bishop gave permission to found Seaman's Club
1941	10		Transferred to Yakima parish, which extended eighty miles to the east into the Cascade Mountain region
1941	10	06–10	St. Paul, Minnesota: Liturgical Conference
1942	01		Restricted to five-mile radius in Yakima
1942			Able to drive to Seattle once every two months
1943	10	13	Mother's death
1943			Requested leave of absence until the end of war
1944	04		Became an American citizen
1944	09	09	Appointed pastor of St. Joseph's Parish, Sunnyside
1944–1945	01	28	Published an eighteen-month-long series of articles in *The Tidings*, the Los Angeles diocesan newspaper
1946			Formed the Vernacular Society, initially a subgroup of members of the Liturgical Conference
1949	08		En route to the Liturgical Week in St. Louis, visited Santa Rosa, New Mexico; Grailville, Ohio; and Gethsemani, Kentucky
1951	06		Received an honorary Doctor of Divinity degree from Saint John's University, Collegeville, Minnesota

1952	08		Made his first trip back to Germany: visited Hamburg, the Rhineland, Bavaria, and "the small German enclave south of the Brenner pass in Italy"
1953	09	14–16	Attended the Second International Congress of Liturgical Studies in Lugano, Switzerland
1954	07	31	Visited Catholic Worker, New York City
1954	09	12–18	Attended the Third International Congress of Liturgical Studies in Lugano, Switzerland
1954	11	07	Made a series of radio broadcasts on the liturgy from Sunnyside
1955	04		Visited New York and stayed at Corpus Christi Rectory "to take care of an ulcer on my vocal chords and of a toxic goiter"
1956	05	01	Left Yakima on a leave of absence
1956			Diagnosed with Parkinson's disease
1961	01	13	Visited Bishop Dougherty, Yakima
1961	03	10	Incardinated in the Diocese of Pittsburgh
1961	06		Received an honorary Doctor of Human Letters degree from Seton Hill College
1961	11	03	Entered the Oratory at Pittsburgh as long-term guest
1961	12	21	Appointed by Bishop Wright to the Diocesan Liturgy Commission
1962	04	12	Received the Dom Odo Casel Award at Fordham
1963	02	20	Underwent brain surgery at St. Barnabas Hospital, New York, New York
1963	08		Refers to recent trip to Maria Laach
1963	10	14	Lectured at the College of Mount St. Joseph, Cincinnati, Ohio, "Revitalizing the Liturgy: Some Observations for Architects"
1963	11	04	Absentee ballot: "afflicted with PD"
1964	04		Spent Holy Week at Mount Saviour
1964	05	07, 09	Spoke at Liturgical Day in Camden, New Jersey, on "The Changes in the Mass"

1964	08	14	Consulted on a renovation of the cathedral in Baton Rouge, Louisiana
1964	11	05–25	Visited Rome (Hotel Michelangelo 5–12), attended session of Vatican II (12–14), visited sister in Hamburg and W. H. Auden in London (23–25)
1964			Received an honorary degree from Duquesne University
1965	12	22	Celebrated fortieth anniversary of ordination Mass at Holy Family Church in New York City, New York
1966	01	09	Celebrated fortieth anniversary of ordination Mass at St. Paul's Cathedral, Pittsburgh, Pennsylvania
1966	04	26–28	Received the Conover Award at the National Conference on Religious Architecture in San Francisco
1967	12		Spent Christmas at Mount Saviour
1968	01	26	Died at Mercy Hospital, Pittsburgh, following surgery for intestinal obstruction
1968	01	30	Funeral: St. Paul's Cathedral, Pittsburgh, Pennsylvania
1968	01	31	Burial at Mount Saviour, Good Shepherd Cemetery

Appendix B

H. A. R.[1]

We had a talk last week with Father H. A. Reinhold, probably one of the best informed and articulate writers on the liturgy of the Church. For many years, his "Timely Tracts" column in *Worship* magazine (formerly *Orate Fratres*) with the familiar by-line "H.A.R.," was the feature readers invariably read first on opening the magazine each month. The 59-year-old German-born priest (he was a refugee from Hitler and Nazism in 1936) has come to see many of the liturgical reforms he was urging with his pen become a reality through Vatican decree.

Father Reinhold was in Davenport briefly on his way to visit with his good friend, Monsignor Martin Hellriegel, pastor of Holy Cross parish in St. Louis. A slightly built man of medium height with sandy, crew-cut hair, Father Reinhold told us he was leaving his St. Joseph's parish at Sunnyside, Washington, after 13 years of pastoral duties there. He has been in delicate health for more than a year.

"I felt I could leave now," said Father Reinhold. "There is no longer a shortage of priests in the Yakima diocese. There is a fully developed Confraternity of Christian Doctrine study club, a parish credit union, a new church. As Dom Godfrey Diekmann (editor of *Worship*) said, 'You have proved to your satisfaction and to your bishop's satisfaction that you can carry out in a parish the things you advocate in writing.'

"I thought it was time," continued Father Reinhold, "to settle down and do some exploring, publishing and writing and I have got my bishop's permission to establish myself where I can do more of this theoretical and scholarly work. I have several prospects on the West Coast, in the Middle West and on the East Coast and I am on my way now to look into each of them."

Father Reinhold said he would like to establish a parish-liturgy center at which, within the limits of rubrics and canon law, the liturgy could be adapted for greater pastoral efficiency.

"It would be similar to the center of pastoral liturgy staffed by the Dominicans at Neuilly, France," said Father Reinhold, "or like those at Klosterneuburg near Vienna and the one at Lugano, Switzerland.

---

[1] *The Catholic Messenger* (Davenport, IA), June 14, 1956. I have taken the liberty of correcting several grammatical errors in the text so as not to confuse the reader. Although no author is listed, I know from my interviews that it was written by Warren Bovée. Used with permission.

"You know there is a great need for what can be called 'parish liturgy.' All liturgy is monastic, it is geared to Cathedral-usage and the clergy. Until the last Holy Week it was not obvious that the people should have a part in it. Parish liturgy should be an interplay between the priest and the congregation. That hasn't been adequately explored yet, though there are some promising signs in France, notably the work being done by Abbe Michonneau. The Dominicans at Neuilly have been looking for ways for the people to participate more effectively in the liturgy.

"Ground-work," said Father Reinhold, "has to be done to make liturgical reforms acceptable. Reform can't be done merely by decree from Rome. The mind of the priests and people has to be prepared. If it isn't, then priests and people may carry out the letter of the reform, but not the spirit of the reform."

We asked Father Reinhold to spell out a few of the details, some of the areas he would explore in his projected parish-liturgy center.

"Well, we have never explored the possibilities of using lay readers, lectors to read the common prayers of the congregation. Although it is being done in individual places it has never been systematically worked out.

"Also, we should have a closer connection with the religious sociologists who are discovering a great many significant things about parish life, men like Father Fichter[2] and Father Houtart[3] who are throwing a considerable amount of light on the social and economic factors which affect the spiritual life of parishioners. We have been working alongside of these men without becoming aware of them. The liturgical movement has suffered from the fact that it has very often been unrealistic, it has not adequately taken into consideration the social and economic context in which the liturgy must live."

"Reforms themselves are sometimes misinterpreted," said the priest. "A parish-liturgy center could help clarify reforms decreed by Rome."

"People believed they were carrying out Saint Pius X's reforms," said Father Reinhold, "by making schoolchildren sing Gregorian High Mass and having the rest of the people listen. Pius X and Pius XII made it quite clear that they wanted the congregation to sing. And whether or not you have a choir, the choir should not sing the parts belonging to the people."

"In rubrics and canon law, there is," said Father Reinhold, "much more latitude than would be assumed."

[2] Fr. Joseph H. Fichter, SJ, noted for his sociological study of a southern parish in 1951, was referenced in H. A. Reinhold, "Simone Weil, Saint of the Churchless," *Commonweal* 55 (October 26, 1951): 65–70.

[3] Born in Brussels in 1925, Fr. François Houtart completed his studies in philosophy and theology in Malines, Belgium, in 1949. Concerns about the situation of the working class, particularly young workers, led him to specialize in the social sciences. After completing a Licentiate in Socio-Political Sciences at Louvain in 1952, Houtart went on to complete a postgraduate course in Urban Sociology at the University of Chicago in 1954. At this writing, he remains active in global social issues.

"Pope Pius XII's reform of the Holy Week is," he said, a "signal development, because it shows a clear line as to which way the new adaptations of the liturgy are going to go. There is no doubt that the aim is pastoral," said Father Reinhold, "not antiquarian, not aesthetical, not monastic, but pastoral. It's the most significant reform since the Council of Trent, not because of the liturgical aspects but because of the pastoral aspects. The trend is irreversible. It may be delayed in certain of its aspects, but it will not go back, it will go forward."

At St. Joseph's parish in Sunnyside, besides the Credit Union and CCD, there is the dialogue Mass, congregationally sung Mass, family Communion. Five members of the parish, public high school teachers, handle the catechetical instruction of 80 high school boys and girls, while 30 laymen and women teach 230 grade school children. Instruction is done in private homes and church buildings. All the catechists were themselves instructed by Father Reinhold before they began teaching.

We wondered whether Father Reinhold had future plans in addition to his hoped-for parish-liturgy center.

"First I have a book to write for Doubleday on the liturgy," said the priest. "It's for those 'who hate it.' You remember that record a few years ago, 'Long-Hair Music for Those Who Hate It'? The record company gathered up a number of attractive, melodic passages from classical compositions, put them on one record and people who thought they 'hated' classical music found that they liked what they heard. My book will attempt, among other things, to show that the liturgy is attractive.

"I would also like to write for priests' periodicals and Catholic magazines like The Commonweal. I am also considering the publication of a booklet of Advent Masses where certain parts, like the Introit of the Mass, are sung in hymn form, similar to the 'Bettsingmesse'[4] where the Proper is sung in hymn-form and the Ordinary is congregationally recited on the monotone, an easy tone. The great difficulty is to find collaborators to provide the texts. We already have the simple Gregorian tones in the traditional Gregorian liturgy; they can be sung by anyone, even by the most primitive congregation. The singing should sound, according to Pius XII, like 'the bursting of a thunderous sea.'"

Father Reinhold, who was the only American pastor at the last international liturgy congress in Lugano, Switzerland, said he will attend the International Congress for Pastoral Liturgy to be held later this summer at Assisi, Italy, with an added pilgrimage of the delegates to Rome.[5]

---

[4] This is a traditional practice of German-speaking Catholics to sing vernacular hymns during the celebration of Mass. See Anthony Ruff, Sacred Music and Liturgical Reform: Treasures and Transformations (Chicago: Liturgy Training Publications, 2007), 235.

[5] Although this was Reinhold's plan, he was not able to attend the Congress due to ill health.

"It is a great advantage to know that instead of three priests going over this year, there will be 30 and that the bishops will be represented by such an outstanding man as Archbishop O'Hara of Kansas City," said Father Reinhold. "The trip to Rome is really a homage to Pius XII at Castelgandolfo; it is a tribute to him for the liturgical reforms he has achieved.

"In this whole business of reform and Rome, some things are not clearly understood. Rome never refuses, irrevocably, a reasonable request. The French asked for evening Mass; the answer was 'no.' The Germans asked for evening mass; the answer was 'no.' The Germans asked a second time; the answer was 'yes.' The point is that you have to ask. Rome is not the initiator of changes. Rome is the solid guardian of dogma and morals. But if you can prove you have a good case and if you get a 'no' and come back like a good boy and ask, respectfully, again, Rome will not refuse. One of the reasons Rome may refuse the first few requests is to test the determination of those asking. Rome will not yield to a fad."

Appendix C
Farewell to Father Reinhold:
Friend and Teacher[1]

The articles and speeches devoted to Father Hans Ansgar Reinhold on the occasion of his death, January 30th, all bring out the fact that he was not only a great liturgist and champion of social justice, but also an exceptionally true and warm friend. This was the intimate, human note that this profound scholar and bold pioneer lent to his contacts with his fellow-priests, lay apostles, ecumenists and students. For he gave them not only a full share of his knowledge and experience, but also his love, thus establishing with them that true communication which is so often sought in our days, and so rarely found.

Father Reinhold was, as we all know, the initiator of all the main changes in the structure of the Mass and other liturgical services, as well as one of the first leaders of the Vernacular Society, whose recommendations have now been fully implemented. But this is not all. His story as an intrepid priest, engaged in Catholic social action, started in the thirties, in Germany, where he was a seamen's chaplain before coming to the United States. He was also at that time already a resolute opponent of Hitler and the Nazis, at a time when many of his compatriots and some Americans still failed to recognize the handwriting on the wall.

It was for this reason that he left his native land and came to America, where he was to serve in the forties as a seamen's chaplain in Seattle. He had observed with interest and sympathy the longshoremen's strike in San Francisco. He was deeply concerned with the Apostolate of the Sea, and had come to the Catholic Worker on earlier visits to America to discuss these problems with Peter Maurin and Dorothy Day. He was to be the friend of the CW during many years and up to his death; the older members of the Catholic Worker were particularly grieved to learn that he had passed away.

As a matter of fact, Father Reinhold never ceased, in the midst of his strenuous liturgical search and long and painful illness, to be concerned with the poor, the underprivileged and oppressed. This rare combination of a strict,

---

[1] Helene Iswolsky, *The Catholic Worker* (March, 1968): 8. Helene Iswolsky (1896–1975), a Russian émigré, was the daughter of the last Tsarist ambassador to France. An associate of Dorothy Day, Iswolsky lived in Pittsburgh and came to know Reinhold there at the end of his life. See Helene Iswolsky, *No Time to Grieve: An Autobiographical Journey* (Philadelphia: Winchell Company, 1983).

sophisticated scholar and an extraordinarily sensitive humanist, did not represent two parallel, but essentially different spheres. It was made possible because the two spheres were inspired by a common love: the love of truth. For in Father Reinhold's mind, liturgy, properly interpreted and understood, was the reflection of Divine Truth, expressed in symbols. And the defense of man's dignity and rights is nothing else but this truth put into action.

The liturgy could be beautiful only if it was genuine and if it told the story of the Incarnation and of Salvation. "Beauty," wrote Dostoevsky, "will save the world." This sentence puzzles the reader who seeks in it a merely esthetic value. For Dostoevsky, the religious philosopher, just as for Father Reinhold, the "liturgical philosopher" as he has been called, the words meant infinitely more. It was the absolute beauty of the New Jerusalem which could be reflected here upon earth, but would be clearly seen at the end of times: the Parousia.

To grasp this other meaning it was necessary to understand the Eucharistic meal as it was instituted by Christ; it was necessary to remove the superfluous and the irrelevant, while preserving the sacred symbolism which really mattered. And in the social sphere as well, it was urgent to uncover the Pharisee, the merciless and covetous bourgeois, who piled up the bricks for the ever rising wall of injustice.

To pursue this dual goal, and to do it unceasingly, was obviously a hard task for one man to perform. Perhaps only a few people knew of the scope of this dedicated life. It passed most of the time unnoticed, because Father Reinhold was an extremely quiet and reserved man. This natural restraint grew even greater during the last years of his life, due to his fatal sickness, Parkinson's disease, which gradually spread over his frail body. His speech, which had been clear and charming, was reduced to a whisper. The friendly smile froze on his lips. He withdrew from our midst, and we could do nothing to bring him back. The last time I saw him was at his anniversary Mass, marking the fortieth year of his priesthood, celebrated at the Church of the Holy Family in New York. He offered the Holy Sacrifice himself and gave us communion. All his friends were there, Catholics and non-Catholics, and there was a party for him afterwards. But he was exhausted and did not speak again.

However, this increasing disability did not prevent Father Reinhold from pursuing his work as a writer. He dictated his articles and books with great difficulty, or somehow managed to operate an electric typewriter. After the anniversary Mass, he published two books: *Liturgy and Art* and his autobiography entitled *H.A.R.* This last book appeared almost on the day of his death. We hope to publish a review in a future issue of the CW. Meanwhile, I shall merely speak of my own reminiscences.

My first encounter with H.A.R., as he liked to call himself, took place at the home of my friend Arthur Lourie and his wife Elizabeth. Lourie was, like myself, a Russian Catholic and a friend of Jacques Maritain, who considered him the finest composer of modern religious music. H.A.R. had planned to commission Lourie to compose a Mass according to an entirely new yet strictly liturgical pattern. Unfortunately this plan never materialized, due to the many difficulties that assailed both the priest and the composer. But at least I had the opportunity to discover a new friend.

At that first meeting, I was happy to learn that Father Reinhold was interested in the Byzantine rite and in ikon-painting and Eastern religious architecture, Greek, Armenian and Russian. He knew a great deal about Russia and had studied my native language, as well as Church Slavonic. This formed a lasting link between us. When he wrote to me, he enjoyed signing his letters "Ivan," and I called him Father Hans.

When I, along with Lourie and a few other friends, started the small ecumenical group called the Third Hour, Father Reinhold attended our meetings and contributed an article to our yearbook. This article, entitled "Hypapante Jesus and Mary," dealt specifically with one feast: The Purification of the Blessed Mary or Candlemas; rereading it today, in the light of H.A.R.'s entire teaching, I realize how clearly he stated the problem of reinterpreting liturgical forms.

As early as the fifties, Father Reinhold had, I believe, completed the blueprint of the liturgical reforms which were implemented by Vatican Two, including of course the introduction of the vernacular, only recently admitted. When he spoke to us about these changes and told us that they would inevitably come, it seemed to us quite incredible. He had the joy of living long enough to see this happen. He had worked and suffered much, for he had been misunderstood and harshly criticized until Bishop John Wright invited him to Pittsburgh, where he could continue his teaching and writing as long as his failing health permitted.

I saw him often in the years 1960–65 when I taught at Seton Hill College, in the Pittsburgh area. He was very eager to hear about my two trips to Russia, for he had a great love of the Russian people and faith in their deep spirituality.

At that time, Dr. Leonard Swidler, of Duquesne University, founded a very dynamic ecumenical seminar, the first of its kind in America, and began publishing the *Journal of Ecumenical Studies*, in which both Father Hans and I participated. He also lectured at the Seminar, as did the theologian Hans Kung. This was the golden age of this ecumenical group. It has since been transferred to Temple University, Philadelphia, and is extremely active. But we shall always miss Father Reinhold and his unique, infinitely inspiring work with us.

What was H.A.R.'s "liturgical philosophy"? It is hard to define, because it was extremely complex and at times paradoxical. To understand it, his books, all his books, should be attentively studied. He would take various elements of the liturgy apart, carefully examine them, discard all that he considered non-essential and non-liturgical, then put all the relevant parts together. He did not care whether the irrelevant parts were old and obsolete, or modernistic, or merely in bad taste. They had to go. His sole concern was whether the new liturgy expressed the Eucharistic sacrifice. He wrote: "The Church claims that the first meal eaten in the upper room in Jerusalem was as liturgical as it is today in the Mass." Everything, old and new, prayers, hymns, music, art itself, must gravitate around the central theme, or else it has no value.

For the rest, Father Reinhold was ever open to change, and more change. He said that we live in an age in which all are "shaken up"; everything is changing, from the interpreters of the scriptures to the astronauts who step out of their capsule into space. He used this metaphor to show that we are entering a new dimension, and he was unafraid of it. All that he demanded was, as he put it, that "the liturgical man should be one of great veracity and insight." And such was our dear friend and teacher, to whom we say a sorrowful farewell.

Appendix D

H. A. Reinhold
The Dynamics of Liturgy
New York: Macmillan, 1961

Contents
Foreword by Rt. Rev. Monsignor Edward G. Murray

1. The Beginnings of the Liturgical Movement

a. The Cloister and Society [pp. 1–6] = "The Closter and Society," *Commonweal* 28 (May 20, 1938): 97–99.

b. Denver and Maria Laach [pp. 7–13] = "Denver and Maria Laach," *Commonweal* 45 (November 8, 1946): 86–88.

2. The Work of the People

c. A Social Leaven [pp. 14–19] = "A Social Leaven?" *Orate Fratres* 25 (October–November 1951): 515–18.

d. Thunderstorm Religion [pp. 19–23] = "Thunderstorm Religion," *Orate Fratres* 16 (November 1941): 33–36.

e. The Dexterity of Missing the Point [pp. 23–28] = "The Dexterity of Missing the Point," *Orate Fratres* 26 (February 1952): 129–34.

f. A Change of Emphasis [pp. 29–38] = "The Family and the Eucharist," *National Liturgical Week Proceedings* 7 (1946): 61–70.

3. Lent: Rebirth and Resurrection

g. Lent in Focus [pp. 39–45] = "Lent in Focus," *Commonweal* 51 (March 17, 1950): 599–601.

h. The Spirit of Lent [pp. 45–51] = "The Spirit of Lent," *Commonweal* 61 (March 4, 1955): 577–80.

i. The Reformed Lenten Liturgy [pp. 52–57] = "The 'Reformed' Lenten Liturgy," *Today* 12 (March 1957): 22–23.

4. The Christmas Cycle

j. Christmas Currents [pp. 58–62] = "Christmas: Anno Domini 1955," *Commonweal* 63 (December 23, 1955): 299–301.

k. Incarnation and Parousia [pp. 62–67] = "Incarnation and Parousia," *Commonweal* 35 (December 19, 1941): 214–16.

l. The Treasures of Christmas [pp. 67–72] = "The Treasures of Christmas," *Commonweal* 60 (December 28, 1956): 327–29.

m. Parousia [pp. 72–78] = "Parousia, 1943," *Commonweal* 37 (January 15, 1943): 318–20.

5. Liturgy and the Arts

n. Fashions in Church Architecture [pp. 79–83] = Unidentified.

o. Art, Architecture and the Christian [pp. 84–92] = "Art, Architecture and the Christian: Some Notes on How to Look at Churches Past and Present," *Jubilee* 5 (April 1958): 17–20.

p. Music in Church [pp. 92–99] = "Music in Church is Part of the Mystery," *Today* 14 (April 1959): 17–20, however it is significantly modified.

6. The Eucharist and the Liturgy

q. A Dangerous Inadequacy [pp. 100–103] = "A Dangerous Inadequacy," *Orate Fratres* 14 (1940): 451–54; [pp. 103–6] = Unidentified.

r. Family Communion [pp. 106–9] = "Family Communion," *Orate Fratres* 16 (1942): 126–29.

7. A Few Reforms

s. Vernacular in the Liturgy [pp. 110–14] = "Vernacular in the Liturgy," *Orate Fratres* 17 (1943): 458–63; and "About English in our Liturgy," *Commonweal* 41 (March 16, 1945): 537–40.

t. Notes on a Breviary Reform [pp. 120–27] = Unidentified.

8. Liturgy and Devotion

u. The Imitation of Christ [pp. 128–34] = "Imitation of Christ," *Jubilee* 5 (January 1958): 17–24.

v. Spiritual Growth: A Progressive Sharing Divine Nature [pp. 134–43] = "Spiritual Growth: A Progressive Sharing Divine Nature," *Spiritual Life* 3 (June 1957): 85–94.

H. A. Reinhold Bibliography

BOOKS AND MONOGRAPHS

Our Parish: House of God and Gate of Heaven. New York: Paulist, 1943.

Speaking of Liturgical Architecture. Notre Dame, IN: Notre Dame Liturgy Program, 1952.

The American Parish and the Roman Liturgy: An Essay in Seven Chapters. New York: Macmillan, 1958.

Bringing the Mass to the People. Baltimore: Helicon, 1960.

The Dynamics of Liturgy. New York: Macmillan, 1961.

Liturgy and Art. New York: Harper and Row, 1966.

H. A. R.: The Autobiography of Father Reinhold. New York: Helicon, 1968.

BOOKS, EDITED

Reinhold, H. A., ed. *The Soul Afire: Revelations of the Mystics*. New York: Pantheon Books, 1944.

Anson, Peter. *Churches: Their Planning and Furnishing*. Introduction, footnotes, and Americanization by H. A. Reinhold. Milwaukee, WI: Bruce, 1948.

ARTICLES

1928

Reinhold, H. A. "Schon Wieder Eine Enttauschung? Gedanken Zu Einer 'Wissenshaftlichen' Kritik." *Die Seelsorge* 6 (1928): 388–96.

1929

"Katholische Deutsche Seemannsseelsorger." *Die Seelsorge* 1929 (September 1929): 433–37.

"Zur Geschichte und Bedeutung des Neuen Herz Jesu-Offiziums." *Jahrbuch Liturgiewissenschaft* 8 (1929): 246–49.

1930

"Das Problem des Epiphanistestes." *Die Seelsorge* 7 (December 1930): 91–94.

1932

"Die Liturgie und Die Pfarrlosen." *Liturgische Zeitschrift* 5 (1932): 97–103.

"Seelsorge und Hichkapitalisches Wirthschaftssystem." *Central-Blatt and Social Justice* 25 (October 1932): 218–20.

1934

"Liturgie, Kunstler und Klerus." *Liturgisches Leben* 1 (1934): 244–50.

1935

"Jungkatholishe Bewegung Allerwegen." *Schweizerische Rundschau* 8 (1935): 727–32.

1936

"Kongress für Seemannsmission in London." *Die Seelsorge* 12 (January 1936): 120–21.

1937

"The Sea for Christ." *Commonweal* 25 (March 12, 1937): 549–51.
"Sakramentales Leben." *Die Seelsorge* 13 (May 1937): 225–31.

1938

"The Catholic Worker Movement in America." *Blackfriars* 19 (September 1938): 635–50.
"Cloister and Society." *Commonweal* 28 (May 20, 1938): 97–99.
"Revolution in Church Architecture." *Liturgical Arts* 6, 3rd quarter (1938): 123–33.

1939

"The Architecture of Rudolf Schwarz." *Architectural Forum* 52 (January 1939): 22–27.
"More or Less Liturgical [#1]." *Orate Fratres* 13 (February 1939): 152–55.
"One Hundred Churches in Seven Years." *Commonweal* 29 (February 10, 1939): 429–31.
"More or Less Liturgical [#2]." *Orate Fratres* 13 (March 1939): 213–18.
"Dom Virgil Michel's Column." *Orate Fratres* 13 (March 1939): 223–25.
"More or Less Liturgical [#3]." *Orate Fratres* 13 (April 1939): 257–63.
"Christian Transients—Transient Christians?" *Orate Fratres* 13 (April 1939): 275–78.
"Use of the Missal by the Laity." *American Ecclesiastical Review* 100 (May 1939): 452–55.
"Liturgy—Medieval or Twentieth Century?" *Orate Fratres* 13 (May 1939): 317–20.
"Catholic Puritanism." *Orate Fratres* 13 (June 1939): 367–69.
"Penance and Penitentiaries." *Orate Fratres* 13 (July 1939): 412–14.
"Christian Spirit and 'Good Manners.'" *Orate Fratres* 13 (September 1939): 461–63.
"Institutionalized Instruction." *Orate Fratres* 13 (October 1, 1939): 513–15.
"Prisons and Penance." *Commonweal* 31 (October 27, 1939): 4–6.
"Christian Radicalism." *Orate Fratres* 13 (October 29, 1939): 554–55.
"ACTU and Liturgy." *Orate Fratres* 14 (November 1939): 32–34.
"House of God and House of Hospitality." *Orate Fratres* 14 (December 24, 1939): 77–78.

1940

"Letter to the Editor." *Liturgical Arts* 8 (January 1940): 39.

"Faith is a Kosmos." *Orate Fratres* 14 (January 1940): 122–24.

"Just War." *Commonweal* 31 (February 9, 1940): 345–47.

"Popular Christianity." *Orate Fratres* 14 (February 1940): 169–72.

"Anglican." *Orate Fratres* 14 (March 1940): 220–22.

"My Dream Mass." *Orate Fratres* 14 (April 1940): 265–70.

"Le 'Catholic Worker' en Amérique I." *La Relève* (April 1940): 7–13.

"The God of the Godless." *Orate Fratres* 14 (May 1940): 312–14.

"Sacrament of Responsibility." *Commonweal* 32 (May 10, 1940): 58–59.

"Le 'Catholic Worker' en Amérique II." *La Relève* (May–June 1940): 49–59.

"Apocalyptic Present." *Orate Fratres* 14 (June 1940): 363–67.

"That Interesting Fiction: The American Standard of Living." *Orate Fratres* 14 (July 1940): 409–12.

"Word for the Fuller Parish Liturgy." *American Ecclesiastical Review* 103 (August 1940): 173–78.

"A Dangerous Inadequacy." *Orate Fratres* 14 (September 1, 1940): 451–54.

"Meaning and Necessity of 'Devotions,'" *Proceedings of the National Liturgical Week* (1940): 169–76.

"Liturgical Parish Mission in Everett, Washington." *Orate Fratres* 14 (September 1940): 463–67.

"Eucharistic Piety." *Orate Fratres* 14 (September 29, 1940): 508–10.

"Anglican." *Liturgical Arts* 9 (October 1940): 4–5.

"Secular and Liturgical Civilization." *Orate Fratres* 14 (October 1940): 558–60.

"Inner Forum: Liturgical Week." *Commonweal* 33 (November 15, 1940): 109–10.

"Dosed Religion." *Orate Fratres* 15 (December 1, 1940): 28–31.

"Liturgy and the 'New Order.'" *Orate Fratres* 15 (December 29, 1940): 77–79.

1941

"Msgr. Franz Xaver Muench." *Orate Fratres* 15 (January 1941): 128–29.

"Thirty Years After." *Orate Fratres* 15 (February 1941): 175–78.

"Collective Ownership is Collectivism?" *Orate Fratres* 15 (March 1941): 225–27.

"Out of the Night?" *Commonweal* 33 (March 28, 1941): 559–61.

"Depersonalized Property." *Orate Fratres* 15 (April 1941): 273–75.

"The Catholic Faith Catechism." *Orate Fratres* 15 (May 1941): 315–18.

"Resisting the Zeitgeist." *Orate Fratres* 15 (June 1941): 371–73.

"Christian Formation Through the Liturgy." *The Wanderer* (June 19, 1941): 5ff.

"The Liturgical Church." *Church Property Administration* 5 (June–July 1941): 7–8, 29.

"Advertising the Mass *a la* Hollywood." *Orate Fratres* 15 (July 1941): 413–15.

"The Sacrament of Extreme Unction in Parish Life." *Proceedings of the National Liturgical Week* (1941): 135–41.

"Periculum in Mora." *Orate Fratres* 15 (September 1941): 464–67.

"The Malvern Conference." *Orate Fratres* 15 (October 1941): 510–12.

"Bible and Liturgy." *Orate Fratres* 15 (November 2, 1941): 561–63.

"Eternal Glory: Sacrament and Treatment of Death in the Christian Tradition." *Commonweal* 35 (November 7, 1941): 66–69.

"Thunderstorm Religion." *Orate Fratres* 16 (November 30, 1941): 33–36.

"Nature Mirrors Supernature." *Orate Fratres* 16 (December 1941): 80–82.

"Incarnation and Parousia." *Commonweal* 35 (December 19, 1941): 214–16.

1942

"Family Communion." *Orate Fratres* 16 (January 1942): 126–29.

"Christian Liberty and Economic Systems." *Orate Fratres* 16 (February 1942): 510–14.

"Inroads of the Bourgeois Spirit." *Commonweal* 35 (February 27, 1942): 458–61.

"Liturgical Fascism?" *Orate Fratres* 16 (March 1942): 217–21.

"Printed in America." *Orate Fratres* 16 (April 1942): 249–56.

"Sacrament of Responsibility: Confirmation." *Sower* 143 (April 1942): 6–7.

"Soren Kierkegaard." *Commonweal* 35 (April 10, 1942): 608–11.

"They Fought a War Over It!" *Orate Fratres* 16 (April 1942): 271–74.

"Three Books." *Orate Fratres* 16 (May 1942): 312–16.

"Nazis and the Germans." *Commonweal* 36 (May 29, 1942): 133–34.

"Paddy the Cope." *Orate Fratres* 16 (June 1942): 365–68.

"Without Spot or Wrinkle." *Orate Fratres* 16 (September 1942): 458–61.

"Christian Responsibility." *Orate Fratres* 16 (October 1942): 510–14.

"Cart and Horse," *Orate Fratres* 16 (October 1942): 523.

"Parable of the Liturgical Priest." *Orate Fratres* 16 (November 1, 1942): 557–61.

"The Two Mentalities." *Orate Fratres* 17 (November 29, 1943): 31–34.

"Body of Christ." *Orate Fratres* 17 (December 1942): 76–79.

"The 'Versus Populum' Altar Again." *American Ecclesiastical Review* 107 (December 1942): 442–50.

1943

"Spirit of the Roman Liturgy." *Commonweal* 37 (January 1, 1943): 270–72.

"How Many Cycles Has the Liturgical Year?" *Orate Fratres* 17 (January 1943): 102–10.

"Hierarchical Value and Beauty." *Homiletic and Pastoral Review* 43 (January 1943): 306–11.

"Freedom of Worship." *Orate Fratres* 17 (January 1943): 130–32.

"Parousia, 1943." *Commonweal* 37 (January 15, 1943): 318–20.

"Let Us Give Thanks for Our Colored Brethren." *Orate Fratres* 17 (February 1943): 172–74.

"Social and Economic Naturalism." *Orate Fratres* 14 (March 1943): 218–23.

"True Humanism." *Orate Fratres* 17 (April 1943): 272–75.

"Don Luigi Sturzo." *Orate Fratres* 17 (May 1943): 313–16.

"The Neatest Trick of the Year." *Orate Fratres* 17 (June 1943): 367–71.

"Styles Do Not Make a Church." *Orate Fratres* 17 (August 1943): 414–18.

"The Vernacular in the Liturgy." *Orate Fratres* 17 (September 1943): 458–63.

"Hallowing of All Life." *Commonweal* 38 (October 8, 1943): 607–10.

"The Menace of the Herd." *Orate Fratres* 17 (October 1943): 505–10.

"The Purists." *Orate Fratres* 17 (October 1943): 559–65.

"Letter to the Editor." *Liturgical Arts* 12 (November 1943): 22.

"High-Pressure Salesmanship." *Orate Fratres* 18 (November 1943): 32–35.

"Choir and/or People." *Orate Fratres* 18 (December 1943): 73–76.

1944

"The Vernacular Again." *Orate Fratres* 18 (January 1944): 127–32.

"Pope's Plea for Personalism." *Commonweal* 39 (January 14, 1944): 323–26.

"Worship in Spirit and Truth." *Tidings* (January 28, 1944–August 18, 1945).

"L'Esprit de la Liturgie Romaine." *Nouvelle Relève* 3 (January 1944): 86–92.

"Allegory vs. Symbol." *Orate Fratres* 18 (February 1944): 180–85.

"Choir and/or People." *Catholic Choirmaster* 30 (March 1944): 10–11, 15.

"City Planning." *Orate Fratres* 18 (March 1944): 217–20.

"Prudence and Timidity." *Orate Fratres* 18 (April 1944): 267–70.

"The Discussion Continues." *Orate Fratres* 18 (May 1944): 314–21.

"What about Germany's Christians?" *Commonweal* 40 (May 19, 1944): 102–5.

"Rural Liturgy." *Orate Fratres* 18 (June 1944): 364–68.

"A Variety of Things." *Orate Fratres* 18 (July 1944): 418–22.

"Letter to the Editor." *Liturgical Arts* 12 (August 1944): 97.

"Liturgy and Maturity." *Orate Fratres* 18 (September 1944): 469–72.

"Music and Other Things." *Orate Fratres* 18 (October 1944): 514–20.

"Perspectives Partielles." *Nouvelle Relève* 3 (October 1944): 385–90.

"I Never Thought of That." *Commonweal* 41 (November 17, 1944): 118–20.

"Some Aspects of Freedom." *Orate Fratres* 18 (November 1944): 558–63.

"Speaking as Saul among the Prophets." *Catholic Choirmaster* 30 (December 1944): 147–49.

"Planning the Spiritual City." *Orate Fratres* 19 (December 3, 1944): 29–34.

"H. A. R. on Vestments." *Catholic Art Quarterly* 81 (Christmas 1944): 24.

"Liturgical Regimentation." *Orate Fratres* 19 (December 31, 1944): 74–81.

1945

"Answering Some Answers." *Orate Fratres* 19 (January 1945): 119–27.

"The Soldiers Are Ahead of Us." *Orate Fratres* 19 (February 1945): 170–74.

"About English in Our Liturgy." *Commonweal* 41 (March 16, 1945): 537–40.
   [Republished as "English in Our Liturgy" in the fiftieth anniversary issue: *Commonweal* 99 (November 16, 1973): 167–68.]

"Celebration of the Paschal Mysteries." *Catholic Choirmaster* 31 (March 1945): 3–5.

"Escapist Worshippers." *Orate Fratres* 19 (March 1945): 222–27.

"Are We Losing Our Identity?" *Orate Fratres* 19 (April 1945): 273–78.

"Germany." *Commonweal* 42 (May 4, 1945): 68–69.

"Return to Worship." *Orate Fratres* 19 (May 1945): 315–19.

"A Radical Social Transformation Is Inevitable." *Orate Fratres* 19 (June 1945): 362–68.

"Liturgical Discernment." *Catholic Choirmaster* 31 (June 1945): 51–53.

"The German Lesson." *Orate Fratres* 19 (July 1945): 411–16.

"To Recite with a Fuller Understanding." *Orate Fratres* 19 (July 1945): 385–90.

"Open Wounds of the Mystical Body." *Orate Fratres* 19 (September 1945): 462–66.

"A Thesis Never Written." *Orate Fratres* 19 (October 1945): 510–14.

"Germany." *Commonweal* 43 (October 26, 1945): 44–45.

"Decent Godless People." *Orate Fratres* 19 (November 1945): 555–58.

"Lesson from Ketteler." *Catholic Digest* 10 (December 1945): 13–15.

"Bigotry and Militant Catholicism." *Orate Fratres* 20 (December 2, 1945): 28–32.

"The Christians and Security." *Orate Fratres* 20 (December 30, 1945): 83–88.

1946

"The Oblates of St. Benedict: A Letter." *Benedictine Review* 1 (January 1946): 34–40.

"How to Defeat the Critic." *Orate Fratres* 20 (January 1946): 129–33.

"Things on My Desk." *Orate Fratres* 20 (February 1946): 175–80.

"Desiderata To Be Prayed For." *Orate Fratres* 20 (March 1946): 230–35.

"Action without Contemplation Is Blind." *Orate Fratres* 20 (April 1946): 276–79.

"Unfathomable Europe." *Orate Fratres* 20 (May 1946): 317–23.

"Hope for Germany." *Commonweal* 44 (May 31, 1946): 158–62.

"Unfathomable Europe II." *Orate Fratres* 20 (June 1946): 364–69.

"Le Pasteur Niemoeller et Les Deux Allemagnes." *Nouvelle Relève* 5 (June 1946): 144–64.

"The Tiger and the Boa Constrictor." *Orate Fratres* 20 (July 1946): 411–14.

"The Family and the Eucharist." *National Liturgical Week Proceedings* 7 (1946): 61–70.

"Copyrighted Churches." *Orate Fratres* 20 (September 1946): 464–67.

"Extramural Liturgical Movements." *Orate Fratres* 20 (October 1946): 503–9.

"Denver and Maria Laach." *Commonweal* 45 (November 8, 1946): 86–88.

"The 'New Parish.'" *Orate Fratres* 20 (November 1946): 558–63.

"Colombes Continued." *Orate Fratres* 21 (December 1946): 21–27.

"Praying Wisely—in Latin and English." *Orate Fratres* 21 (December 1946): 75–79.

"Catholic Art, Reply to M Lavanoux with Rejoinder." *America* 76 (December 21, 1946): 335.

1947

"Catholic Art." *America* 76 (January 4, 1947): 392.

"Things to Think About." *Orate Fratres* 21 (January 1947): 123–29.

"French Catholic Thinking." *Orate Fratres* 21 (February 1947): 168–75.

"German Mentality." *Commonweal* 45 (February 7, 1947): 420.

"Two Suggestions." *Orate Fratres* 21 (March 1947): 229–32.

"Mail from the Enemy Defeated." *Commonweal* 46 (May 23, 1947): 134–37.

"Ruminating on Rubrics." *Orate Fratres* 21 (May 1947): 312–17.

"A Long Question and a Short Answer." *Orate Fratres* 21 (June 1947): 363–69.

"Europe's Troubled Mind." *Commonweal* 46 (June 20, 1947): 233–35.

"Renouveau Liturgique." *Nouvelle Relève* 5 (June 1947): 603–14.

"Vernacular Problem in 1909." *Clergy Review* 27 (June 1947): 361–72.

"Participation in What?" *Orate Fratres* 21 (July 1947): 414–17.

"The Liturgical Movement to Date." *National Liturgical Week Proceedings* 8 (1947): 9–20.

"From the Vernacular Front." *Orate Fratres* 21 (September 1947) 459–66.

"Liturgical Parish Missions." *Commonweal* 46 (September 12, 1947): 520–22.

"Work of the People." *Commonweal* 46 (September 26, 1947): 571–73.

"Jube d'Asnieres." *Orate Fratres* 21 (October 1947): 513–17.

"Remarks about Minor Items." *Orate Fratres* 21 (November 2, 1947): 556–60.

"Streamlining an Old Idea." *Orate Fratres* 22 (November 30, 1947): 29–33.

"The Vernacular." *Orate Fratres* 22 (November 1947): 92–93.

"Committee on Un-Liturgical Activities." *Orate Fratres* 22 (December 1947): 76–80.

1948

"Philistinism and Education." In *The Philosophy of Catholic Higher Education*, edited by Roy J. Deferrari, 13–27. Washington, DC: Catholic University of America Press, 1948.

"Father Remillieux." *Orate Fratres* 22 (January 1948): 114–21.

"Meaning of the Church Year." *Orate Fratres* 22 (January 1948): 135–37.

"Pastor to His People." *Catholic Mind* 46 (February 1948): 119–20.

"First Impressions: *Mediator Dei*." *Orate Fratres* 22 (February 1948): 176–79.

"A Great New Book." *Orate Fratres* 22 (March 1948): 219–23.

"What about England?" *Orate Fratres* 22 (April 1948): 267–70.

"Bible and Liturgy." *Orate Fratres* 22 (May 1948): 315–18.

"The Present at Maria Laach and Klosterneuburg." *Liturgical Arts* 16 (May 1948): 70–71.

"Dom Odo Casel." *Orate Fratres* 22 (June 1948): 366–72.

"Scandal of Christians Being Separated." *Commonweal* 48 (July 9, 1948): 301–3.

"Lost Cause of the Epiphany." *Homiletic and Pastoral Review* 48 (July 1948): 731–36.

"Which Is the Cart and Which the Horse?" *Orate Fratres* 22 (July 1948): 413–17.

"Pioneering at Notre Dame." *Orate Fratres* 22 (September 1948): 465–67.

"Return of the Nazis." *Commonweal* 48 (September 3, 1948): 497–98.

"Inflation's Human Aspect." *Commonweal* 48 (September 17, 1948): 538–41.

"Pastor to His Employer-Parishioners." *Catholic Mind* 46 (September 1948): 592–93.

"Sectarianism and Departmentalism." *Orate Fratres* 22 (October 1948): 508–14.

"News from Europe." *Orate Fratres* 22 (October 1948): 557–61.

"Liturgical Arts at Notre Dame." *Liturgical Arts* 17 (November 1948): 13.

"East and West." *Orate Fratres* 23 (November 1948): 22–27.

"Clama, Ne Cesses!" *Catholic Choirmaster* 34 (December 1948): 147–49.

"Towards the Breviary Reform." *Orate Fratres* 23 (December 1948): 74–79.

1949

"Missarum Sollemnia." *Orate Fratres* 23 (January 1949): 122–27.

"Spiritually Semites." *Orate Fratres* 23 (February 1949): 169–73.

"Monolithic Catholicism?" *Orate Fratres* 23 (March 1949): 210–15.

"Our Lenten Liturgy." *Commonweal* 49 (March 25, 1949): 582–85.

"St. Radbert and St. Bernard." *Orate Fratres* 23 (April 1949): 260–65.

"Vernacular in our Liturgy." *Catholic Mind* 47 (April 1949): 200–207.

"Growing Liturgy." *Orate Fratres* 23 (May 1949): 313–17.

"Explanation." *Commonweal* 50 (May 27, 1949): 172.

"Gleanings from Scholars." *Orate Fratres* 23 (June 1949): 363–67.

"Commencing to Live." *Orate Fratres* 23 (July 1949): 418–25.

"A Thousand Faces, But Who Cares?" *Commonweal* 50 (July 8, 1949): 331–34.

"Christian Meaning of Sunday." *Proceedings of the National Liturgical Week* (1949): 62–75.

"Threshold and Interior." *Commonweal* 50 (August 26, 1949): 480–83.

"Leads from Germany." *Orate Fratres* 23 (September 1949): 462–67.

"Thoughts on Church Planning." *Orate Fratres* 23 (October 1949): 509–14.

"Tourist and Pilgrim." *Commonweal* 51 (October 14, 1949): 6–9.

"Cultural Lag." *Commonweal* 51 (November 4, 1949): 103–5.

"Grailville." *Orate Fratres* 23 (November 1949): 544–48.

"A Liturgy for Labor Peace." *Orate Fratres* 24 (December 1949): 22–25.

1950

"The New Knox Missal." *Orate Fratres* 24 (January 1950): 70–75.

"Vereinigte Staaten Von Amerika." In *Liturgische Erneuerung in Aller Welt*, edited by Theodor Bolger. Maria Laach: Verlag Ars Liturgica, 1950.

"An Epochal Document on Church Building." *Liturgical Arts* 18 (February 1950): 29–32.

"Offertory Processions." *Orate Fratres* 24 (February 1950): 116–20.

"Sir, We Would See Jesus." *Orate Fratres* 24 (March 1950): 172–76.

"Lent in Focus." *Commonweal* 51 (March 17, 1950): 599–601.

"A Significant Rescript." *Orate Fratres* 24 (April 1950): 211–15.

"Social Change?" *Orate Fratres* 24 (May 1950): 259–64.

"The Breviary in the Vernacular." *Priest* 6 (June 1950): 428–35.

"Question of Culture." *Orate Fratres* 24 (June 1950): 312–16.

"Collectivized Education." *Orate Fratres* 24 (July 1950): 361–64.

"Works of Faith." *Orate Fratres* 24 (August 1950): 408–11.

"Orthodox or Heterodox?" *Orate Fratres* 24 (September 1950): 450–55.

"The Right Moment." *Orate Fratres* 24 (October 1950): 506–11.

"Thy Kingdom Come." *Orate Fratres* 25 (December 1950): 29–33.

1951

"Reevaluating Epiphany." *Orate Fratres* 25 (January 1951): 72–75.

"Mother Tongue: Pro's and Foes." *Orate Fratres* 25 (February 1951): 121–27.

"Long Loneliness of Dorothy Day." *Commonweal* 55 (February 29, 1951): 521–22.

"Our Lady of Fatima." *Orate Fratres* 25 (March 1951): 166–70.

"Kerygmatic Pastoral Theology." *Orate Fratres* 25 (April 1951): 220–24.

"Re-presenting the Whole of Redemption." *Orate Fratres* 25 (May 1951): 260–67.

"State as Monster." *Commonweal* 54 (June 8, 1951): 217–18.

"Rite and Tongue." *Orate Fratres* 25 (June 1951): 311–16.

"Strange Things Happen!" *Orate Fratres* 25 (July 1951): 356–62.

"The Christian in the World." *Orate Fratres* 25 (August 1951): 405–11.

"Celebrating Marriage." *Orate Fratres* 25 (September 1951): 453–56.

"Simone Weil, Saint of the Churchless." *Commonweal* 55 (October 26, 1951): 65–70.

"A Social Leaven?" *Orate Fratres* 25 (October–November 1951): 515–19.

"Don Luigi Sturzo: A Memoir." *Commonweal* 55 (November 30, 1951): 193–95.

"More about the New German Ritual." *Worship* 26 (December 1951): 26–30.

1952

"Father of the World to Come." *Worship* 26 (January 1952): 74–81.

"European Union: Reply." *Commonweal* 55 (February 8, 1952): 449.

"The Dexterity of Missing the Point." *Worship* 26 (February 1952): 129–34.

"Past and Present." *Worship* 26 (March 1952): 179–86.

"Back to—What?" *Worship* 26 (April 1952): 248–56.

"All that Rest in Christ." *Worship* 26 (May 1952): 298–303.

"The Lure of Communism." *Worship* 26 (June 1952): 358–65.

"Toward Christian Unity." *Commonweal* 56 (July 4, 1952): 320–22.

"Coming Breviary Reform." *Worship* 26 (September 1952): 469–75.

"Life of Christ in the Liturgy." *Worship* 26 (October 1952): 516–20.

"Notes on Spain." *Commonweal* 57 (October 17, 1952): 31–33.

"Asking Rome." *Worship* 26 (November 1952): 574–78.

"Scriptural Green Pastures." *Worship* 27 (December 1952): 31–35.

1953

"Germany: Shadows of Tomorrow: Replies." *Commonweal* 57 (January 2, 1953): 323–26.

"Who is Missing the Boat?" *Worship* 27 (January 1953): 89–94.

"Liturgical Art." *Liturgical Arts* 21 (February 1953): 32–35.

"The Trials of a Reader of Translations." *Worship* 27 (February 1953): 138–41.

"Matter of Tradition." *Commonweal* 57 (March 6, 1953): 556–60.

"The New Eucharistic Decrees." *Worship* 27 (March 1953): 187–90.

"New Easter Vigil." *Today* 8 (April 1953): 15ff.

"The Resurrection." *Worship* 27 (April 1953): 244–46.

"Pastorale Problem des Grundonnerstages." *Liturgisches Jahrbuch* 3 (1953): 253–59.

"Search for the New Man." *Social Order* 3 (May–June 1953): 195–206.

"Yearnings of a Reformer." *Worship* 27 (June 1953): 353–55.

"Frequent Communion, Accessible and Integrated." *Proceedings of the National Liturgical Week* (1953): 65–70.

"Which Foot Forward?" *Worship* 27 (September 1953): 460–64.

"Public Relations." *Worship* 27 (October 1953): 506–10.

"Future of the Liturgy." *Commonweal* 59 (November 6, 1953): 111–13.

"A Turing Point: Lugano." *Worship* 27 (November 1953): 557–63.

1954

"Praying Over a Mike." *Worship* 28 (May 1954): 292–94.

"Understanding the Mass." *Today* 9 (May 1954): 10–11.

"Spain 1954: Franco's Achievements Reply and Rejoinder." *Commonweal* 60 (July 2, 1954): 319–21.

"Liturgical Reform." *Commonweal* 60 (July 30, 1954): 407–9.

"Lugano and Holy Week." *Worship* 28 (September 1954): 426–32.

"Speaking of Liturgical Architecture." *Church Property Administration* 18 (October 1954): 27–29, 139–43.

1955

"No Time to Push Alien Compromises." *Caecilia* 82 (February 1955): 74.

"Spirit of Lent." *Commonweal* 61 (March 4, 1955): 577–80.

"New Ritual." *Worship* 29 (April 1955): 265–70.

"Return to Liturgy." *Commonweal* 62 (August 26, 1955): 521–23.

"Research of Un-Liturgy." *Worship* 29 (November 1955): 613–14.

"Advent: A Time of Longing." *Today* 11 (November 1955): 13–15.

"Revealing Example of Charity and Hope." *Commonweal* 63 (December 16, 1955): 288.

"Christmas: Anno Domini 1955." *Commonweal* 63 (December 23, 1955): 299–301.

"Modern Parish." *Priest* 11 (December 1955): 991–97.

1956

"One Pastor's Reaction." *Worship* 30 (February 1956): 180–85.

"Lesson of Assisi." *Commonweal* 65 (October 5, 1956): 7–10.

"Challenges of Our Time." *Commonweal* 65 (December 7, 1956): 262–64.
"Treasures of Christmas." *Commonweal* 65 (December 28, 1956): 327–29.

1957
"Cross and Resurrection." *Crosier Missionary* 32 (1957): 2–7.
"The 'Reformed' Lenten Liturgy." *Today* 12 (March 1957): 22–23.
"Worker Priests." *Commonweal* 65 (March 1, 1957): 561–64.
"The Way of the Cross." *Altar and Home* 24 (March 1957): 15–24.
"Spiritual Growth: A Progressive Sharing of Divine Nature." *Spiritual Life* 3 (June 1957): 85–94.
"Christ Living in the Church." *Ave Maria* 86 (August 17, 1957): 9–11.
"Johannes Pinsk R.I.P." *Worship* 31 (November 1957): 605–8.
"Is Liturgy a Panacea?" *Worship* 32 (December 1957): 12–16.

1958
"Imitation of Christ." *Jubilee* 5 (January 1958): 17–24.
"Meaning of Assisi." *Voice of St. Jude* 23 (March 1958): 5–7.
"Art and the Liturgy." *Commonweal* 67 (March 21, 1958): 631–34.
"The Assisi Congress and our Greatest Parochial Problem." *Pastoral Life* 7 (March–April 1958): 11–17.
"Art, Architecture and the Christian: Some Notes on How to Look at Churches Past and Present." *Jubilee* 5 (April 1958): 17–20.

1959
"Music in Church is Part of the Mystery." *Today* 14 (April 1959): 17–20.
"Parousia and Etimasia: A New Emphasis of the Beliefs of the Early Church about Advent." *Jubilee* 7 (December 1959): 14–17.

1960
"Liturgy and Contemplation: A Rebuttal." *Spiritual Life* 6 (1960): 207–17.
"The One Church, A Challenge to Us as Catholics." *Proceedings of the North American Liturgical Week* (1960): 106–12.

1961
"Celebrating Easter." *Jubilee* 8 (April 1961): 12–15.
"Liturgy, Architecture and the Arts." *Irish Ecclesiastical Record* 95 (May 1961): 299–305.
"The Silence and Singleness of Prayer." *The Current: A Review of Catholicism and Contemporary Culture* 1 (May 1961): 61–64.
"What is Benediction?" *Ave Maria* 94 (July 15, 1961): 5–9.
"Why Worship?" *The Lamp* 8 (July 1961): 9ff.
"Celebration of Baptism and the Eucharist." *Proceedings of the North American Liturgical Week* (1961): 157–59.
"Liturgy and Church Architecture." *Good Work* 24 (Fall 1961): 112–18.

H.A. Reinhold Bibliography

1962

"Liturgy and Ecumenism." In *Dialogue for Reunion*, edited by Leonard Swidler, 38–53. New York: Herder and Herder, 1962.

"Expectations of the Faithful." In *Looking Toward the Council*, edited by Joseph Cunneen, 82–89. New York: Herder and Herder, 1962. [Reprint of *Cross-Currents* article above of the same name.]

"Liturgy and Reunion." *Commonweal* 75 (January 5, 1962): 379–82.

"Liturgy and Church Architecture." *Jubilee* 9 (February 1962): 17–19.

"Worship in Spirit and Truth." *Way* 2 (April 1962): 115–20.

"Expectations of the Faithful." *CrossCurrents* 12 (Spring 1962): 204–11.

"Do We Need Liturgical Reforms?" *Life of the Spirit* 16 (June 1962): 509–18.

"Importance of the Liturgical Program at Colleges and Universities." *Proceedings of the North American Liturgical Week* (1962): 142–45.

"Christmas in the Liturgy." *Commonweal* 77 (December 28, 1962): 355–57.

1963

"Eucharistic Bread." In *Sunday Morning Crisis: Renewal in Catholic Worship*, edited by Robert W. Hovda, 89–97. Baltimore: Helicon, 1963.

"Gift for Father Godfrey Diekmann on His Jubilee as Editor of *Worship*." In *The Revival of the Liturgy*, edited by Frederick R. McManus, 9–14. New York: Herder and Herder, 1963.

"The Pyrrhic Victory of Florus of Lyons." In *Liturgy for the People: Essays in Honor of Gerald Ellard, S.J., 1894–1963*, edited by William J. Leonard, 206–14. Milwaukee, WI: Bruce, 1963.

"Historical Analysis of Ecumenical Councils' Influence on Sacred Architecture." *Proceedings of the North American Liturgical Week* (1963): 92–96.

"Maria Laach Revisited." *Commonweal* 78 (August 23, 1963): 497–500.

"Worship or Pretenses?" *Today* 19 (October 1963): 7–9.

"Revitalizing the Liturgy: Some Observations for Architects." Address, Festival of the Arts, sponsored by the Diocese of Cincinnati at Mount St. Joseph College, Cincinnati, OH, October 14, 1963.

"In These Ecumenic Times." *The Lamp* 61 (November 1963): 10–11, 22, 24.

1964

"Spiritual Life in the Parish." *Ave Maria* 99 (February 15, 1964): 14–15.

"Liturgy and the Second Vatican Council: Constitution on the Sacred Liturgy." *Catholic World* 198 (March 1964): 347–56.

"The Cardinal of Vienna and the Nazis." *Jubilee* 12 (May 1964): 22–23.

"Timely Questions [Active Participation]." *The Living Light* 1, no. 1 (Spring 1964): 130–34.

"Why Active Participation in the Mass." Keynote address, Liturgy Conference, Camden, NJ, May 7–9, 1964.

"Timely Questions [Concelebration]." *The Living Light* 1, no. 2 (Summer 1964): 162–65.

"The Mass of the Future." *Commonweal* 80 (August 21, 1964): 565–68.

"Timely Questions [Penance]." *The Living Light* 1, no. 3 (Fall 1964): 142–45.

"Vatican II: Some Unfinished Business." *Priest* 20 (December 1964): 1035–40.

"Timely Questions [Vernacular]." *The Living Light* 1, no. 4 (Winter 1964):
134–37.

1965

"Foreword." In *The Mass Reformed: A New Draft Liturgy of the Mass with Commentary*, by Roger P. Kuhn, 3–7. Notre Dame, IN: Catholic Action Office, 1965.

"Timely Questions [Music]." *The Living Light* 2, no. 1 (Spring 1965): 142–45.

"A Liturgical Reformer Sums Up." *New Blackfriars* 46 (July 1965): 554–61.

"Timely Questions [Music]." *The Living Light* 2, no. 2 (Summer 1965): 142–45.

"The Future of the Liturgy." *Continuum* 3 (Summer 1965): 258–61.

"No Time to Stop." *Commonweal* 82 (August 20, 1965): 583–85.

"Timely Questions [Translation]." *The Living Light* 2, no. 3 (Fall 1965): 122–24.

"Timely Questions [Vernacular]." *The Living Light* 2, no. 4 (Winter 1965):
118–20.

1966

"Reputation of the Council at Stake." *Journal of Ecumenical Studies* 2 (1966): 474.

"Mary in the Liturgy." *Jubilee* 13 (February 1966): 10–13.

"Timely Questions [Penance]." *The Living Light* 3, no. 1 (Spring 1966): 82–85.

"The Mass: Proposals for Further Reform." *Jubilee* 14 (May 1966): 3.

"Timely Questions [Adult Baptism]." *The Living Light* 3, no. 2 (Summer 1966):
121–23.

"Implementing the Reform of Worship." *Continuum* 3 (Winter 1966): 525–27.

1967

"Abbot Ildefons Herwegen." *New Catholic Encyclopedia* (1967).

"Allegorical Interpretation of Liturgy." *New Catholic Encyclopedia* 8 (1967):
937–38.

"Joseph Kramp." *New Catholic Encyclopedia* 8 (1967): 261.

BOOK REVIEWS

1938

Review of *The Eastern Branches of the Catholic Church: Six Studies on the Oriental Rites*, by Liturgical Arts Society. *Commonweal* 28 (September 9, 1938): 509.

Review of *Contemporary Continental Theology: An Interpretation for Anglo-Saxons*, by Walter Marshall Horton. *Commonweal* 28 (October 7, 1938): 621.

1939

Review of *World Communism*, by F. Borkenau. *Commonweal* 29 (March 31, 1939): 640.

Review of *The Church and Mankind*, vol. 1 of *Concilium: Theology in the Age of Renewal*. *Commonweal* 82 (May 21, 1965) 298–99.

Review of *Cross and Swastika*, by Arthur Fey. *Commonweal* 30 (May 26, 1939): 136.

Review of *The Believer's Christ*, by Ludwig Kosters, trans. by J. W. Grunder. *Commonweal* 30 (June 9, 1939): 192–93.

Review of *The Eucharist*, by Peter Skarga. *Commonweal* 30 (July 14, 1939): 302–3.

"A Bad, Bad Book." Review of *Perpetual Peace*, by Immanuel Kant. *Commonweal* 30 (August 4, 1939): 360.

Review of *Germany Rampant: A Study in Economic Militarism*, by Ernest Hambloch. *Commonweal* 31 (December 1, 1939): 142–43.

1940

Review of *The Church and Social Problem of Our Day*, by Karl Barth. *Commonweal* 31 (January 12, 1940): 271.

Review of *The Church before Pilate*, by Edward Leen. *Commonweal* 31 (January 26, 1940): 310–11.

Review of *Seventy Stories of the Old Testament*, ed. Helen Slocum Estabrook. *Liturgical Arts* 8 (April 1940): 77–78.

1941

Review of *Hugh Sophia*, by Emerson Howland Swift. *Commonweal* 33 (January 31, 1941): 378.

Review of *Living Religions and a World Faith*, by William Ernest Hocking. *Commonweal* 33 (April 11, 1941): 625–26.

1942

Review of *Thus Speaks Germany*, by W. W. Coole and M. F. Potter. *Commonweal* 35 (April 3, 1942): 594–95.

Review of *The Dialog Mass: A Book for Priests and Teachers of Religion*, by Gerald Ellard. *Commonweal* 36 (July 3, 1942): 259–60.

Review of *Sonnets to Orpheus*, by Rainer Maria von Rilke. *Commonweal* 36 (August 14, 1942): 404.

Review of *Man and Society in Calamity*, by Pitirim Aleksandrovich Sorokin. *Commonweal* 37 (October 30, 1942): 45.

1943

Review of *Can Our Cities Survive: An A.B.C. of Urban Problems, Their Analysis, Their Solutions: Based on the Proposals Formulated by the C.I.A.M.*, by José Luis Sert. *Commonweal* 37 (February 5, 1943): 402.

Review of *A Short Life of Kierkegaard*, by Walter Lowrie. *Commonweal* 37 (February 26, 1943): 475–76.

Review of *The Church in Disrepute*, by Bernard Iddings Bell. *Commonweal* 38 (May 7, 1943): 79–80.

Worship in Spirit and Truth

Review of *Force and Freedom, Reflections on History*, by Jacob Burckhardt, ed. James Hastings Nichols. *Commonweal* 38 (May 28, 1943): 149–50.

Review of *The True Life: Sociology of the Supernatural*, by Luigi Sturzo. *Commonweal* 39 (November 5, 1943): 76–77.

Review of *Arrival and Departure*, by Arthur Koestler. *Commonweal* 39 (December 24, 1943): 255–56.

1944

Review of *Der Fuehrer: Hitler's Rise to Power*, by Konrad Heiden. *Commonweal* 39 (February 11, 1944): 428.

Review of *Germany: A Self-Portrait*, by Harlan R. Crippen. *Commonweal* 40 (June 2, 1944): 162.

Review of *The Altar and the World*, by Bernard Iddings Bell. *Commonweal* 40 (June 16, 1944): 210.

Review of *Either/Or*, by Søren Kierkegaard [vol. 1, trans. David F. Swenson and Lillian Marvin Swenson; vol. 2, trans. Walter Lowrie]; *For Self Examination and Judge for Yourselves*, by Søren Kierkegaard, trans. Walter Lowrie; *Training in Christianity*, by Søren Kierkegaard, trans. Walter Lowrie. *Commonweal* 40 (June 30, 1944): 260.

Review of *Omnipotent Government: The Rise of the Total State and Total War*, by Ludwig von Mises. *Commonweal* 40 (July 21, 1944): 329–30.

Review of *Christian Counter-Attack: Europe's Churches Against Nazism*, by Hugh Martin, Douglas Newton, Herbert Montague Waddams, and R. R. Williams. *Commonweal* 40 (August 4, 1944): 379.

Review of *The Eucharist, the Mystery of Holy Thursday*, by Francois Mauriac. *Liturgical Arts* 12 (August 1944): 96.

Review of *Slavery and Freedom*, by Nicolas Berdiaev. *Commonweal* 41 (October 27, 1944): 44.

Review of *The Concept of Dread*, by Søren Kierkegaard, trans. Walter Lowrie. *Commonweal* 41 (November 17, 1944): 133.

1945

Review of *The Biography of a Cathedral: The Living Story of Man's Most Beautiful Creation . . . Notre Dame of Paris*, by Robert Gordon Anderson. *Liturgical Arts* 13 (February 1945): 43–44.

Review of *A History of the Dominican Liturgy*, by William R. Bonniwell. *Commonweal* 41 (February 2, 1945): 404.

Review of *Radical State*, by Gerhard Jacoby. *Commonweal* 41 (February 16, 1945): 451.

Review of *Catholic Art and Culture*, by E. I. Watkin. *Liturgical Arts* 13 (May 1945): 66.

Review of *Re-Educating Germany*, by Werner Richter. *The Review of Politics* 7 (July 1945): 379–82.

Review of *The Yogi and the Commissar and Other Essays*, by Arthur Koestler. *Commonweal* 42 (July 27, 1945): 362–63.

1946

Review of *Rembrandt, the Jews and the Bible*, by Franz Landsberger. *Commonweal* 44 (September 13, 1946): 533.

Review of *Journal from My Cell*, by Roland DePury. *Commonweal* 45 (November 22, 1946): 149.

1947

Review of *Dear Fatherland, Rest Quietly*, by Margaret Bourke-White. *Commonweal* 45 (January 10, 1947): 327–28.

Review of *In Time and Eternity: A Jewish Reader*, ed. Nahum N. Glatzer. *Commonweal* 45 (January 17, 1947): 356.

Review of *The Story of Jesus in the World's Literature*, ed. Edward Wagenknecht. *Commonweal* 45 (February 14, 1947): 452.

Review of *A Kierkegaard Anthology*, ed. Robert Bretall. *Commonweal* 45 (February 28, 1947): 498–99.

Review of *How It Happens: Talk about the German People, 1914–1933*, by Pearl Buck. *Commonweal* 45 (March 7, 1947): 525.

Review of *Ibsen: The Intellectual Background*, by Brian Westerdale Downs. *Commonweal* 46 (June 27, 1947): 268.

Review of *Ferdinand Lassalle, Romantic Revolutionary*, by David Footman. *Commonweal* 47 (October 24, 1947): 53.

Review of *Autobiography*, by Solomon Maimon. *Commonweal* 47 (November 28, 1947): 177.

Review of *From the Land of Sheba: Tales of the Jews of Yemen*, ed. Solomon Dob Fritz Goitein. *Commonweal* 47 (November 28, 1947): 177.

Review of *Galut*, by Yitzhak Fritz Baer. *Commonweal* 47 (November 28, 1947): 177.

Review of *Rabbi of Bacherach: A Fragment*, by Heinrich Heine. *Commonweal* 47 (November 28, 1947): 177.

Review of *The Language of Faith: Selected Jewish Prayers*, ed. Nahum N. Glatzer. *Commonweal* 47 (November 28, 1947): 177–78.

Review of *The Von Hassell Diaries, 1938–1944*, by Ulrich Von Hassell. *Commonweal* 47 (December 5, 1947): 204.

1948

Review of *Art in the Early Church*, by Walter Lowrie. *Commonweal* 47 (January 9, 1948): 332.

Review of *In Darkest Germany*, by Victor Gollancz. *Commonweal* 47 (January 16, 1948): 358.

Review of *Transformation in Christ: On the Christian Attitude of Mind*, by Dietrich Von Hildebrand. *Commonweal* 49 (February 11, 1948): 451.

Review of *On the Marble Cliffs*, by Ernst Junger. *Commonweal* 48 (April 16, 1948): 639.

Review of *The King and the Corpse: Tales of the Soul's Conquest of Evil*, by Heinrich Robert Zimmer. *Commonweal* 48 (July 23, 1948): 356.

Review of *Death of Socrates: An Interpretation of the Platonic Dialogues, Euthyphro, Apology, Crito and Phaedo*, by Romano Guardini. *Commonweal* 48 (August 13, 1948): 432–33.

Review of *Behold the Spirit: A Study in the Necessity of Mystical Religion*, by Alan Wilson Watts. *Commonweal* 48 (August 20, 1948): 454.

1949

Review of *And the Third Day . . . A Record of Hope and Fulfillment*, ed. Herbert John Clifford Grierson. *Commonweal* 49 (March 11, 1949): 49.

Review of *Cathedrals and How They Were Built*, by David Herbert Somerset Cranage. *Commonweal* 49 (April 1, 1949): 621.

Review of *Seeds of Contemplation*, by Thomas Merton. *Commonweal* 50 (April 15, 1949): 19.

Review of *Hero with a Thousand Faces*, by Joseph Campbell. *Commonweal* 50 (July 8 1949): 321.

Review of *Theologia Germanica*, by Anonymous Frankfurt Priest. *Commonweal* 50 (July 15, 1949): 347.

Review of *Wisdom of Catholicism*, ed. Anton Charles Pegis. *Commonweal* 50 (August 19, 1949): 466.

1950

Review of *Goethe and the Modern Age*, by Arnold Bergstrasser. *Commonweal* 53 (December 1, 1950): 212.

1951

"State as Monster." Review of *Origins of Totalitarianism*, by Hannah Arendt. *Commonweal* 54 (June 8, 1951): 217–18.

Review of *Memoirs*, by Ernst Heinrich Freiherr Von Weizsacker. *Commonweal* 55 (November 23, 1951): 177.

1952

"The Long Loneliness of Dorothy Day." Review of *The Long Loneliness*, by Dorothy Day. *Commonweal* 55 (February 29, 1951): 521–22.

Review of *One Shepherd: The Problem of Christian Reunion*, by Charles Boyer. *Commonweal* 56 (July 4, 1952): 320–22.

1953

Review of *Two Roads to Truth: A Basis for Unity Under the Great Tradition*, by Edmund Ware Sinnot. *Commonweal* 57 (March 6, 1953): 556.

Review of *Saint Paul*, by Henri Daniel-Rops. *Commonweal* 58 (August 21, 1953): 496.

1954

Review of *Russian Assignment*, by Leslie C. Stevens. *Commonweal* 59 (January 15, 1954): 383.

Review of *Aspects of Buddhism*, by Henri de Lubac. *Commonweal* 59 (March 19, 1954): 607–9.

Review of *God, Man and the Universe: A Christian Answer to Modern Materialism*, ed. Jacques de Bivort de La Saudee. *Commonweal* 61 (November 12, 1954): 173.

Review of *The Lord*, by Romano Guardini. *Commonweal* 61 (November 19, 1954): 192–93.

1955

Review of *Human Element in the Church of Christ*, by Paul Simon. *Commonweal* 61 (February 25, 1955): 560.

Review of *Catholic Approach to Protestantism*, by George Henry Tavard. *Commonweal* 63 (December 16, 1955): 288.

1956

Review of *Contemporary Church Art*, by Anton Henze and Theodor Filthaut. *Commonweal* 65 (December 7, 1956): 262.

1957

Review of *God the Unknown, and Other Essays*, by Victor White. *Commonweal* 65 (February 22, 1957): 547.

Review of *Worker-PRIESTS: A Collective Documentation*, by Robert John Petrie Hewison. *Commonweal* 65 (February 22, 1957): 548.

Review of *The Bible and the Liturgy*, by Jean Danielou. *The Catholic Art Quarterly* 20 (Easter 1957): 61–63.

Review of *Golden Gospels of Echternach* [*Codex aureus Epternacensis*]. *Commonweal* 66 (September 27, 1957): 641.

1964

"Tension between Individualism and Community in the Church." Review of *The Variety of Catholic Attitudes*, by Theodore Westow. *Commonweal* 79 (March 13, 1964): 724–25.

1965

Review of *The Church and Mankind*, vol. 1 of *Concilium: Theology in the Age of Renewal*. *Commonweal* 82 (May 21, 1965): 298–99.

Selected Bibliography

Adam von Bremen. *History of the Archbishops of Hamburg-Bremen.* Edited by
    Francis Joseph Tschan. New York: Columbia University Press, 1959.
Adolph, Walter. *Geheime Aufzeichnungen aus dem nationalsozialistischen Kirchen-
    kampf 1935–1943.* Mainz: 1979.
Ahlers, Rolf. "The Confession of Altona." *Harvard Theological Review* 77 (July /
    October 1984): 377–94.
Albers, Jan. "Tage im Kloster: Maria Laach Abbey." In *Ecclesia Lacensis,* edited
    by Emmanuel von Severus, 593–99. Münster, Germany: Aschendorff,
    1993.
Anson, Peter F. *The Church and the Sailor: A Survey of the Sea-Apostolate Past and
    Present.* London: Catholic Book Club, 1948.
———. *Churches: Their Plan and Furnishing.* Milwaukee: Bruce, 1948.
———. *Harbour Head: Maritime Memories.* London: John Gifford Limited, 1944.
Augustine, Dolores L. "The Business Elites of Hamburg and Berlin." *Central
    European History* 24, no. 2/3 (1991): 132–46.
Barrett, Michael. *Rambles in Catholic Lands.* New York: Benziger Brothers, 1914.
Barrett, Noel Hackmann. *Martin B. Hellriegel: Pastoral Liturgist.* St. Louis, MO:
    Central Bureau of the Catholic Central Union of America, 1990.
———. "The Contribution of Martin B. Hellriegel to the American Catholic Li-
    turgical Movement." PhD diss., St. Louis University, 1977.
Berger, Teresa. *Women's Ways of Worship: Gender Analysis and Liturgical History.*
    Collegeville, MN: Liturgical Press, 1999.
Bethune, Adé. "Font and Altar; Footnotes on Sacred Architecture." *The Catholic
    Art Quarterly* 15 (Pentecost 1954): 88–105.
Boler, Martin. "The Influence of Maria Laach on Mount Saviour Monastery."
    In *Ecclesia Lacensis,* edited by Emmanuel von Severus, 436–48. Münster,
    Germany: Aschendorff, 1993.
Botte, Bernard. *From Silence to Participation: An Insider's View of Liturgical Re-
    newal,* trans. John Sullivan. Washington, DC: Pastoral Press, 1988.
Bourke-White, Margaret. *Dear Fatherland, Rest Quietly: A Report on the Collapse
    of Hitler's "Thousand Years."* New York: Simon & Schuster, 1946.
———. *Portrait of Myself.* New York: Simon & Schuster, 1963.
Bovée, Warren G. "Cyclone with a Calm Center." *The Catholic School Editor* 25
    (January 1956): 6–8.
———. "H. A. R." *Davenport Messenger* (June 14, 1956).
———. "H.A.R., Front Line Fighter." *Today* 10 (December 1954): 3–5.
Brand, Eugene L. "Worship and the Ecumenical Movement." *Ecumenical Re-
    view* 51 (1999): 184–92.

Bredeck, Martin J. *Imperfect Apostles: The Commonweal and the American Catholic Laity, 1924–1976.* New York: Garland, 1988.

Brehany, Blane. "Aspects of the Liturgical Renewal as seen in the Writing of H. A. Reinhold and the Constitution on the Sacred Liturgy." Master's thesis, Catholic University of America, 1965.

Brendon, Piers. *The Dark Valley: A Panorama of the 1930s.* New York: Alfred A. Knopf, 2000.

Breuilly, John. "Hamburg: The German City of Laissez-Faire." *The Historical Journal* 35 (September 1992): 701–12.

Bugnini, Annibale. *The Reform of the Liturgy: 1948–1975.* Translated by Matthew J. O'Connell. Collegeville, MN: Liturgical Press, 1990.

Burleigh, Michael. *The Third Reich: A New History.* New York: Farrar, Strauss and Giroux, 2000.

Busch, William, trans. "Directives for the Building of a Church," *Orate Fratres* 24 (December 1949): 3–12.

Caldecott, Stratford, ed. *Beyond the Prosaic: Renewing the Liturgical Movement.* Edinburgh: T&T Clark, 1998.

Casey, George W. Review of *Bringing the Mass to the People*, by H. A. Reinhold. *Worship* 35 (December 1960): 66–68.

Clancy, William C. "In Memoriam: H.A.R." *Worship* 42 (March 1968): 130–33.

Clark, Stephen L. "C. P. E. Bach and the Tradition of Passion Music in Hamburg." *Early Music* 16 (November (1988): 533–41.

Connell, Martin. *Guide to the Revised Lectionary.* Chicago: Liturgy Training Publications, 1998.

Conzemius, Victor. "German Catholics and the Nazi Regime in 1933." *Irish Ecclesiastical Record* 108 (1967): 326–35.

Corrin, Jay P. *Catholic Intellectuals and the Challenge of Democracy.* Notre Dame, IN: University of Notre Dame Press, 2003.

———. "H. A. Reinhold, *America*, and the Catholic Crusade Against Communism." *Records of the American Catholic Historical Society* 105 (Spring–Summer 1994): 47–69.

———. "H. A. Reinhold: Liturgical Pioneer and Anti-Fascist." *The Catholic Historical Review* 82 (July 1996): 436–58.

Davies, John G. "The Influence of Architecture upon Liturgical Change." *Studia Liturgica* 9 (1973): 230–40.

De La Bedoyere, Michael. *The Cardijn Story: A Study of the Life of Msgr. Joseph Cardijn and the Young Christian Workers' Movement which He Founded.* London: Longmans, Green and Co., 1958.

Deedy, John G., Jr. "Restless Ambassador of Christ." *Jubilee* 8 (November 1961): 7–11.

———. Review of *H. A. R.: The Autobiography of Father Reinhold. Commonweal* 87 (February 16, 1968): 598–99.

Diekmann, Godfrey. "H.A.R.'s Sabbatical Leave." *Worship* 27 (1953): 569–70.

———. "Is there a Distinctive American Contribution to the Liturgical Renewal?" *Worship* 45 (1971): 578–87.

———. "Monsignor Martin B. Hellriegel: Holy Cross Church. St. Louis." *Worship* 38 (August–September 1964): 497–98.

———. "Ten Years of H.A.R." *Orate Fratres* 23 (April 1949): 275–77.

Dietrich, Donald. *Catholic Citizens in the Third Reich: Psycho-Social Principles and Moral Reasoning*. New Brunswick, NJ: Transaction Books, 1988.

———. "Catholic Theologians in Hitler's Third Reich: Adaptation and Critique." *Journal of Church and State* 29 (1987): 19–45.

Dixon, John W. "The Iconic Architecture of Rudolph Schwarz: An Essay on Architectural and Theological Method." http://www.unc.edu/~jwdixon/articles/schwarz.html (accessed January 24, 2009).

Ducey, Michael. "Maria Laach and Liturgy." *Orate Fratres* 9 (January 1935): 108–13.

———. "The National Liturgical Weeks and American Benedictines." *American Benedictine Review* 6 (Summer 1955): 155–67.

———. "The National Liturgical Weeks and American Benedictines (II)." *American Benedictine Review* 8 (Autumn 1957): 235–42.

———. "The National Liturgical Weeks and American Benedictines (III)." *American Benedictine Review* 9 (Autumn and Winter 1958): 227–33.

Ebel, Karen E. "German American Internees in the United States during WWII." http://www.traces.org/timeline.aftermath.html (accessed January 24, 2009).

Ellard, Gerald. "The American Scene 1926–1951." *Orate Fratres* 25 (October–November 1951): 500–508.

———. *The Dialog Mass: A Book for Priests and Teachers of Religion*. New York: Longmans, Green and Co., 1942.

———. *Mass of the Future*. Milwaukee, WI: Bruce, 1948.

———. *The Mass in Transition*. Milwaukee, WI: Bruce, 1956.

———. "'A Spiritual Citadel of the Rhineland': Maria Laach and the Liturgical Movement." *Orate Fratres* 3 (October 6, 1929): 384–88.

Ellis, John Tracy. "American Catholicism in 1960: An Historical Perspective." *American Benedictine Review* 11 (September 1960): 1–20.

Ellis, Vincent Patrick, Jr. "Bearing the Weight of the Mystery: The Pictorial Arts and Liturgical Renewal in the Roman Catholic Church in the United States of America, 1926–1963." PhD diss., Drew University, 2003.

Evans, Richard J. *Death in Hamburg: Society and Politics in the Cholera Years, 1830–1910*. New York: Oxford University Press, 1987.

Farrell-Vinay, Giovanna. "The London Exile of Don Luigi Sturzo (1925–1940)." *Heythrop Journal* 45 (2004): 158–77.

Feld, Frederick William. "Is Purgatory Inevitable?" *Ecclesiastical Review* 88 (June 1933): 581–89.

———. "Why be Anointed?" *Ecclesiastical Review* 84 (May 1931): 484–91.

Frederick, J. B. M. *The Future of Liturgical Reform*. Wilton, CT: Morehouse-Barlow, 1987.

Gallin, Alice. *Midwives to Nazism: University Professors in Weimar Germany 1925–1933*. Macon, GA: Mercer University Press, 1986.

Galloway, David D. "Happening in Hamburg." *Art in America* 78 (May 1990): 77–89.

Gannon, Arthur. *Apostolatus Maris 1920–1960: The Personal Record of Arthur Gannon*. New Orleans, LA: Apostleship of the Sea, 1965.

Garner, Joel Patrick. "The Vision of a Liturgical Reformer: Hans Ansgar Reinhold, American Catholic Educator." EdD diss., Columbia University, 1972.

Gass, Robert. *Chant: Discovering Spirit in Sound*. New York: Broadway Books, 1999.

Hall, Jeremy. *The Full Stature of Christ: The Ecclesiology of Virgil Michel*. Collegeville, MN: Liturgical Press, 1976.

Hallinan, Paul. "A Time to Create." *Commonweal* 87 (October 13, 1967): 47–49.

Havemann, Joel. *A Life Shaken: My Encounter with Parkinson's Disease*. Baltimore: Johns Hopkins University Press, 2002.

Hayes, John M. "Review of *The Dynamics of Liturgy* by H. A. Reinhold (New York: Macmillan, 1961)." *Worship* 36 (May 1961): 403–4.

Hecht, Ingeborg. *Invisible Walls: A German Family Under the Nuremberg Laws*. New York: Harcourt Brace Jovanovich, 1984.

Hughes, Kathleen, ed. *How Firm a Foundation: Voices of the Early Liturgical Movement*. Chicago: Liturgical Training Publications, 1990.

———. *The Monk's Tale: A Biography of Godfrey Diekmann, O.S.B.* Collegeville, MN: Liturgical Press, 1991.

Hurd, Madeline. "Education, Morality, and the Politics of Class in Hamburg and Stockholm, 1870–1914." *Journal of Contemporary History* 31 (October 1996): 619–50.

International Commission on English in the Liturgy. *Documents on the Liturgy 1963–1979: Conciliar, Papal and Curial Texts*. Collegeville, MN: Liturgical Press, 1982.

Iswolsky, Helene. "Farewell to Father Reinhold: Friend and Teacher." *The Catholic Worker* (March 1968).

———. *No Time to Grieve: An Autobiographical Journey*. Philadelphia: Winchell Company, 1983.

Jordan, Patrick, and Paul Bauman, eds. *Commonweal Confronts the Century: Liberal Convictions, Catholic Traditions*. New York: Simon & Schuster, 1999.

Jungmann, Joseph A. *The Early Liturgy*. Notre Dame, IN: University of Notre Dame Press, 1959.

———. *The Mass of the Roman Rite*. Translated by Francis A. Brunner. 2 vols. New York: Benziger, 1951–55.

Keegan, John. *The First World War*. New York: Random House, 1998.

Kern, Joseph. *De Sacramento Extremae Unctionis Tractatus Dogmaticus*. Regensburg: Friderici Pustet, 1907.

Klauser, Theodor. *A Short History of the Western Liturgy: An Account and Some Reflections*. Translated by John Halliburton. London: Oxford, 1969.

Krieg, Robert A. *Catholic Theologians in Nazi Germany*. New York: Continuum, 2004.

———. *Romano Guardini: A Precursor of Vatican II*. Notre Dame, IN: University of Notre Dame Press, 1997.

———. "Romano Guardini's Theology of the Human Person." *Theological Studies* 59 (1998): 457–75.

Kverndal, Roald. *The Way of the Sea: The Changing Shape of Mission in the Seafaring World*. Pasadena, CA: William Carey Library Publishers, 2008.

Lawrence, Emeric A. "H. A. R.—Death of a Friend." *Commonweal* 87 (March 8, 1968): 686–88.

Lieberman, Abraham. *Shaking Up Parkinson Disease: Fighting Like a Tiger, Thinking Like a Fox*. Sudbury, MA: Jones and Bartlett, 2002.

Liturgical Conference, ed. *Church Architecture: The Shape of Reform*. Washington, DC: The Liturgical Conference, 1965.

Madden, Lawrence J., ed. *The Awakening Church: 25 Years of Liturgical Renewal*. Collegeville, MN: Liturgical Press, 1992.

———. "The Liturgical Conference of the U.S.A.: Its Origin and Development: 1940–1968." PhD diss., Universität Trier, 1969.

Manley, Thomas E. "The Purists." *Orate Fratres* 18 (December 1943): 93–95.

Marini, Piero. *A Challenging Reform: Realizing the Vision of the Liturgical Renewal 1963–1975*. Collegeville, MN: Liturgical Press, 2007.

Martindale, C. C. *The Sea and its Apostolate*. London: Catholic Truth Society, 1929.

Mathis, Rev. Michael A. "The Notre Dame Liturgy Program." *Liturgical Arts* 16 (1947–48): 3–7.

McMahon, L. M. "Towards a Theology of the Liturgy: Dom Odo Casel and the 'Mysterientheorie.'" *Studia Liturgica* 3 (1964): 129–54.

McManus, Frederick, ed. *The Revival of the Liturgy*. New York: Herder and Herder, 1963.

Mills, William Christopher. "In the World, of the Church, for the Kingdom: A Study of Alexander Schmemann's Pastoral Theology." Union Institute and University, 2004.

Moriarty, M. "William Palmer Ladd and the Origins of the Episcopal Liturgical Movement." *Church History* 64 (September 1995): 438–51.

Murray, Gregory. Review of *Bringing the Mass to the People*, by H. A. Reinhold. *Theological Studies* 22 (1961): 128–30.

Neuberger, Richard L. "Plutonium and Problems." *The Nation* (July 30, 1949): 104–6.

Neunheuser, Burkhard. "Die 'Krypta-Messe' in Maria Laach, Ein Beitrag zur Frühgeschichte der Gemeinschaftemesse." *Liturgie und Mönchtum* 28 (1961): 70–82.

———. "Maria Laach Abbey: A Double Jubilee 1093–1993; 1892–1992." *Ecclesia Orans* 10 (1993): 163–78.

———. "Report on Liturgical Activities in Germany During the War." *Orate Fratres* 21 (1946–1947): 114–22.

Nolan, Francis. "Pro and Con." *Orate Fratres* 18 (March 1944): 221–29.

Nyhart, Lynn K. "Civic and Economic Zoology in Nineteenth-Century Germany: The 'Living Communities' of Karl Mobius." *Isis* 89 (December 1998): 605–30.

O'Brien, David J. "When It All Came Together: Bishop John J. Wright and the Diocese of Worcester, 1950–1959." *The Catholic Historical Review* 85 (1999): 174–95.

O'Meara, Thomas Franklin. *Church and Culture: German Catholic Theology, 1869–1914.* Notre Dame: University of Notre Dame Press, 1991.

Quitslund, Sonya. *Beauduin: A Prophet Vindicated.* New York: Newman Press, 1973.

Pecklers, Keith. *Dynamic Equivalence: The Living Language of Christian Worship.* Collegeville, MN: Liturgical Press, 2003.

———. *The Unread Vision. The Liturgical Movement of the United States of America 1926–1955.* Collegeville, MN: Liturgical Press, 1998.

Petrek, William. "Liturgical Awareness." *Commonweal* 74 (March 31, 1961): 22–23.

Repgen, Konrad. "German Catholicism and the Jews: 1933–1945." In *Judaism and Christianity Under the Impact of National Socialism,* edited by Otto Dov Kulka and Paul R. Mendes-Flohr, 197–226. Jerusalem: Historical Society of Israel and the Allman Shazar Center for Jewish History, 1987.

Roarke, J. Madeleva. *Father Damasus and the Founding of Mount Saviour.* Pine City, NY: Madroar Press, 1998.

Ruff, Anthony. *Sacred Music and Liturgical Reform: Treasures and Transformations.* Chicago: Hillenbrand Books, 2007.

Ruttinger, Josephine. "History of the Seamen's Apostolate in the Harbor of New York." Master's thesis, St. John's University, 1953.

Sagarra, Eda. *A Social History of Germany 1684–1914.* New York: Holmes & Meier, 1977.

Saint-Severin. *The Liturgical Movement.* New York: Hawthorn Books, 1964.

Schloeder, Steven Joseph. "The Church of the Year 2000: A Dialogue on Catholic Architecture for the Third Millennium." PhD diss., Graduate Theological Union, 2003.

Schwarz, Rudolf. *The Church Incarnate: The Sacred Function of Christian Architecture.* Translated by Cynthia Harris. Chicago: Henry Regnery, 1958.

Searle, Mark. *Called to Participate: Theological, Ritual and Social Perspectives.* Edited by Barbara Searle and Anne Y. Koester. Collegeville, MN: Liturgical Press, 2006.

Senn, Frank C. *The People's Work: A Social History of the Liturgy.* Minneapolis: Fortress Press, 2006.

————. "What Has Become of the Liturgical Movement: Its Origins, Current Situation and Future Prospects." *Pro Ecclesia* 6, no. 3 (1997): 319–32.

Shannon, Robert L. "Damasus Winzen: A Voice for Liturgical Reform in the United States." PhD diss., Catholic University of America, 2004.

Sherwood, Polycarp R. "*In Memoriam*: Dom Lambert Beauduin." *American Benedictine Review* 10 (June 1959): 195–204.

Smith, Randall. "Speaking of Liturgical Architecture: Modernism and Modern Church Architecture," *Christian Literature and Living* 2, no. 9 (August 2003), http://www.christianliteratureandliving.com/aug2003/rsmitharchitecture.html (accessed January 24, 2009).

Sorg, Rembert. "In Defense of Latin." *Orate Fratres* 19 (January 1945): 113–19.

Stafford, R. H. Review of *H. A. R.: The Autobiography of Father Reinhold. Perspective* 9 (Summer 1968): 190–91.

Stehlin, Stewart A. *Weimar and the Vatican 1919–1933: German-Vatican Diplomatic Relations in the Interwar Years.* Princeton, NJ: Princeton University Press, 1983.

Swidler, Leonard. "In Memoriam." *Journal of Ecumenical Studies* 5 (Winter 1968): i.

Timascheff, Nicholas S. *The Sociology of Luigi Sturzo.* Baltimore: Helicon Press, 1962.

Tucker, Spencer C. *The Great War 1914–18.* Bloomington: Indiana University Press, 1998.

Tuzik, Robert L. "H. A. Reinhold: The Timely Tract to the American Church." In *How Firm a Foundation: Voices of the Early Liturgical Movement*, edited by Kathleen Hughes, 174–83. Chicago: Liturgy Training Publications, 1990.

Tyldesley, Mike. *No Heavenly Delusion?: A Comparative Study of Three Communal Movements.* Liverpool: Liverpool University Press, 2003.

Upton, Julia A. "Carpe Momentum: Liturgical Studies at the Threshold of the Millennium." In *At the Threshold of the Millennium*, edited by Francis A. Eigo, 103–38. Villanova, PA: Villanova University Press, 1998.

————. "H. A. Reinhold: Architect of the Liturgical Movement in America." In *Benedict in the World: Portraits of Monastic Oblates*, edited by Linda Kulzer and Roberta Bondi, 187–99. Collegeville, MN: Liturgical Press, 2002.

Van Allen, Roger. *The Commonweal and American Catholicism: The Magazine, the Movement, the Meaning.* Philadelphia: Fortress Press, 1974.

Von Klemperer, Klemens. *The German Resistance Against Hitler.* Oxford: Clarendon Press, 1992.

Weakland, Rembert G. "Liturgical Renewal: Two Latin Rites?" *The Catholic Historical Review* 176, no. 20 (June 14, 1997): 12–16.

Weiner, William J., Lisa Shulman, and Anthony E. Lang. *Parkinson's Disease: A Complete Guide for Patients and Families*. Baltimore: Johns Hopkins University Press, 2001.

Whaley, Joachim. *Religious Toleration and Social Change in Hamburg, 1529–1819*. New York: Cambridge University Press, 1985.

White, Susan J. *Art, Architecture, and Liturgical Reform: The Liturgical Arts Society (1928–1972)*. New York: Pueblo, 1988.

Winzen, Damascus. "Progress and Tradition in Maria Laach Art." *Liturgical Arts* 10 (November 1941): 19–24.

———. "The Church Alive in Her Liturgy." *Benedictine Review* 14 (1959): 87–100.

Wright, John. "The Liturgical Movement: An Appraisal." Review of *The American Parish and the Roman Liturgy*, by H. A. Reinhold. *America* 98 (February 1, 1958): 516.

Zahn, Gordon. *German Catholics and Hitler's Wars*. New York: Sheed & Ward, 1962.

Zeender, John. "The Genesis of the German Concordat of 1933." In *Studies in Catholic History in Honor of John Tracy Ellis*, edited by Nelson H. Minnich, Robert B. Eno, and Robert F. Trisco, 617–65. Wilmington, DE: Michael Glazier, 1985.

Zolberg, Aristide R. "The Ecole Libre at the New School 1941–1946." *Social Research* 65 (Winter 1998). http://findarticles.com/p/articles/mi_m2267/is_4_65/ai_54098124/pg_1?tag=artBody;col1 (accessed January 24, 2009).

Index